D1251906
DAILY
TELEGRAPH
Longmans
BERNADETTE

PHOENIX OF FLEET STREET

To C.C. Clawson
with warm wishes
David Morgan
at St Bride's
17 July 1979

PHOENIX OF FLEET STREET

2000 years of St Bride's

by Dewi Morgan

CHARLES KNIGHT & CO. LTD

Designed by Ruari McLean and Terence Ridley-Ellis

Charles Knight & Co. Ltd
11/12 Bury Street, London EC3A 5AP
Dowgate Works, Douglas Road, Tonbridge, Kent

First published in 1973

Set in Monophoto Sabon semi-bold and printed by offset-lithography
in Great Britain by BKT Printers Ltd, Tonbridge

ISBN 0 85314 196 7

endpapers St Bride's day and night. Taken on Kodak film

over Panorama of Fleet Street, 1838. Tallis

facing John Douswell engraving, 1753

Contents

Chapter	Page
1. The Background	1
2. Celtic and Roman Christians	11
3. The Middle Ages	22
4. The Sixteenth Century	49
5. New Thoughts and the New World	77
6. Commonwealth and Restoration	109
7. Wren's St Bride's	139
8. Print, Parsons and Prison	164
9. The Eighteenth Century	181
10. The Nineteenth Century and after	203
11. A Phoenix again	249
Appendix	277
Notes	279
Sources of illustrations	281
Index	282

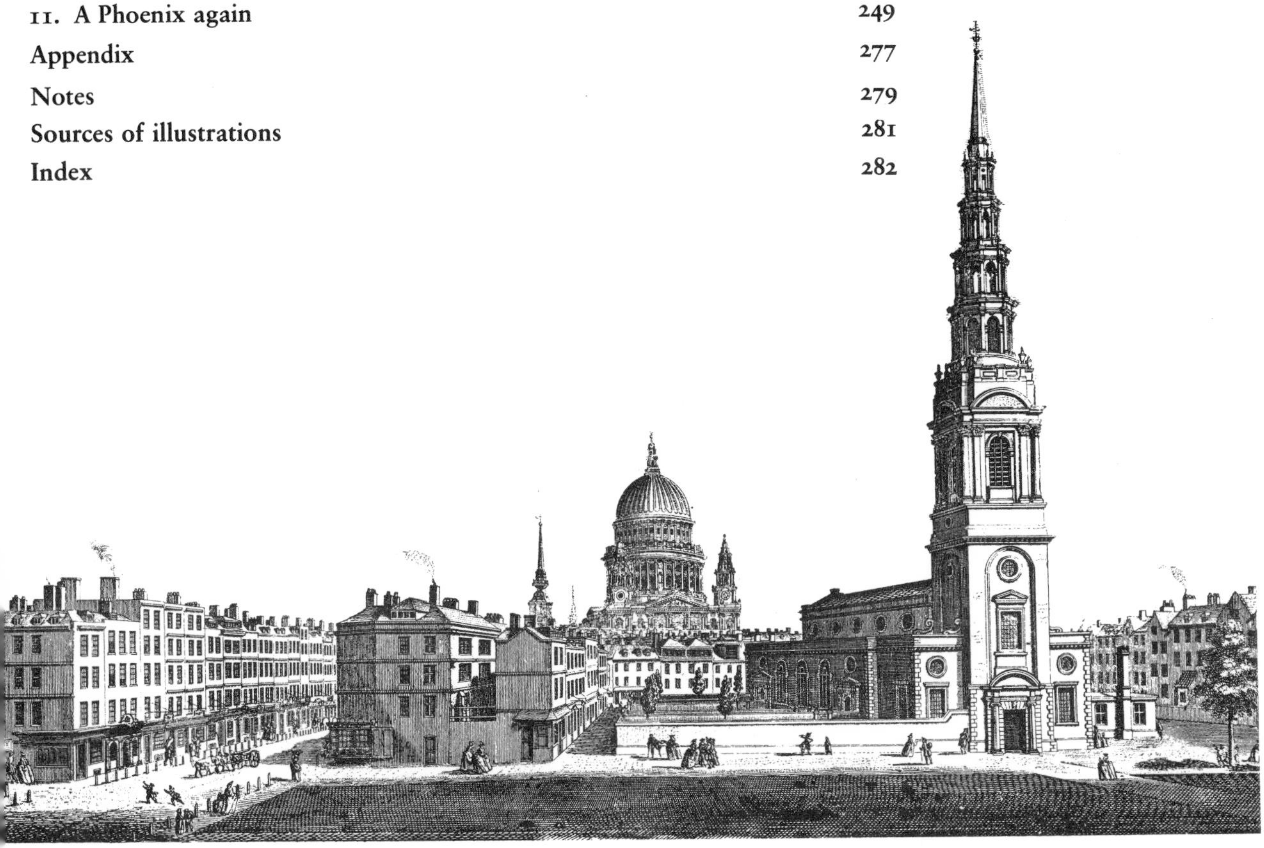

Nor shall this peace sleep with her; but as when
The bird of wonder dies, the maiden phoenix,
Her ashes new-create another heir
As great in admiration as herself.

Shakespeare,
King Henry VIII, Part III.

Preface

The Romans used to make much of the *genius loci*, the spirit of a place. Few spots can be more instinct with their own characteristic personality than St Bride's and its neighbourhood, parish pump to the world. The Rector, who lives, so to speak, 'over the shop', is permanently exposed to all this. It is enough to make him want to write a book about it.

Furthermore, the Rector of St Bride's is exposed to a constant barrage of questions, from many parts of the world, about Fleet Street and its inhabitants over the centuries. Rather than forever doing disjointed bits of research, then, it proved expedient for him to produce a coherent manuscript, even if it were never published. It was at least a self-protective source of reference.

Such factors are the genesis of this book. But no Rector of St Bride's could claim that a book like this is all his own work. I have indeed borrowed shamelessly from the efforts of men of many centuries. Among my contemporaries I must thank Ruari McLean for his gifted efforts, Victor Bonham-Carter for ensuring that a Welshman's prose – and punctuation – conformed to an Englishman's standards, the staff of the British Museum and the Guildhall Library, the St Bride's Print Historical Library, Fianach Jardine and a host of others for expert help in tracing the superb illustrations as well as the facts, and my wife and my colleagues for putting up with the temperament which seems the usual companion of gestation especially when literary parenthood must let parish priesthood constantly take priority. Last, but not least, I am grateful to Henry Bailey-King who came to my study a few years ago for quite another purpose but left it with yet another Fleet Street phoenix finding a new source of life.

Dewi Morgan
St Bride's
Fleet Street
1972.

1. The Background

'The man must have a rare recipe for melancholy, who can be dull in Fleet Street', said Charles Lamb. The remark was made in 1802, but it would be no less true in any age. For this street, now parish pump to all the world, has always been a willing conscript of the forces that make history.

Towards the eastern end – and the orientation is significant – is a pocket handkerchief of land which, sensitised by topography and its involvement in human affairs, has reflected every nuance of the centuries. On this tiny plot stands St Bride's Church. Here once was a well, invested with all the meaning, human and divine, that a well can have. Here too was the no-man's-land between the Government in Westminster and the commerce of the City. Along Fleet Street have surged a host of men and events. St Bride's has watched – and often participated – as English history has been made. And when the first English printing press was brought from the precincts of Westminster Abbey to alongside St Bride's churchyard, this place became the eye of the typhoon of communication, which has influenced the minds of men and moulded the pattern of their actions. Fleet Street must be one of the best documented places in the British Isles. But the story begins before documents.

Romans walked here

In St Bride's crypts you can see the line of a first century Roman ditch which, being 15-16 feet wide and more than 7 feet deep, was larger than that eventually dug around the Roman city itself. It may have been part of a military enclosure set up by the invading armies to guard the first builders of imperial Caesar's Londinium. Or perhaps the Romans started to build Londinium here, and then – changing their minds – sought a new site across the Fleet river. You can also see the remains of a red and yellow tesserae pavement and some masonry of the Roman period. It defies accurate dating, but is the only undoubted Roman building recorded on the north bank of the Thames between the City wall and Westminster. Here too were found well-preserved skeletons suggesting burial at a very early Christian date.

This site was occupied far back in time. The remains we see are the founda-

The main crypt seen from the steeple, 1954

2

Roman foundations

tions that support the high rise of the last 2000 years. Yet they can hardly be the start of the story, for an essential feature of the place was the Bride Well, now dehydrated and dead, cloaking a brood of ghosts that hint at its origin. London must have had many wells. Few of them have greater claims to antiquity than Bride Well, since it suggests a link with prehistoric man, whose theology enabled him to find a spirit to worship in a well. Animism was a respectable creed, and Christianity had no difficulty in choosing saints to patronise wells and mountains and streams, once cherished as places of pagan reverence. It was a Celt, Brigid-Bridget-Bride, who, when the Christian era was well started, gave her name to a church and a well whose story would grow together. Significantly, when in 1962 the remains of an ancient ship were found in Thames gravel at Blackfriars, a hundred yards or so from St Bride's, scholars decided it was of Celtic, not Roman, workmanship; and that, like much else in Romano-British culture, it was probably made in Britain. 'There is every reason' said *The Times*, 'to believe it was built by native shipwrights according to a native tradition which survived the Roman occupation.' This ship has also 'proved to be the earliest sailing-vessel discovered in north-west Europe', and it belongs to the second century.

As to the dating of St Bride's, Professor W. F. Grimes – who investigated its bombed site after the war – made this comment:

> 'These excavations have produced no result which can be said to comment on the early association of the Celtic St Bride or Bridget with this site. There is no evidence that can be used to link the Roman building beneath the east end of the church with the church itself, except that

which says that the church-builders used the Roman building as a quarry. Yet a continuity there may have been; and it comes from the use to which this part of the city outside the walls was put in Roman times. The evidence of burials found in the angle of Shoe Lane and Fleet Street in 1927 shows that here was a cemetery which was in use at least well into the third century AD.

The burials in question were by cremation in urns and the cremation rite gave way gradually to the burial of the body during the second and third centuries. It cannot be claimed for any of the simple inhumation burials recorded at St Bride's that they are certainly of Roman date; they nevertheless display features which would be considered "early Christian" rather than mediaeval, and they are supported by the finds of human bones in the pit at the east end of the early church, which shows that there must have been many inhumation burials in and about the area in pre-Norman times. The gap between those burials and those of the earlier Roman period may well be filled in due course by some lucky chance. In the meantime the theory that the presence of an early church here with a Celtic dedication owes something to the use of the area as a burial ground since Roman times has much in it that is attractive.'[1]

The first London Wall was built at some date before the year AD 200. Over a million cubic feet of ragstone were brought from Maidstone and erected into a wall two miles long. The Thames beside it must have been thick with little

Roman London about A.D. 100. Reconstruction drawing Alan Sorrell

left Roman woman's burial discovered west end of crypt. Position implies Christian influence

below Early Iron Age craftsmanship, first century B.C. © *British Museum*

First century A.D. pottery jug inscribed LONDIM AD FANUM ISIDIS. The earliest use of the name London. © *London Museum*

Roman wall and tesserae.
East end of crypt

ships, like the one found near St Bride's. It had a coin of the Emperor Domitian (AD 81-96) in its mast step. It was St Bride's position, just outside the Wall, that gave it literally so close an insight into historical events; but there are contingent reasons, even if our appreciation of them must be partly conjectural. One was the fact that City business and State affairs overlapped at this point – a possible explanation why newspapers would eventually flourish here, at the centre yet outside the Establishment. Another builds on Professor Grimes's speculation. Roman custom reinforced by Roman law decreed that burials should take place away from habitation; and the discovery of the cremation urns stimulates the imagination to see mourners coming here, perhaps, from the beginning of the Roman occupation. In any event burial places evoke religious associations, hence their possible link in this area with the animist origins of Bride Well. In one way or another worship may have taken place here since a date that has never emerged from the mists of time. As to the origins of Christianity in Britain, although tradition far outweighs fact, that is no reason for dismissing historical conjecture. No one knows when Christianity first reached this country or who brought it. Perhaps Joseph of Arimathea did visit Glastonbury. Perhaps, even less likely, St Paul did preach on the site where his cathedral now stands. Such traditions may only tell us that the faith came as early possibly as the first century AD. Certainly Tertullian knew about Christians in this country. In his tract against the Jews, written AD c. 208, he speaks of parts of Britain inaccessible to Romans which had yet been conquered for Christ. And Origen, writing some thirty years later, includes Britain in a list of places where Christians might be found. Some of them may have been refugees from the persecutions that broke out in Gaul in AD 177. Whoever they were, when and whenever to be found, they were not at first likely to have been noticed – either humble people whom history

Early Bronze Age beaker
found in City of London.
© *Guildhall Museum*

The Landing of Julius Caesar. Engraved by L. P. Boitard

has not mentioned, or secret believers in the ranks of the army or civil society; for while Rome tolerated many sects so long as the sects recognised Rome, Christianity was exclusive.

In the City there were gods who could make concessions to divine Caesar, notably the high-minded Mithras. He was a great one. Had he not set free all the forces of creation by slaying the great bull? Had he himself not emerged from the egg of eternity, and were not the signs of the zodiac his familiars? His attendants were themselves gods and they knew inner secrets. In his temple were practised mysterious ceremonies, veiled from all but the initiates. Yet Mithras had the heavenly wisdom to allow a mortal to throw Caesar a passing bone of obeisance. He was also a god who encouraged the virtues of endurance, much approved by Caesar among his soldiers. Thus Mithras was permitted a public temple. Jesus, however, had to be worshipped in private. He was unique, supreme, not to be shared with any other god. Is it therefore too much to surmise that in days when to profess Christ meant risking persecution, if not martyrdom, it would have been common sense to leave the forum and the basilica, and cross the Fleet at the bottom of Ludgate Hill to say your corporate prayers 'outside the wall'? Bride Well may have been the cradle of London's Christianity.

The Christian religion had to remain clandestine until the fourth century when Constantine, though unbaptised until his death, recognised the potential of a powerful Church as a spiritual counterpart to and practical support of his empire. Official recognition made possible public organisation and assembly, international as well as domestic. Restitutus, a bishop from London, attended the Synod of Arles in 314. Although there seem to have been no British representatives at Nicaea in 325, Athanasius reported that the Church in Britain accepted the Nicaean decisions. British bishops were present at the Council of Rimini in 359, but they were so poor that the State had to meet their expenses. Other historical figures include the martyr Alban, who gave his life for a fugitive priest in c. 304; and that attractive heretic Pelagius, a Celtic monk active towards the end of the fourth century – if it is true that his name is the Latinised form of Morgan, then the writer must be forgiven for having a special interest in him. Pelagius, 'an elusive and gracious figure, beloved and respected wherever he goes . . . silent, smiling, reserved',[2] created a furore by enunciating what has since come to be regarded as a peculiarly British heresy. Convinced that man has a natural human dignity, he thought him capable of perfection largely by his own efforts. The doctrine of Original Sin, he said, had been exaggerated and so had man's need for supernatural grace. The degree to which he aroused the passions of St Augustine indicates that Pelagius was no remote, negligible provincial, and by implication that the Church from which he came was no rude handful. Heretics do not arouse passions until they show signs of becoming influential.

With the life of Pelagius we have moved from the fourth into the fifth century. The period is a great watershed (Augustine used stronger words to describe it). Christianity was established as the official religion, but the Roman empire was on the wane in the west. A major barbarian invasion had occurred in Britain in 360, and there had been a series of raids long before this. Roman rule was periodically re-established, latterly by Theodosius who made London his base and renamed it Augusta. The citizens were unimpressed, so that Augusta was forgotten while

Roman London, early fourth century. Reconstruction drawing Alan Sorrell. © *London Museum*

London remained. Then came the day in 410 when, by tradition at least, the legions finally departed. London was left to itself, its population a cosmopolitan mixture of Celt and Roman, spiced with a dash of the exotic blood of traders from overseas. Perhaps some Celtic Roman sat by the wall – which means where these words are being written – looked about him and pondered the future. Beyond Ludgate he would have become familiar with the startling contrasts between civilisation and barbarism which London now exhibited – the great stone buildings intermingled with wooden and wattle huts, where trade continued despite the periods of chaos. Would even this survive without the army that had defended Britain for nearly 400 years? We know almost nothing about London after the Romans left it. Odd shafts of light illumine the darkness now and then. In 429, to combat the Pelagian heresy, the British bishops called in St Germanus, Bishop of Auxerre, and St Lupus, Bishop of Troyes. Germanus had been a soldier before entering the Church, so that in England he was able to spend as much of his time in military deeds against barbarians as in theological debate with heretics. It is on record that, shouting 'Alleluia' at the head of a British band, he routed the enemy and drove them off the field. In 446 he was summoned again, on this occasion to restore the faith, rather than resort to arms. The darkness then closed in again. What happened to London in the 'dark ages' is guesswork. Some say that it remained the seat of a bishop, that it had sufficient social order to maintain a mint, that Bede's eighth century description of it as 'the mart of many nations resorting to it by sea and land' went on unbroken as the Romans went, or that years passed while it existed as a ghost town, with all its inhabitants scattered or living in suspended animation until the barbarian had acquired enough civilisation to revive it. If we know nothing of London after Germanus's second visit, we do know one thing that belongs strictly to this part of the story – that Brigid-Bridget-Bride was born about the year 453.

Anglo-Saxon jewelled disc brooch, sixth to seventh century. © *British Museum*

2. Celtic and Roman Christians

Bride was born about half a century after a bewildered boy named Patrick had been captured, enslaved, and taken from Britain to Ireland. It was a country of seven kingdoms much given to fighting, except apparently when the warriors exchanged their swords for harps and indulged in the Spring Festival, an eisteddfod under the High King's presidency. Christianity seems to have made little impact in Ireland up to this time, and the druids held sway. There, among the fortified camps, the life of the Irish was a strange mixture of light and dark. They had their colourful tartans and their magnificent metalwork. They also had leprosy. They had their passion for the arts of words and music. They also had slavery.

Bride herself was the daughter of an Irish prince and a slave, fruit of the union between the aristocratic but pagan Dubthach and his bondmaid Brotseach, who had probably already become a Christian, perhaps as a result of the efforts of Patrick. Dubthach's wife was angry about the liaison. Brotseach had to go and was sold to a druid; and in this heathen household Bride was born. She remained, however, the property of her natural father and to his house she was returned at the age of ten, no doubt having learned much druidic lore. During a brief visit Bride made to her mother, so we are told, the druid was converted to Christianity. Bride was brought up by her father, but she found it hard to conform to his ideas. In fact she gave away to the poor so many of his possessions that he determined to sell her. She was offered to the local king but he, learning of her charitable activities, tactfully decided that she was too good for him to buy or for her father to sell. Her hand was then sought in marriage. She refused to contemplate the idea. Her father could see no alternative but to allow her to follow her bent and enter the religious life. She was professed – together with eight other virgins – and made famous the monastery at Kildare.

The name means 'church of the oak' and so suggests a druid grove alongside, merging of pagan and Christian. It was a community of both sexes where, strange to modern ears, the monastic bishop was subject to the orders of the

Eighth-century cast bronze plaque, Irish style, from Co. Roscommon

St Brigid's Well, Tully, Co. Kildare. © *Bord Failte Eirean*

abbess, and where the liturgy derived not from Rome but, via Gaul, from eastern Mediterranean Christianity.

> 'The influence of the traditional Christianity of Western Europe upon the training of St Brigid can only have been of the very slightest, and whatever contact there was with the Patrician mission was established when the disciples of St Patrick were fast passing away, and the work was passing into the hands of a native clergy, only recently emerged from heathendom, and dependent for guidance on their own judgements and the help which came from the Celtic-speaking districts of Britain.'[1]

Perhaps the most remarkable characteristic of the Irish Church at this time related to the status it conferred on women. They were missionaries, teachers and administrators. There is even a tradition, strong enough to rate mention in the *Oxford Dictionary of the Christian Church*, that episcopal orders were conferred on Bride, 'the Mary of the Gael . . . accounted with St Patrick the second patron saint of Ireland'.[2] And there, in that deference to the more influential sex, possibly lies the reason why Ireland was so rapidly evangelised. The hands that rocked cradles were linked with tongues which spoke Christ.

Bride, equally at home amid the rustic aristocracy or tending pigs and brewing beer in the company of village slaves, aware of the nature religion of her people throughout generations and awake to the power of God in Christ, was an astonishingly complete person. There is an eighth century manuscript which con-

Shrine of St Brigid's Shoe.
© *Bord Failte Eirean*

tains a poem ascribed to her. Whether she actually wrote it or not, it must have been in keeping with her character:

'I long for a great lake of ale
I long for the meats of belief and pure piety
I long for flails of penance at my house
I long for them to have barrels full of peace
I long to give away jars full of love
I long for them to have cellars full of mercy
I long for cheerfulness to be in their drinking
I long for Jesus too to be there among them.'

Baring-Gould gives a slightly different version:

'I should like a great lake of ale
For the king of kings
I should like the whole family of heaven
To be drinking it eternally.'[3]

Bride was a rounded person and well equipped to build a rounded life for her monastery. That monastery became a major influence in Irish life. Yet, in a sense, it was only a part-time commitment, for Bride was a persistent traveller – usually, if her biographers are to be believed, at the most breakneck speed her chariot could sustain. Dotted over the map of Ireland are Kilbrides, Tubberbrides and Kilbreedys, all of which proclaim 'Bride came here'. Without question, she was the best-known woman in Ireland – and beyond. She stood high in the calendar of mediaeval Europe. But did she ever leave Ireland in person? History has hidden the answer. None the less numerous ancient church sites in Wales, Scotland, the West of England, Brittany, Belgium, down the Rhine and even as far as Czechoslovakia and Italy, accepted, retained and honoured her name. But how did it reach Fleet Street? Before the early 1950s there was no clue. St Bride's church, according to all the records, dated back only to the twelfth century.

Post-war reconstruction, however, revealed beneath the Wren floor nearly a thousand years of forgotten history. And the revelation included the remains of a stone church which may well date back to Bride's day. The grounds for assuming that a Romano-Celtic community existed on the site after 410 are strong. In fact, such a community could have been a major rallying point. The *Anglo-Saxon Chronicle* states that in 457 the Britons of Kent fled to London from the advancing Saxon invaders, and that their London kinsmen succoured them. Because the invaders preferred the countryside to the town, and were suspicious of Roman relics, they may have left London Christianity alone. So the first stone church here could be considered as tangible evidence of continuity. It belongs to the sixth century and therefore pre-dates St Augustine's arrival in England. According to *The Universe*, 'St Augustine may have known this church'. Its Celtic affinities are manifest for it had a significantly narrow entry to the chancel reminiscent of the rood screen in the church at Kildare, recalling a faith which knew the eastern insistence on concealing the holy of holies from profane eyes. Was the liturgy first celebrated on this spot in the Celtic language? Did Mellitus on his arrival in London in 604 find something which already had long Christian roots, possibly a stone successor to a still earlier wattle-and-daub edifice in use when Pelagius

Remains, probably Celtic, found at low level in the crypt

St Patrick

Ninth-century wall

was causing his furore? It is unlikely that a Celtic patron would have been chosen *after* the Roman Mellitus had assumed leadership. More than that we cannot say.

All this suggests that St Bride's existed before that great crossroads in English church history, the Synod of Whitby in 664, which ensured that England should relinquish the old ways of the Celtic Church and follow the Roman rule. The Celtic dating of Easter, related to Asia Minor and St John, was to be abandoned in favour of the authority of St Peter, and the Roman fashion of hair cutting – the tonsure – was accepted. Then came the incomparable Theodore of Tarsus, Archbishop of Canterbury from 668, who gave his full allegiance to Rome. Perhaps because of his Greek background, he was able to lead the Celts with such gentleness and tact that they accepted his leadership and the Roman authority he stood for. 'He was the first of the archbishops to whom the whole English church consented to submit' said Bede, whose lifetime overlapped Theodore's. The change was not without its advantages, for the Celtic Church was essentially monastic, not diocesan. The Celtic system suited missionary work but not consolidation. The first council of the English Church, held at Hertford in 673, was one result, and significant in that religion knew no barriers in a politically fragmented country. There was a Church of England before there was a Kingdom of England.

By this time, London was again becoming a place of note. Once again the city had begun to count in international trade – with Holland, for example, as indicated by the many coins inscribed 'London' and found in The Low Countries. One of the commodities handled by the London market was slaves – as Pope Gregory knew. He must have thought London important. At the time of Augus-

facing The ninth-century apse and Norman tomb

tine's arrival in 597, it had seemed to him the right place for the seat of church government in England. It was possibly Londoners themselves who refused the honour. Is Canterbury therefore the centre because seventh century Londoners preferred the Celtic to the Roman church? By the time the Synod of Whitby had established Rome, Canterbury was secure in its precedence, but it is difficult to accept the suggestion that it had been chosen because London was still a pagan city. The succession of London bishops was already long when Mellitus arrived, and only three years later Ethelbert, King of Kent, began building St Paul's Cathedral and creating the laws which gave Christianity a favoured position. Londoners were also sufficiently interested in Christianity for St Paul's to be rebuilt in stone, 675-85, by Erconwald, saint, Bishop of London and founder of monasteries at Barking and Chertsey. His building was to last until one of London's periodic fires demolished it in 961.

The seventh century was critical for Christianity in Britain. Fifty years passed before an English king risked the destruction of idols and enforced the observance of Lent while, another fifty years later, Wihtred of Kent still found it necessary to attack heathen worship. Yet retrospectively the pattern is a clear one. Reckoning from 597, W. Levison writes:

> 'The conversion was finished after nearly ninety years, when all England had accepted Christianity, at least superficially. These were not years of continual progress: there were moments of reaction, particularly when wars broke out among the Anglo-Saxons, some of whom clung to the gods of their forefathers, and between the Anglo-Saxons and Britons in the west, who were Christians too, but detested the invaders of their native soil. The aim of Gregory seemed to be frustrated for a while not only by these opponents but also by the zeal of the Irish offspring of the

> Old British Church; its monks regained ground lost by the Papal emissaries, and won over the larger part of England to the Christian faith and to the peculiarities which the Celtic Churches had kept in their separation, and which were opposed by the followers of Rome. But the Synod, or rather debate, of Whitby gave the victory to the Roman cause.'[4]

far left Ivory Pen Case. Late eleventh century. © *British Museum*

left King Ethelbert and the Saxons converted to Christianity by St Augustine. How it might have happened.

Among these 'Irish offspring' Bride was by no means the only great name. Columba (521-597) missionary to Iona, and Columbanus (550-615) missionary to Gaul, certainly deserve mention. The Book of Kells and the Lindisfarne Gospels, both written in the Irish style and both belonging to the eighth century, reveal the force and persistence of their influence.

Meanwhile the number and eminence of English missionaries to the Continent were a sure proof of the country's religious vitality. Wilfrid (634-709), Willibrord (658-739), Boniface (675-754), Alcuin (730-804) were all men who contributed to the conversion and civilisation of northern Europe, although they would not have considered themselves 'foreign' missionaries in any modern sense for they re-

The Synod of Whitby, 664

imago ui tuli
O AGIOS
LUCAS

garded the Germanic peoples as kinsfolk. And the regard was reciprocated. 'We are of one blood and one bone with you', said Charles Martel to the English. It was the heyday of Anglo-Saxon missions. Yet even here the Celtic influence was relevant.

> 'It is impossible to tell how far the incentive to missionary enterprise on the part of the Anglo-Saxon Church was derived from the Celtic Church in Ireland. But in the year 590 St Columbanus with his twelve companions had initiated the monastic and missionary migrations of the Irish to the Continent. A century later, St Willibrord set sail for Friesland: and it can hardly be without significance that he spent the preceding twelve years – since 678, the year of Archbishop Wilfrid's deposition – in Ireland, devoting himself in voluntary exile to the monastic life.'[5]

By the seventh century St Paul's had become the pride of Londoners – it was some time before the Abbey Church of Westminster was to rival it – and by the eighth, so Bede tells us, London was the capital of the East Saxons and a busy emporium. At least one other church – All Hallows, Barking-by-the-Tower – had also been founded, for in the ninth century the Danes found it worth sacking. Their defeat in 882 enabled Alfred to restore London and make it habitable once more. Was it at this time that the second St Bride's church was built? Archaeologists date it to this period, and Alfred's reconstruction makes it more than a coincidence.

left A page from the Lindisfarne Gospels. © *British Museum*

below A King Alfred penny. © *Guildhall Museum*

3. The Middle Ages

The second St Bride's stood for over 200 years. It was replaced in the twelfth century by a third stone building for one of two reasons. It may have been destroyed in the fire of 1135, recorded in the City's *Liber Album* as having burned from London Bridge to St Clement Danes. Or it may have been altered in order to accord with liturgical changes, which demanded a different shape of building. What does stand out from the archaeological diagrams is that the third church implies a different theological concept from the second church, especially in regard to the extension of the east end and the lengthening of the chancel: a change entirely consistent with the increasing emphasis placed on the mystery of the Mass, a theology which was to remove the happening to a distant east end, far from the congregation, and increasingly to make it the concern of the priest alone – while the man in the pew said his rosary. This was a period of doctrinal debate – a time when a belief in the Real Presence of our Lord in the sacrament through transubstantiation was being articulated, and when the chalice was being denied to the laity. It was also a time when Pope Hildebrand was making an unprecedented demand, namely that all priests must be celibate. New doctrines demanded new buildings. The remains of various centuries on St Bride's site are not merely of stone. They are mute reminders that when men alter their thoughts about God, they alter the appearance of God's house.

The long period of speculation about St Bride's was now giving way to fact. The first *documentary* evidence refers to the year 1134 when Henry I, son of William the Conqueror, granted two forges to the Master and Brethren of the Temple. One was in the parish of St Dunstan, the other in the parish of St Brigide. Is it too fanciful to suppose that, at these forges, weapons were tempered for the Crusades; or horses shod for the jousting field of the Knights Templars, roughly where Lincoln's Inn Fields are now? And, if tradition speaks truly, spades made to dig the soil of the Temple garden where, in due course, were plucked the symbols that gave their name to the Wars of the Roses – wars planned at Baynard's Castle, at the other corner of St Bride's parish?

East end of crypt, including ninth-century apse and Norman tomb after excavations

Two views of Norman base of curfew tower

The third St Bride's church had one of the four curfew towers in London. When its bell rang each evening, law-abiding citizens covered their fires. 'No man shall be so daring, on pain of imprisonment', proclaimed Mayor John de Barnes in 1370, 'as to go wandering about the city after the hour of curfew rung out at St Mary-le-Bow, Barking Church in Tower Ward, St Bride's and St Giles without Cripplegate, unless he be some man of the city of good repute or his servant, and that with reasonable cause, and with light.'

Why should a church or parish, important enough to boast a curfew tower, lack any written record until so late as 1134? In the first place records can get lost. In the second place because Domesday Book, compiled in 1086, did not include London. There is however a third, more interesting, reason, and it stems from the fact that from early times St Bride's belonged to the Abbot of Westminster, who denied allegiance – and therefore reports and accounts – to anyone except the Pope himself. Westminster was an exempt house. It had no need to request confirmation of its estates, and it did not have to render account to the Bishop of London. For that reason it did not appear in diocesan records. Under a Charter of 951, the monks of Westminster had title to lands as far as the Fleet river, these being occupied by 'twenty-five houses of the Abbot's knights and of other men who render eight shillings yearly'. Although St Bride's is not mentioned by name, it lay within the territory designated, and is likely to have figured in other supporting documents or accounts, which no monastic institution was ever without. But these have simply vanished in the course of history. Accordingly we have to wait until the twelfth century for the evidence we need: first, the reference to the two forges in 1134; next, at some date between 1163 and 1189 when Gilbert Foliot, Bishop of London, confirmed to the monks of Westminster certain of the churches in their jurisdiction, including the church of St Brigide which carried a pension of one mark; then in 1188 when lands in the parish in the street of Flete next to the cemetery of St Brigide were 'granted by the leprous brethren of St Giles' Hospital, Master Walter, their Warden, and Ralph, son of Adam, to their benefactor, Herbert, Archdeacon of Canterbury'. The value of these lands stood at 15*s*. 3*d*. a year. A few years later, in 1214, the Abbot of Westminster granted the Bishop of London certain tenements and rents in St Bride's; but he carefully safeguarded his right to appoint the incumbent – and the twentieth century still honours the fact.

The thirteenth century suddenly reveals St Bride's as a centre of important business, not only ecclesiastical. For example, in 1205, the Curia Regis, the King's inner council, sat in the church during the third week after Easter and gave judgment about land and inheritance disputes in a number of English counties. In the same place in 1210, King John granted a Charter to Rogarde Mari and Isabell his wife to hold a market on Tuesdays and a fair on the eve day and morrow of St Lawrence at Licchelad (Lechlade) in the County of Gloucester. But if Matthew Paris is to be believed, the occasion was much more important than that. He describes it as a Parliament, the primary purpose of which was for the King to extract from clergy and religious persons the sum of £100,000.

To do business in church was a commonplace, at least until the end of the Middle Ages. The nave was probably the only place large enough to accommodate a public meeting – one reason why until the end of the nineteenth century the parish church was the headquarters of local government. Any church was the heart of the local community, and its special function as a place of worship took

Model of Old St Paul's Cathedral

its place among a host of lesser functions in one indistinguishable whole. The twelfth century had not learned the distinction between sacred and secular, which seems to hypnotise modern man. St Bride's was clearly a useful place of assembly in the western liberties of the City, and suitable on occasion for a wider national purpose.

Yet to see the church merely as a formal meeting place is to miss its heartbeat. Even a mediaeval church, caught up in civic functions as it was, knew how to rejoice with a bride and comfort a widow. Thus the building would put away its regal air and make itself gay for the wedding of someone like the improbably named Cassandra. John de Flete was her bridegroom's name and he seems to have prospered at his trade of making caps, for he owned a tenement and wharf on the Fleet and rents in the parish. The marriage in church being complete, there came the customary ceremony in the porch by which a husband endowed his wife with property. It was a simple matter, just a few words spoken in the presence of witnesses. John died in 1280 and Cassandra's inheritance was not contested.

Not long before John and Cassandra were wed, Fleet Street, which was one day to thrive on recording sensations, had its first recorded crime of violence. On 11 October 1228, Henry de Buke slew Le Ireis le Tyulour ('the Irish Taylor' – Celts were still around) in the street of Fleetbrigge with a knife. The incident comes into history not because violence was rare, but because the assassin fled across London Bridge and was pursued by the Mayor and Sheriff who took his oath to quit the realm. The dignitaries were fined for their trouble, for by apprehending a man outside the City's confines they had trespassed the king's right.

By 1222, seven years after John had conceded defeat by signing the Magna Carta, and a year after the Dominicans had arrived in England, the ownership of the lands around St Bride's was again in dispute. Stephen Langton must have been a busy man, for he acted as a judge in this case, and was simultaneously promulgating the decrees of the Fourth Lateran Council and special decrees for the English Church. The man who was 'perhaps the greatest of our mediaeval archbishops' was joined in this lands tribunal by Richard Poore, the Bishop of Salisbury and finaliser of the Sarum Use, Thomas of Merton, Richard of Dunstable, and Peter de Rupibus, Bishop of Winchester. It must have been a lawsuit of major importance to attract such a galaxy. The disputants were the Bishop of London and the Dean and Chapter of St Paul's on one side and the Abbot and Convent of Westminster on the other. On this occasion, Westminster's title and jurisdiction were reaffirmed and the Bishop of London was excluded. But one wonders if Richard Poore was a wholly disinterested person. The Abbot of Westminster had already made him a grant of tenements in St Bride's parish 'except the advowson of St Bride's, which we retain' at a rental of ten shillings at Easter

left Henry the First

right Richard the First

left King John

right Edward the First

and a similar amount at Michaelmas; and this had been reiterated in 1214 with the proviso that the Bishop of Salisbury 'impart to the Abbey and its officers in their joint business a joint counsel when the opportunity requires'. The Inn of the Bishops of Salisbury, subsequently the house of the Earls of Dorset, recalled in Salisbury Square, E.C.4, saw some complex happenings.

Such, for example, as the question: what did Edward I do with the 10*s.* he received from St Bride's in 1293 (not that we are suggesting he filched it as he apparently filched money and valuables from the Temple in 1263)? The record states that it was for his 'expedition to the Holy Land'. Now Edward had undoubtedly *been* to the Holy Land twenty-two years before when he successfully negotiated a ten-year truce with the sultan, Baibars. But the year 1291 saw the final Mameluke attack on Acre, and when it fell the rest of the area went with it. Western Christians were allowed to evacuate as many as they could get into their ships – and not come back. However Edward used his 10*s.*, it was not for the purpose stated. Perhaps he devoted it to the costs of the Parliament he held in 1296 when in answer to Pope Boniface VIII's insistence that clergy should pay no tax without his permission, Edward outlawed the clergy who came to heel by throwing over the Pope.

English monarchs in the Middle Ages seemed to keep well in touch with St

Bride's. It was Edward II who in 1300 ordered his Escheator (the man responsible for the lapsing of land titles) 'to empanel a jury of eighteen good and lawful men of the venue of Scholane [Shoe Lane] to appear before the King or a person holding his place in the church of St Brigide'. They were to decide the rights of Maude de Caumpeville in Shoe Lane in regard to property the Abbot of Rievaulx was alleged to have appropriated. The good burghers of the City, however, would not have such goings-on. No Escheator, they said, could empanel their citizens. Every borough in England, and London above all, was ready to defend its rights against all comers, whether outsiders trying to settle and trade, or the monks of an expanding monastery, or even the king himself. The wealthy merchants of London were quite prepared to lend their money to the monarch to pursue his Hundred Years War, but it had to be on their terms. And the King's need was a financier's opportunity – even if the object of the war was to keep open the Continental market for the wool which was the staple of the merchant's trade.

One wealthy family with a town house in Fleet Street were the Norfolk Pastons, whose letters (1422-1509) provide unique material for our national history, revealing the domestic conditions of the day.

Tomb of Edward the Second, Gloucester Cathedral

The Canterbury Pilgrims at the Tabard Inn

The size of the fourteenth century St Bride's and the esteem in which it was held may be seen from the fact that in 1337, 1338, and 1357 the Convocation of Canterbury, which usually met in St Paul's Cathedral, met in the church. The membership of Convocations at the time included all bishops, abbots, deans and archdeacons as well as two representatives from the clergy of each diocese and one representative of the chapter. It must have been a very large and important gathering.

But it was not only the size of the church which attracted such events. It was also highly convenient for men of religion, for this area was becoming a focal point for churchmen. Nor was this fact always popular. Edward II, for example, had to adjudicate a complaint from the citizens who objected to the religious orders owning land worth one-third of the rental value of the City, without any obligation to contribute to the cost of repairing the City wall. Fitz-Stephen tells us of thirteen conventual churches and 126 parish churches (an average parish was about three acres) while some of the larger houses also had private chapels. Within a hundred yards of St Bride's, town houses were held by the Bishops of Salisbury and St David's, the Abbots of Winchcombe, Tewkesbury, Faversham, Peterborough, Rievaulx and Cirencester. Not far away were the town houses of the Bishops of Bangor (Shoe Lane), Chichester (Chancery Lane), Norwich (Fetter Lane) and Ely (Ely Place). Such town houses, too, were large by any standards. When it took several days for a bishop to get from his see to London and there were highwaymen en route, he needed a retinue of priests, soldiers and servants who all had to be accommodated. It was the Bishop of Ely's house which was to be coveted by Sir Christopher Hatton, Elizabeth's handsome Chancellor, who 'danced so divinely'. He must have overawed the bishop who gave him a very favourable lease – 'a red rose, ten loads of hay and ten pounds per annum'. Shakespeare in Richard III mentions Ely Place and its strawberries. Hatton, of course, is commemorated in today's Hatton Garden. And the Bishop of Ely's chapel is now St Etheldreda's Roman Catholic Church.

Also in the vicinity of St Bride's, first the Knights Templars and then, after their suppression in 1308, the Knights Hospitallers held 'an orchard and twelve gardens'. The Carmelite Friars had a local convent from 1245, while religious orders held the whole of Thameside from the Dominican Priory across the Fleet at Blackfriars as far as Exeter House (now Essex Street) in the Strand. Ecclesiastical property was extensive. And, for the most part, its size was matched by its sumptuousness. The houses of mediaeval prelates were among the finest in London and the king who wanted to impress a foreign ambassador and his entourage could do no better than rent or borrow such a mansion.

This part of London, accordingly, had some famous visitors – not all of them voluntary. It was along Fleet Street that the Black Prince brought his prisoners, the French King John and the young Prince Philip, after the battle of Poitiers. Chaucer merits mention too, for he first bore arms in the army that went to France to collect John's ransom. He had been born – as had Thomas Becket – up the road from St Bride's.

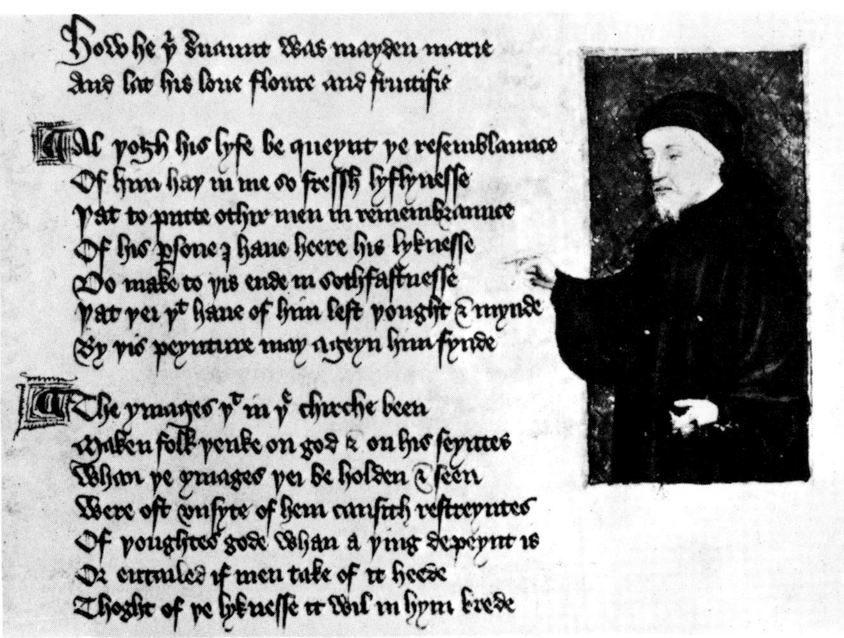

Geoffrey Chaucer in old age from Thomas Hoccleve's fifteenth-century ms.
© *British Museum*

Another royal visitor was Emperor Charles V who lodged at Blackfriars when he visited Henry VIII in 1522.

This part of London, then, had its wealthy, both lay and cleric, and they were not averse to ostentation. Ecclesiastics were no exception. In 1192 Geoffrey, Archbishop of York, was staying at the New Temple. Setting out for Westminster he ordered that his archiepiscopal cross should head the procession. He was outside his province and therefore outside his rights. A complaint was made, so Richard I suspended the divine offices and the bell ringing in the Temple until Geoffrey acknowledged his fault and promised amendment.

The earliest trade centering in Fleet Street seems to have been hat making. During the post-war excavations there was found a sculpture of the arms of the Haberdashers Company which had once been in the mediaeval St Bride's church. The building appears to have had six altars, including one in honour of St Catherine, patron of haberdashers, and one in honour of St Nicholas, patron of milliners. Most craftsmen worked in shops open to the street, yet it was hardly a healthy life. The Fleet river – also known as 'London's sewer' – saw to that. Not only did it carry the offal of Smithfield, the contents of open street drains, and all the household refuse in days when there were no scavengers, but its right bank was the home of the leather workers, who collected raw hides from animals slaughtered at Smithfield nearby. The stench of tanpits must have upset many a sensitive ecclesiastical nostril in what are now Shoe Lane and Leather Lane.

Equally unpleasant was the spectacle of the butchers, granted a quay in 1343 at a rent of one boar's head a year, washing the entrails in the stream. No less distressing was the presence of the Fleet Prison and the wretches confined there for debt and other errors. Its origin is lost in antiquity but it comes on the record as early as 1197, when Richard I confirmed its custody to Nathaniel de Leveland and his son in a document, which suggests this had been the right of the Leveland family 'ever since the conquest of England'.

The environs of the Fleet were such that in 1290 the Carmelites, supported by the Bishop of Salisbury and the Black Friars, complained to the King and Parliament. The putrid odours, they said, were even obliterating the smell of incense at their altars. And, worse still, they caused the death of some of the brothers. In 1307 Henry de Lacy, Earl of Lincoln, who lived in Shoe Lane, grumbled that because of filth ships could not come up the Fleet. 'It was wont to be so full, broad and deep that ten or twelve ships laden with divers wares and merchandize used to come as far as Fleet Bridge and some of them as far as Holborn Bridge.' The complaints, however, had little permanent effect. Fifty years later, in 1356, an Inquisition was held in St Bride's church which learned that the filth of the laystalls and sewers discharging into the rivers had quite choked its course. There was yet another nuisance, since the Fleet – as the modern adjacent street name, Seacoal Lane, shows – was the depot for coal brought in ships from Tyneside. The prejudice against coal, as it began to replace wood and

(From left) Chaucer, Second Nun, Nun's Priest, Manciple, Reeve, all from the Ellesmere ms. of *Canterbury Tales*

The north walls of the Wren (right), Medieval (left), and pre-Medieval churches (centre)

charcoal, was remarkable. Apparently the 'clergy and nobility' were foremost in complaining against 'the stench of burning sea-coal'. In the time of Edward I a man was hanged for the crime of burning it.

The ecclesiastics certainly had reasons for living elsewhere, but they did not do so. The reason is again largely because of the topographical relationship of St Bride's parish with the ancient City. They were days when the arm of the law was short. Merchants, who had prospered, were careful to find a residence inside the relative safety of the City wall. Men of religion had no such need. Even if they had money and possessions, a felon would be careful about harming them. In the first place he appreciated the fact that they helped the sick and the poor. But a still more powerful safeguard was that, whether or not they could punish the wrongdoers in this life, they held supreme powers of damning him in the next. In any case, they were 'held sacred persons whom nobody would hurt'.

As the ecclesiastics had less need of a City wall, they set up their establishments outside it. Moreover, thanks to their near-monopoly of literacy, it was they who provided the majority of statesmen and civil servants. This fact explains, in part, the importance of the Tudor Palace of Bridewell to be referred to later. It also explains why Wynkyn de Worde moved Caxton's printing press from Westminster to a site alongside St Bride's churchyard. Fleet Street became the centre of mass communications in the first place because of the number of churchmen who had settled there.

But we go ahead of our story. Before we reach the year 1500, a uniquely important date in the history of Fleet Street, we must pay the mediaeval Rectors of St Bride's the courtesy of a few words.

They were a curious mixture of men. The church must have had its own minister from the earliest days, but history hides their names until 1255 when Rector Robert Bat decided to become a hermit. In that year Henry III made him a grant of a well-known anchorite's cell near Cripplegate, once held by Richard I's Chaplain. The next Rector worthy of mention is William de Aula who could have added little lustre to the place. It seems he was a mere teenager, and the lowest form of ecclesiastical life, an acolyte, not qualified to say Mass nor hear confessions. Not long after his induction in 1302, the Bishop of London gave him leave of absence to attend a university and acquire a little more learning. No doubt the Rectory income, less a pittance for a resident chaplain who did his work, made Aula's undergraduate days more comfortable. Perhaps he found the secular life so enjoyable that he never came back to St Bride's.

One other Rector of interest was Thomas de Loppedelle, 1313-24. In the year 1317 his name was listed on the roll of 'The Secret Confederation of London Rectors' – an organisation which appears to be a fascinating example of ecclesiastical trade unionism. The objects of the Confederation would have been approved by the Tolpuddle Martyrs, for they included proper care for the members' material interests – not least against unjust archdeacons! The members took a solemn oath, met four times a year and wore livery. The fee was a penny a week. It was in de Loppedelle's day that we find an early reference to a royal patronage of a Fleet Street shopkeeper. In 1321 Edward II was supplied with 'six pairs of boots with tassels of silk and drops of silver gilt, price for each pair, 5*s*.'.

By and large the fourteenth century Rectors of St Bride's did not last long. There were eleven of them in sixty years (as contrasted with only eight incum-

The re-discovery of the crypt

The medieval half-window seen from outside the church

The fourteenth-century chalk tunnel roof and sandstone ribs

bents from 1802 to the present day). The exception was Thomas de Hayton, in office for 34 years. He built a parsonage house on land given in 1380 by Sir John Knyvet and his wife, with a parcel added by the Bishop of Salisbury. And when he died, in 1396, he left all his 'church books' to St Bride's. His successor but one, John Skarle, who subsequently became Master of the Rolls and Archdeacon of Lincoln, left a silver thurible and incense boat to the church which he had served for seven years.

It would be interesting to know whether de Hayton sided with the City Fathers or with John Walworthe, vintner, in a controversy which occurred in 1388. Fleet Street's first water-bearing conduit, 'the London aqueduct', had arrived in 1246 – evidence of the City's enterprise. The conduit, however, had brought trouble as well as water and John Walworthe was one of the sufferers. Breaks in the pipe had flooded his cellars and spoiled his wine. He appealed to the City and eventually was given permission to build a 'penthouse' to safeguard his goods. Since his address was given as 'situate near to the hostel of the Bishop of Salisbury' he must have lived beside St Bride's. He was buried in the church in 1396, bequeathing to one Richard Janock 'his leasehold tavern in Fletestrete called fourdelys [fleur-de-lis], charged with the maintenance of a conduit which the testator had erected in Fletestrete'. He left a considerable fortune.

But a handful of names gives little idea of the number of clerics who in the fourteenth century clustered round a church like St Bride's. There would have been the parish priest with perhaps as many as five assistant priests. Mediaeval wills show no fewer than twenty-three chantries – bequests for Masses to be said for the departed – founded in this church. They alone would have demanded a large staff, though few of them were likely to be well off. Unlike a country church, St Bride's had no glebe – for land has always been at a premium in London. The parsons had to depend on the customary payments from houses and shops in proportion to their rent, a system which some of the City churches continue today though now it is based on rates. There were, of course, donations from the faithful but people had little cash in those days and city folk, unlike their rural counterparts, had little to give in terms of produce. Even with an occasional wedding or burial fee, the total still suggests frugality.

Perhaps money meant little to a body of men whose vows required them to live in chastity and to eschew gluttony whether in food or drink, who were required to wear neither 'cuffed' clothes nor 'pyked' shoes, who were forbidden to carry a dagger or engage in wrestling or other manly sports, who were not allowed to indulge in trade and for whom a tavern was out of bounds. Their main expenditure was probably on hospitality – to both rich and poor – which was a requisite of their office. There were, of course, priests who fell short of all their ideals. They remained in the minority – and attracted publicity, no less in those days than does an erring parson nowadays. Some of their names are to be found in the Guildhall Letter Book.

One was Sir William Nechtone (it was commonplace for the complimentary title of knighthood to be bestowed on clergymen). On 29 September 1414 – the feast of St Michael and All Angels, when churchmen had dragons on their minds – he was arraigned before the Mayor (William Crowmere), the Recorder of London and the Aldermen. The offence was that he, a chaplain of St Bride in Fleet Street, had been taken in adultery with Matilda de la Mare. Other than an offence of treason, however, the civil authority could impose no penalty. Accordingly

William was handed over to his bishop for punishment, and the worthy burghers issued a proclamation that anyone in future hiring William would pay a fine to the Guildhall treasure equal to twice the hire fee. Nechtone's misdemeanour must have supplied fuel for the fire of the anti-clerical Lollards, who in 1414 met in nearby Lincoln's Inn Fields. Thirty-seven of them were hanged and seven burnt by royal command as a result of that meeting.

facing The fourteenth-century chapel

Then there was Sir John Canesby, 'the Morrowemasse prest of St Bride's, Flete Strete' whose crime was forgery, made still more grave in the eyes of the Church by his denying it 'on the word of a priest'. Canesby's offence – the year was 1423 and Fleet Street had just had its first artificial lighting by lamps hung on ropes – was too complex to unravel here; but broadly it consisted of counterfeiting a document which would oust William Gauntbrigge, a grocer, from his tenement. And so St Bride's had to find a new priest to say the Morrow Mass – the very early service designed for travelling merchants and their servants, who set off with their pack animals at the break of dawn.

Another cleric who seemed little more enthusiastic as a priest – but impeccable as a man – was Alexander Legh or Lee. In 1470 he was able to prove his loyalty by telling Edward IV of the treason of John Neville, Marquis of Montagu. The monarch was grateful. In 1471, Legh became rector of St Bride's. He resigned in 1475 and is next heard of as the King's Almoner and Ambassador Residentiary to Scotland.

Nechtone and adultery, Canesby and forgery, Legh and diplomacy. It seems a remote world. And perhaps the story of the lovely Eleanor Cobham and her procession through Fleet Street, barefooted and robed in a sheet, in 1441 brings it into focus. She had been chief lady-in-waiting to Jacquelaine, Duchess of Gloucester, and had replaced her in her husband's affections. Humphrey the Duke was in line for the throne and the delicate Henry VI seemed too slight a barrier to impede his progress. Eleanor, by now the Duke's wife, decided, so it was alleged, to resort to witchcraft to hasten her progress to a crown. Necromancy and unholy rites and wax images slowly melted were the hoped-for means. Discovery and condemnation were the result. The beautiful but discredited Eleanor made her penitential procession, carrying a 'tall candel two pounds in weight' to St Paul's. Just a few years before, in 1431, the Fleet had its first stone bridge, built by John Wels, Mayor.

No doubt some of the chantry priests looked on, meditating on the ways of the wealthy and the great. The average parson lived an unsung life. Yet the Church was also the way by which men could rise to high office and wealth. It is worth noting that Thomas Cardinal Wolsey, doyen of all ecclesiastical careerists, once held St Bride's parsonage. Without doubt the way to high office lay in escaping a country cure and getting to London – and becoming the sort of man Chaucer despised, for he

'. . . ran to London, unto seynt Poules
To seken him a chaunterie for soules.'

In 1471 one Master Henry Steven left his house in St Bride's Alley (Salisbury Court) as such a 'chaunterie' to the priests then dwelling there and their successors. Quite frequently a chantry priest had few duties other than those at the altar and was consequently able to take other employment. John Ulsthorpe, however, was one who did not approve of this, for when he founded his chantry in St Bride's Church (1433) he expressly directed that the priest chosen 'shall be looking after and helping as far as he is able at divine service there done, without having any other service'. Thus did the Rector acquire an extra curate, also additional income of 8*d.* a year, for Ulsthorpe laid it down that such a sum should be paid to the incumbent on each anniversary of his death, while each chantry priest should have 6*d.*, each stipendiary chaplain 4*d.*, clerks together and for the bells, 20*d.*, and the churchwardens, for their labour, the princely sum of 2*s.*

Ulsthorpe is one of the characters who comes out of mediaeval mists as a clear-cut figure. He was a prosperous tailor, able on his death to leave three properties in trust to Thomas Faux (Faukys), Rector of St Bride's, and to Henry Bagley and Nicholas Overton, Churchwardens. One tenement, the *Tabard*, stood in Fleet Street two doors east of Shoe Lane. The second, the *Ravyne*, was across the street close to St Bride's Church and the third, nameless, adjoined it.

In return the Rector and Wardens and their successors were to provide

> 'a chaplain, of good fame and honest conversation, to be celebrant in that same church for my soul, and for the soul of my parents and benefactors, and for the soul of Alice, late my wife, and that of Reymund my son and our other children, and for the soul of Thomas Duke and for the good estate of Isabell my wife while she shall live, and for her soul when she has departed this life, and for the souls of the faithful dead.'

Perhaps Ulsthorpe felt he had special reason for needing a chaplain in St Bride's. For Thomas Faux gave less than all his time to Fleet Street. In addition to being Rector of St Bride's, he held another benefice, was a canon of Heytesbury, a canon of Bangor, and a prebend of Swalclyff – all at the same time. But he must have had a special affection for St Bride's for he directed he should be buried there and made gifts to it. The first chaplain appointed was Thomas Rede and he held office for life. His reward was ten marks a year, payable quarterly. He was to have his chamber and dwell in the parish and he was to say Mass daily at the altar of St Anne within the church. To this altar Ulsthorpe gave a missal, a chalice and paten, a chasuble of red velvet with apparels for the principal feasts as well as two other chasubles and a processional. The celebrant was 'to have the use of my great antiphonary noted for the use of Sarum, a great gradual of the aforesaid use, a pair of phials and a paxbrede of silver'. On the anniversary of his death there were to be *placebo* and *dirige* and 'beating of bells', while he also provided for a 'candel weighing one pound to be lighted and kept burning before the Sacrament of the Altar every day and night forever'. He also left much to St Bride's for other purposes.

This is a good example of how mediaeval man was ridden with thoughts of mortality. Equally it is a good example of mortality that none of the gifts remain to the present day. The moths and rust of history have corrupted them as they have those gifts attached to twenty-six other (though not quite so wealthy) chantries which St Bride's acquired before 1500. Those who aimed at perpetuity of public remembrance have been disappointed. Perhaps William de Bathe, who died in 1375 and was buried in St Bride's, was wiser in trying to secure early release from purgatory by a crash programme. His will called for a thousand Masses to be said on his soul's behalf within a month of his decease.

above left Henry VIII (after Holbein). © *National Portrait Gallery*

above right Catherine of Aragon (attr. L. Hornebolte). © *National Portrait Gallery*

left Head from Funeral Effigy of Elizabeth I. © *London Museum*

Sir Walter Raleigh with his son. © *National Portrait Gallery*

St Bride's also had gifts for the improvement of the fabric. William Venor, a vintner and sometime Warden of the Fleet prison, was one such donor. About 1480 he either added or rebuilt the nave and side aisles, and acquired a magnificent screen (costing £160) from the Duke of Somerset's mansion in the Strand. For some reason this screen was not erected until 1557, and forty years later it was damaged by some 'wilful bodie'.

Mediaeval man's concern about his soul did not blind him to the need for concern about the welfare of his neighbour. When Mistress Isabell Ulsthorpe came to die, perhaps because she was assured that adequate chantry arrangements had already been made for her, she willed to the poor of Newgate Gaol for bread and ale £4, to those of Ludgate £3, and to those of the Fleet Prison 40 shillings; to the clerks of the prison of the Abbot of Westminster, 40 shillings; to the Hospital of Bethlehem (Bedlam) 13*s.* 4*d.*; £20 towards the marriage of

King Richard delivered to the citizens of London.
© *British Museum*

poor girls, namely to each £1; and to sixty poor shopkeepers near Fleet Street, 6*s*. 8*d*. each.

William Trippelowe was another who considered the poor (5*d*. per year to give to poor men in honour of the five joys of the Blessed Virgin was one item in his will), the prisoners, the sick and the widows. His bequests also included money for the repair of roads near London. In days when there was no public authority to undertake the task, the repair of a road or a bridge was public service indeed and held as highly meritorious.

But not everyone could afford to establish a chantry and maintain a chantry priest. Poor people wanted their souls prayed for too. The way to do it was to create a co-operative. A care for the after-life was not the only reason for the growth of the parish gilds. Indeed they were among England's earliest examples of organisations set up for the social welfare both of their own members and of other people. Today these parish gilds have been largely forgotten and the word always suggests the trade fraternities and city companies. Yet St Bride's still has its parish gild and it likes to see its origin somewhere before 1375 when Edward III (who, interestingly enough, had a daughter called Bride) confirmed by charter the Gild of St Bride. In the same year London citizens were admonished by proclamation (in both Latin and Norman French) to keep the streets clear and prevent pigs from wandering freely round the City. In 1379, Matilda Chatham left 3*s*. 4*d*. to the 'Fraternity of St Brigide', and in the following year, Henry Fabian, a stainer, left 6*s*. 8*d*. The only other reference in wills is a bequest by Simon Pettigue alias atte Nax, a cutler, who also endowed the Brotherhood of St Mary, in 1391. The first purpose of the Gild, apparently, was to maintain a light to burn before the statue of St Brigide the Virgin, in whose honour the church was founded. Towards this, the members of the gild paid 4*d*. yearly at the rate of 1*d*. a quarter. Later on the members, aided by supporters from neighbouring parishes, decided to employ a chaplain to say Mass before St Bride's statue, i.e. the high altar, and the yearly subscription was raised to 2*s*. 2*d*. to find the wax light, the chaplain's stipend and the expenses of two torches at the procession attending each member's funeral. The Gild of St Bride continued until 1545 when it was swept away by the avalanche set in motion by Henry VIII. It was restored by Cyril Armitage in the twentieth century.

At one time St Bride's had four gilds and no doubt they had a full share in the activities which made gilds such a feature of mediaeval church life. They would raise funds to extend or beautify a church, supply its candles and acquire their own chaplains, relieve brothers and sisters who fell on hard days and attend a member's funeral – and be fined if they failed to do so. They wore a special livery – as members of the Gild of St Bride do today – paid their dues and built up their resources.

The gilds had their share of misfortune. The records show, for example, how in 1348 the Black Death struck one of St Bride's gilds – named after St Mary. With many of its members swept into a plague pit, its funds languished, its altar light could not be maintained, its chaplain's stipend could not be found. When happier times came, the members agreed to a payment of 1*d*. a week toward gild funds and a bequest of a parishioner, John Wye, once more provided for a chaplain.

Just forty years after the Black Death, gilds were in trouble again. In 1381 (the year in which Wycliffe's teaching was repudiated at Oxford and a year before

The medallion of the Guild of St Bride has a Celtic cross on the flame-coloured emblem of St Bridget's perpetual fire encircled with grapes and vine leaves and surmounted by a representation of the medieval curfew bell. Designed by H. Litterick

The Tower of London, fifteenth century

Wycliffe came along Fleet Street for his trial by the 'Earthquake Council' at Blackfriars) John Ball had made his speech: 'We be all come from one father and one mother, Adam and Eve', and had drawn contrast between privilege and under-privilege. Wat Tyler and Jack Straw, the men of action, were ready and the peasants revolted. The trouble was nationwide but London was its focus. The scene in Fleet Street was grim as, joined by prisoners from the Fleet gaol which they had burned down, the mob surged towards the Temple to attack the lawyers whom they regarded as the source of much of their misery. The two forges destroyed in Fleet Street remained blackened ruins for a hundred years.

Many of the troublemakers were feudal retainers of the great houses, and discharged soldiers from the French wars. They too formed gilds and distinguished themselves with their own livery. The result was that drastic penalties were proposed against gilds of all kinds. The Wardens of St Bride's were eager to protest their innocence, and no less eager to maintain their gilds. This 'was not out of any wicked intention to maintain a confederacy. The gild had no oaths, congregations, conventions, meetings or assemblies'. They maintained that their gild had no possessions beyond the wax to be made into torches and candles; and they were six marks in arrears of payment of their chaplain. The royal antipathy to gilds had persuaded the less eager members to renege; and it seemed that their religious work must cease 'perchance to the peril of many souls'.

In the event the organisation survived, and St Bride's maintained its parish gilds until they were lost in the convulsions of the Reformation.

It was an age when the Christian faith was pre-eminently the centre of community life. The Church was beginning to display new vigour. The arrival of the Friars (London was their centre) shook a somnolent parish clergy into wakefulness.[1] 'The Friars illuminate our whole country with the bright light of their preaching and teaching . . . Oh, if your holiness could see with what devotion and humility the people run to hear from them the Word of life', wrote Robert Grosseteste to Pope Gregory in 1238. The Church supplied not only spiritual needs, but also intellectual excitement. In 1465 a major disputation at St Paul's Cross between Franciscans, Carmelites and secular clergy, attracted vast crowds who listened intently. Some laid bets about the outcome of the contest.

Other pastimes, such as archery, were less pacific. It was on the Feast of Epiphany – a holy day and so a holiday – that John de Burton of Fleet Street, using a crossbow instead of the more usual long bow, shot an arrow into the air. It hit a pear tree, glanced off and killed a spectator named William. The verdict was death by misadventure. Even more serious was a wrestling match in 1222 between the youths of Westminster and those of the City. It led to a brawl which led to a bigger brawl and so escalated. It ended in a riot. The ring leaders were executed and the City had to pay a heavy fine to the king for breaking his peace. The tension between the City and Westminster has taken many forms and Fleet Street has seen them all.

London

Brute & his men wente forth / & sawe abowte in dyuers places. where that they myghte. fynde a gode place & couenable / that they myghte

ne name/
tons. And
wyf Gen
worthy of
lid Lotrin
thyrd La
ne in the
tyme that
re he mad
holde. An
wel belou
tes sones
gyder. An
all the lo
he fonde
tayne/ th
londe B
ne. And l
name/ þ
Brute fo
de the we
his other
after his
lys. And
yere/ as

4. The Sixteenth Century

'In the beginning was the Word, and the Word was with God, and the Word was God.' John the Evangelist began his supreme statement about God not by talking of his love or even of his power, but by asserting that he communicates. Jesus commanded his followers to hear that divine Word and take it to the ends of the earth. That the Church should be a major user of words on paper is an ineluctable response to its own inner calling. Hence there developed a relationship between the printer and the Church quite unlike that between the Church and any other trade. In mediaeval times you could be a goldsmith or buy his goods, a tailor or the wearer of a suit, without being able to read. But to be a printer or a printer's customer, reading was essential. And the Church had a near-monopoly of literacy, not because the Church refused to teach reading to others, but because most of those who learned the art became 'clerks in holy orders'.

This unique relationship of Church and printer has left many marks on the industry, which survive even in a secularised twentieth century. In almost every other trade you will find shop stewards as agents of the relevant Trade Union; but not in printing or any of its ancillaries. There they are styled 'Fathers of the Chapel'.

According to Joseph Moxon's classic *Mechanick Exercises* of 1683-4:

> 'Every *Printing-house* is by the Custom of Time out of mind, called a *Chappel*: and the Oldest Freeman is *Father of the Chappel*. I suppose the stile was originally conferred upon it by the courtesie of some great Churchman, or men (doubtless when Chappels were in more veneration than of late years they have been here in *England*) who for the Books of Divinity that proceeded from a *Printing-house*, gave it the reverend title of *Chappel*.'[1]

Moxon also felt that a 'chappel' ought to attract the right kind of respect by means of the penalties imposed for any breach of its laws, the appropriate term being 'solace'.

Woodcut of London from *The Chronicles of England*, printed by Wynkyn de Worde, 1497. © *London Museum*

William Caxton, 1422–91

'1. Swearing in the *Chappel*, a *Solace*.
2. Fighting in the *Chappel*, a *Solace*.
3. Abusive Language, or giving the Lye in the *Chappel*, a *Solace*.
4. To be drunk in the *Chappel*, a *Solace* . . .'

Any man failing to observe these rules became an 'excommunicated person', also known as a 'Brimstone', in which state he had no redress for any mischief done him.

Moxon was hardly a man who would be predisposed to favour any ecclesiastical traditions. He had spent some years of infancy in Holland with a father who had gone there in order to print Puritan, Independent, anti-Establishment episcopacy-defying 'Libellous books', as Laud called them. The word 'chappel' can hardly be attributed to any legend that the first English user of moveable type had his press in part of a consecrated building. Not that such a thing was impossible, with consecrated buildings used as they were in those days, but because researches have made it clear that Caxton worked in an outlying tenement which belonged to Westminster Abbey and not in the church itself.

Of *Depositio Cornuti Typographici*, 'a mirthful play performed at the Confirmation of a Journeyman' (printer), a reviewer wrote:

> 'When apprenticeship had ended, the young workman was called a "Cornute", a horned brute beast who had to undergo the ritual cleansing of this ceremony before taking his place as a journeyman. The deposition ceremony has ancient antecedents and indeed it resembles in certain particulars the rites of primitive tribes – the apprentice is treated roughly with an axe, a plane, and a saw, he has a tooth "pulled", and his face is daubed with black soapsuds. The mock-religious nature of the rite – the apprentice is "baptised" and renamed by the "priest" who, after hearing his confession, finally admits him to membership in the Printers' Guild.'[2]

Printing sprang from the side of the Church and the Church was its bulwark. Thus the first two European printers to set up a press outside Germany chose a Benedictine abbey (Subiaco) as their site. The first printed advertisement, not only for English publishing but apparently for any product in England, was designed to sell a highly technical *ecclesiastical* book. Nor is the chapel the only ecclesiastical word adopted by printers, who 'justify' a line to get it all square in its place and to fill up the space neatly. Theologically, justification is getting all square with God and having all one's spaces filled up with Christ. Again, 'font' or 'fount' is a word as familiar to printers as to parsons. When type is distributed after use, it often first goes into 'hell-boxes' which recalls doctrines of purgatory. And everyone has heard of a printer's devil, the one with the ink-smudged face and hands – also called, by Moxon, a 'spirit'. If that devil was to become an apprentice he was first given the status of 'deacon'. Perhaps most intriguing of all, in terms of etymology, are monks (splotches of black ink on a page) and friars (patches which are left white because the ink failed to take). Is there an echo of the habit and the tonsure there? In the light of all this, it seems appropriate that when a building was first used for printing, the Father of the Chapel was called upon to 'consecrate' it. The Church connection was also something more than a matter of vocabulary. In writing of the customs of the chapel, Moxon

Here begynnyth the treatyse of fysshynge wyth an Angle.

Salamon in his parablys ſayth that a good ſpyryte makyth a flourynge aege / that is a fayre aege & a longe. And ſyth it is ſoo: I aſke this queſtyon / whiche ben the meanes & the cauſes that enduce a man in to a mery ſpyryte.: Truly to my beſte dyſcrecõn it ſemeth good dyſportes & honeſt gamys in whom a man Ioyeth wythout ony repentaunce after. Thenne foloweth it ẏ gode dyſportes & honeſt games ben cauſe of mannys fayr aege & longe life. And therfore now woll I choſe of foure good diſportes & honeſte gamys / that is to wyte: of huntynge: hawkynge: fyſſhynge: & foulynge. The beſte to my ſymple dyſcrecõn whyche is fyſſhynge: callyd Anglynge wyth a rodde: and a lyne

left Wynkyn de Worde

right The Book of St Albans, printed by Wynkyn de Worde, 1496. © *British Museum*

makes it clear that the annual feast must be preceded by a church parade compulsory for everyone. No doubt they went to some trouble in choosing 'the Divine (whom the Stewards before ingag'd to Preach them a Sermon) and his Reader'.

When printers began to get together, therefore, they looked for their own religious centre and, as far as England was concerned, St Bride's was a natural focus for reasons to which we shall return. Here they would have had their own particular chapel and, by constant familiarity, the word chapel got transferred from the place where they met to their concept of togetherness.

So much for what might be called the philosophy of relationship. Now to the historic facts. To the European, Johann Gensfleisch zum Gutenberg is the 'father of printing' and his child was born in 1440 though there are those who contest this judgement and give credit to Waldvogel in Avignon or Coster in Haarlem or Brito in Bruges. Print historians will know that the Chinese were able to block-print nearly a thousand years before, and the precisionist will know that 'printing' is a complex word covering a variety of processes. Yet no one can deny to Gutenberg the flash of inspiration which enabled him to synthesise many bits of craftmanship, to make possible the production of infinite numbers of movable type units and secure the reproduction of their images an infinity of times. Maybe paper had been known for centuries, maybe the winepress which Gutenberg used had been known to the Romans, maybe a multitude of men had impressed wood blocks on some readable surface. Gutenberg joined them all together to make mass communications possible; moreover the use of interchangeable parts pointed the way to mass production in other industries.

Gutenberg had flair, but he also lived at the right moment. Europe was hungry for reading. Men's minds were waking. The half-century which followed the installation of Gutenberg's press is bright with names like Donatello, Fra Angelico, Fra Lippo Lippi, Leonardo da Vinci, Verocchio, Michelangelo, Dürer, Francois Villon, Nicholas of Cusa, Thomas à Kempis, John Bessarion, Thomas Malory. Such intellectual energy demanded communication. By the time Gutenberg had been dead fifteen years, printing presses had been set up in every country of western Christendom and they were already making their contribution to internationalism – though at the same time paying a curious tribute to ancient conservatism in that, because the customer demanded it so, printers did all they could to suggest their products were handwritten.

'Germany's most important single contribution to civilisation' spread fast, and the Church was prominent along the lines of communication. 'The church, and especially the monastic orders with their far-flung connections, provided easy ways of transmitting the art regardless of political frontiers.'[3] It was not that printers were unusually religious. It was rather that they were good business

The coffin on the left, discovered during excavations, is believed to be that of Wynkyn de Worde

An English Printing Office, 1619

men, while the Church not only had a consuming appetite for print, but was also powerful enough to finance printing and ensure its distribution. Thus print-shops were often found alongside monasteries. In Italy, for example, Subiaco was its first point and, to generations who regard Torquemada, the Grand Inquisitor, as the arch suppressor of free thought, it is of interest that the abbey where the press was set up was under the supervision of that redoubtable cardinal.

The abbeys were foci, so it was natural that the precincts of Westminster should be the place that William Caxton chose. And natural, too, that the first modern advertisement in the English language should be a Caxton poster urging 'ony man, spiritual or temporal' to buy a 'good chepe' and 'wel and truly correct' festival calendar according to the Sarum use. The year was 1477. And the poster showed an instinct for self-preservation by including the words 'Please do not tear'. Caxton, of course, did not confine himself to religious books. Romances and educational works came from his press. And he also deserves no small reputation as a writer of prose. He also had something of the character of the moralist in every generation in that he had serious doubts about youth:

> 'I see that the children ben borne within the sayd cyte encrese and prouffyte not like their faders and olders; but for the mooste parte, after that they ben comeyn to theyr perfight yeres of discretion and rypnes of age, kno well that theyre faders haue lefte to them grete quilite of goodes, yet scarcely among ten two thrive. O blessed Lord! when I remember this, I am al abashed; I cannot judge the cause.'

Caxton died in 1491 and his business went to his assistant Wynkyn who added to his name his place of birth, Worth in Alsace (he sometimes wrote it Wynkyn de Worth). Wynkyn de Worde 'excelled in quantity rather than in quality, for by 1535, the year of his death, he had published about 800 items . . . about two-fifths of his output was intended for the use of grammar school boys . . . he may justly be called the first publisher who actually made the schoolbook department the financial basis of his business.'[4]

Caxton was first and foremost a merchant but he was also a scholar, a gentleman and something of an aesthete. He could afford to be, for his cloth business was prosperous. Wynkyn de Worde had no means of income except from his printing press. But he was an entrepreneur and he had a native commercial wit. He consequently followed the formula which has always been good business practice. He took his goods to the customer – beside St Bride's.

Wynkyn looked at London and saw that around St Bride's had grown a heavy concentration of the ecclesiastics who had a monopoly of literacy. The prelates thus congregated were Wynkyn's magnet. It was because the Church was there that the press came to Fleet Street and Fleet Street has retained a lively folk memory of the fact.

If Caxton was the father of English printing, Wynkyn was the progenitor of mass communications. He owned and occupied two houses at the sign of the Sun in Fleet Street, one as his dwelling and the other as his printing works, probably with a shopfront bookstore or a stall outside it. St Bride's church, beside which he set up his press, became the godparent of a cultural and sociological revolution. In its nave Wynkyn's bones were buried. The Gild of St Bride was directed, in his will, to attend his funeral in their russet gowns. To that Gild he left 10*s*. to ease his soul's passage to peace, to St Bride's poor he bequeathed a yearly sum of

Caxton type

facing William Lily.

20*s.*, and he gave £36 to buy land whose profits should maintain an obit for his soul.

Wynkyn's tithe rent in Fleet Street was 66*s.* 8*d.* – no small sum. Business must have been good. But then, in addition to its resident luminaries, Fleet Street would have been a regular thoroughfare for men like Thomas Linacre, who founded the Royal College of Physicians at his house a hundred yards away; Colet who became Dean of St Paul's in 1505 and who in 1510 founded St Paul's School with the image of Jesus in the classroom and its miraculous draught of 153 pupils; William Lily, master at St Paul's School and author of a Latin Grammar which was a best-seller for three centuries; Thomas More, who was born in the City, read law at Lincoln's Inn, and whose *Utopia* is one of the few books which gave a new and permanent word to the English language.

Wynkyn therefore had plenty of distinguished customers. But he also catered for the mass market and his wealth is a sobering reminder that mass production need not involve quality. Indeed, he can justly be accused of carelessness – such as, for example, reprinting Caxton's *The Horse, the Shepe and the Ghoos* from a copy which had a leaf missing and, by failing to notice the omission, making nonsense of the whole. He quite cheerfully used the same woodcut more than once in the same book in the conviction that any illustration was better than none. Indeed, he went further. He had a series of blocks of men and women with a blank space left so that any appropriate name could be inserted. Thus Caiaphas could easily become Joseph and vice versa. Misprints, too, seemed to matter little to him. 'Get the paper out' was his motto and Fleet Street has never despised him for it. Like contemporary Fleet Street, he produced volumes on nearly every subject and for every class of person. He was not squeamish about sensation. Wynkyn's own title, 'Father of Fleet Street', has more than a merely geographical connotation.

H. S. Bennett lists 829 Wynkyn publications – a truly phenomenal number, for it represents some 15 per cent of all known works printed before 1557 – and sums up his publishing policy:

> 'Briefly it was to give the public a variety of books on subjects known to have a popular appeal – religious and homiletic, practical and instructional – and to issue these in easily handled volumes likely to attract readers who would recoil from large and expensive volumes.'[5]

Wynkyn, then, was the publisher who anticipated our great mass circulation papers in seeing that money was to be made by catering for the common man. While Caxton had to find a royal patron, Wynkyn relied on his own business acumen – although in 1508, when Richard Pynson became the King's Printer (at a salary of 40*s.* a year, less than Wynkyn's rent, though it subsequently became £4), Wynkyn insured against the future by securing the appointment of printer to the Countess of Richmond, the King's mother. Perhaps the rivalry was a reality. Certainly Wynkyn and Pynson were the giants. Between them, in the first decade of the sixteenth century, they were responsible for 70 per cent of all books printed in England; in the next decade, 73 per cent, and in the third 55 per cent.

To return to the comparison with Caxton. His works were expensive. Wynkyn published some of his for as little as a penny for a popular market. Caxton, the 'fine art printer', established the techniques of his craft not least in order to publish a book according to his own taste. Wynkyn did all he could to match

William Lilly

First master of Saint Pauls school

Henry VII and Henry VIII (attributed to Holbein). © *National Portrait Gallery*

Oliver Cromwell.
© *National Portrait Gallery*

John Douswell engraving, 1753

Model of a frost fair on the Thames. © *London Museum*

everyone's taste. It was the contrast of the artist and creator with the technician and the populariser.

Wynkyn de Worde arrived in Fleet Street in the year 1500. One reason for the move derived from a family quarrel. Caxton's daughter Elizabeth had found her husband, Gerard Croppe, intolerable and gained a deed of separation from him in 1496. Croppe seems to have been particularly hostile to Wynkyn and instituted a series of proceedings against him. Westminster therefore acquired unpleasant associations for Wynkyn. Besides this, his wife Elizabeth had died there in 1498, and his son in 1500. In such a situation, he could well have wished to make a fresh start elsewhere. Again, a building in an abbey's precincts big enough to suit a fine art printer would hardly have satisfied an energetic and ambitious business man. Wynkyn wanted elbow room. Another attraction was the presence of bookbinders – for whom Shoe Lane had long been a centre – and who in turn relied on the tanners and leather workers, all of them customers of the butchers of Smithfield. Above all, as explained, Wynkyn moved to Fleet Street because he had the good sense to go where the customer was. The monks of Westminster needed but few books (perhaps fifty or so); and they were few and relatively poor compared with the number of clergy to be found between St Paul's and Temple Bar. Furthermore, the great humanist surge was under way. Knowledge was news, and, through books, becoming accessible to people of moderate means.

As a body, however, the clergy supplied the best market, for they were all literate; and they were becoming aware that the long serenity of the Middle Ages was over. The Lollards had already made a broad impact, while Colet and Erasmus were influencing Oxford, and indeed probably strolled together in Fleet Street when Colet was Dean of St Paul's. Within a few years – in 1521 – Henry VIII

Model of mouth of Fleet River as seen from Baynard's Castle about 1550. Made by J. B. Thorp. © *London Museum*

was to secure for himself and his successors the title of *Fidei Defensor* from Pope Leo X, by refuting Luther in his *Assertio septem sacramentorum*. Our coins have commemorated the fact ever since. Henry's words, incidentally, are so violent that no printer or publisher today would risk using them. Having no printing devices to indicate emphasis, the lines were broken up lest any of Henry's loving subjects missed some of the vitriol:

> 'So wretched
> So vyle
> So detestable
> provokynge man to myschefe encoragyng the world to syn
> preaching an unsaciat lyberte
> and finally
> so farre against all honesty
> virtue and reason
> that never was there erst any heretyke so farre voyde of
> all grace and wyt that durst for shame speke them.'

But Henry did not concede to others the same freedom of speech as he enjoyed. His anti-Lutheranism, for example, sounded an echo in Fleet Street in 1524 when Wynkyn de Worde was one of those warned by Bishop Tunstall against importing Lutheran literature into England. Nor was he free to print whatever he liked. To quote James Moran's monograph:

> 'In 1525, he was again summoned before the bishop with John Gough to answer a charge of having published a work called *The Image of Love*. De Worde confessed that he was one of those present in the previous year and that since that date he had printed *The Image of Love*, which was alleged to contain heresy, and had sent sixty copies to the nuns of Syon and had sold as many more. The two men were warned not to sell any more and to get back those they had sold.'[6]

The art of printing had already shown itself capable of upsetting the Establishment. Not only were books being printed – to acquire them had become *de rigeur*. Even the most unacademic felt constrained to read at least one book to find out what was going on. It is little wonder that the booksellers settled in numbers around St Paul's Cathedral and down Ludgate Hill to Fleet Street. And little wonder that Caxton's press soon had rivals. One of them was Johannes Lettou (of Lithunia) who came to the City of London in 1480. He was joined by William de Machlinia who described himself as living near 'Flete-Bridge' and printed there the Bull of Pope Innocent VIII granting dispensation for the marriage of Henry VII and Elizabeth of York. One of Machlinia's few titles is a delight: *A passing gode lityll boke necessary and behoveful agenst the Pestilence*. It was written by a Swedish bishop. What little he and the others printed was not done in Fleet Street proper, so – to quote James Moran – they 'cannot challenge de Worde either in the geographical or the metaphorical sense as "Father of Fleet Street".'

By the time Wynkyn was established, competition had begun in Fleet Street. There was the Frenchman Guillaume Faques, anglicised to William Fawkes and appointed King's Printer in 1503, an office in which he was succeeded in 1508 by

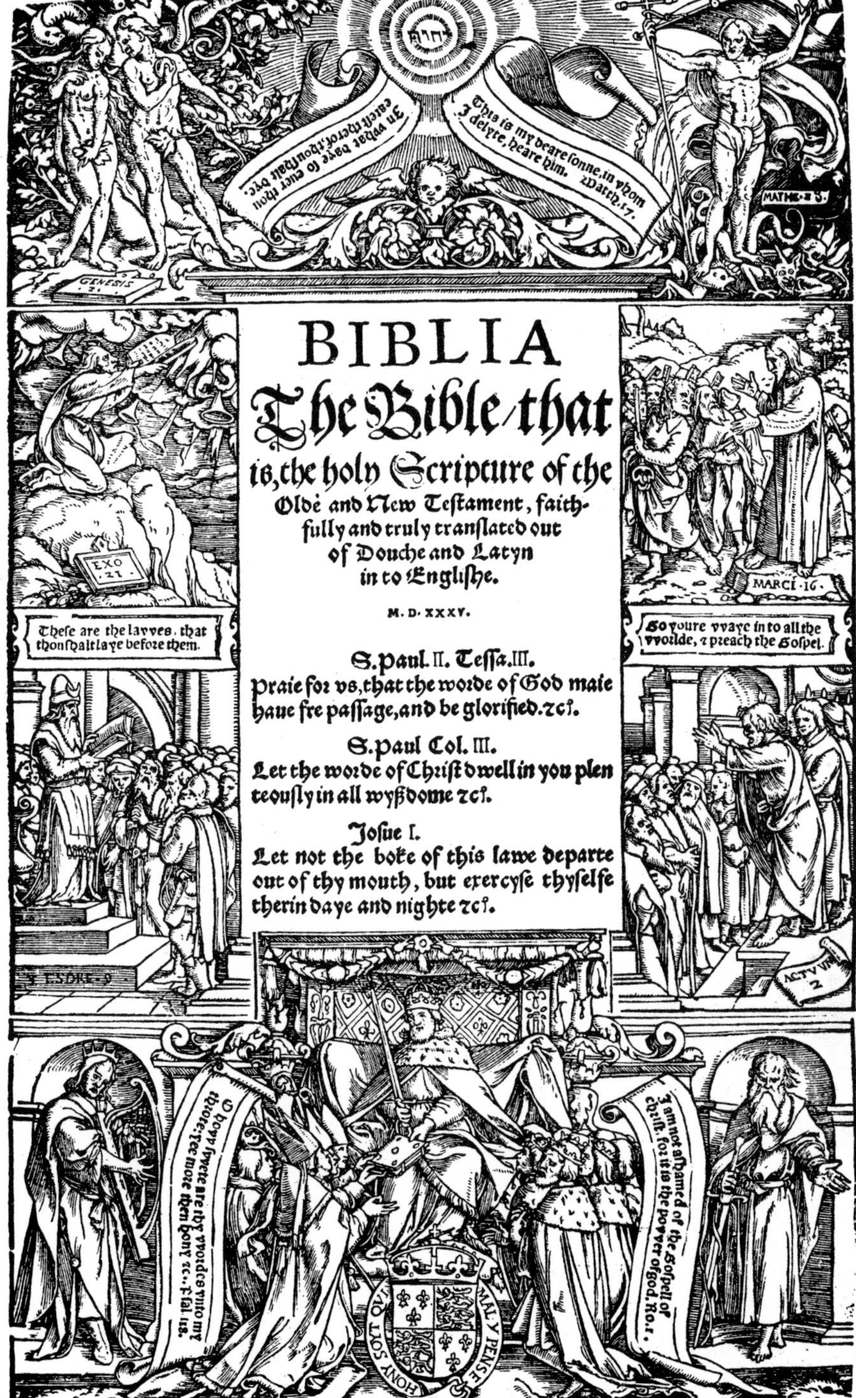

BIBLIA
The Bible/that
is, the holy Scripture of the
Olde and New Testament, faithfully and truly translated out
of Douche and Latyn
in to Englishe.

M.D.XXXV.

S.Paul. II. Tessa. III.
Praie for vs, that the worde of God maie
haue fre passage, and be glorified. &c.

S.Paul Col. III.
Let the worde of Christ dwell in you plen
teously in all wysdome &c.

Josue I.
Let not the boke of this lawe departe
out of thy mouth, but exercyse thyselfe
therin daye and nighte &c.

Title page of first printed English Bible (Coverdale's translation), 1535. © *British Museum*

William Tyndale. © *Bodleian Library*

the great Richard Pynson, a Norman by birth. His place of business was at the sign of St George where Chancery Lane joins Fleet Street. It was Pynson who printed the *Assertio* which brought Henry VIII the papal honour. He also printed a very fine Sarum Missal for Cardinal Morton (its borders and initials include punning allusions to the name with MOR surmounting a tun, or barrel), and the first English translation of the *Imitatio Christi*. He was the first printer to use roman type. Wynkyn died in 1535. His premises were taken over by John Byddell, one of his assistants and an executor of his will, who also called himself John Salisbury. He in his turn was succeeded by Whitchurch.

Wynkyn, Fawkes and Pynson, together with lesser fry, produced a wide range of titles, predominantly religious; and yet they did not print a single Bible. For Henry's thinking which made him *Fidei Defensor* also caused him generally to oppose English translations of the Scriptures, though he was not inflexible about this. The earliest *printed* English Bibles (Wycliffe's were hand-written) were printed in Germany (ironically, Tyndale's was printed on presses belonging to devout Roman Catholics). Coverdale's Bible (the first complete English version) was printed in Antwerp in 1536.

> 'Its revised edition would have been published in Paris, had not the French inquisition intervened and forced the printer to flee across the Channel. The Great Bible, as it came to be called, was thus finished in London in 1539 after Thomas Cromwell had succeeded in acquiring the Paris press and matrices. Seven editions were called for in two years. Owing to the king's vaccillating policy, its printer, Richard Grafton, was thus actually commissioned by Henry to publish a work for which Tyndale had, only two and a half years earlier, been burned at the stake.'[7]

Most English Bibles were circulated in secret though it was possible for an educated man to get episcopal permission to have a copy, provided it did not carry the heretical Lollard preface. Tyndale, when in Germany, had smuggled leaves of his English Bible into England in bales of wool. He had compounded his crime, in the view of conservative Englishmen, by adding his own strongly Protestant notes to the text. So, betrayed by a friend, he went to the scaffold and his last words were memorable 'Lord, open the King of England's eyes'. The prayer was less necessary than he realised, for Henry, as well as Cranmer and Thomas Cromwell, were already set on producing an English Bible; and Coverdale, whose Psalms have become part of our language through the Book of Common Prayer, was already at work. His English Bible, dedicated to the King, was complete a year before Tyndale died. In 1536 Henry issued a decree for the provision of a Bible in Latin and English in every parish. The difficulty lay in reaching agreement about a translation.

For about eighteen months in 1523-4 Tyndale had actually lived in Fleet Street, where he was a chaplain at St Dunstan's. In two thousand years the Street has played many roles in English history. The conduit opposite St Bride's, with its image of St Christopher, patron of wayfarers, on top, its 'sweet chiming bells' and its internal mechanism capable of playing a hymn, was one of London's wonders. Never has it been nearer the centre of the stage than in the formative years when Henry VIII was on the throne. Down Fleet Street went the new king, joyful as any bridegroom, with Katherine, former sister-in-law and now his new

MARTYR
AVLA MAGD:
Hac ut luce tuas dispergam Roma tenebras
Sponte extorris ero Sponte Sacrificium
REFERT HÆC TABELLA QVOD SOLVM POTVIT ARS GVILHELMI TYNDAIL., HVIVS OLIM AVLÆ ALVMNI, SIMVL
ET ORNAMENTI, QVI POST FÆLICES PVRIORIS THEOLOGIÆ PRIMITIAS HIC DEPOSITAS ANTVEPIÆ IN NO=
VO TESTAMENTO NEC NON PENTATEVCHO IN VERNACVLAM TRANSFERENDO OPERAM NAVAVIT, ANGLIS
SALVTIFERAM, VT INDE NON IMMERITO ANGLIÆ APOSTOLVS AVDIRET MARTYRIO WILFORDÆ PROPE
CORONATVS A° 1536. VIR SI VEL ADVERSARIO (PROCVRATORI NEMPE IMPERTORIS GENERALI) CREDAMVS PERDOCTVS PIVS ET BONVS.

Queen Catherine pleading with Henry before the two papal legates

queen in 1509. And perhaps it was the crowds drawn by such an occasion who helped Wynkyn make the year the record for the whole of his life in terms of output. They could not have known that Katherine would also be a record holder – as Henry's longest-lasting Queen. One of the places where she went shopping was at the sign of The Coppe, Fleet Street.

Down Fleet Street, nearly twenty years later, went two Cardinals, Wolsey and Campeggio. The latter, ordained after the death of his wife who had borne him five children, had been made Bishop of Salisbury in 1525 and so, like Wolsey, had a house nearby. He was probably glad of it for, racked with gout, he had to be carried in a chair (of crimson velvet), the poles supported by four attendants. 'I wish', wrote Gerado Moeza to the Marchioness of Mantua, 'that you could have seen the Cardinals abreast, one on his mule, the other in his chair, the rain falling so fast that we were all drenched.'

The weather would have reduced the crowds. In any case, probably few people knew that they were going to discuss with the king whether she was his legal wife or not. 'The 8th of November', says Stow, 'in his great chamber, he [Henry] made unto them an oration touching his marriage with Queen Katherine.'[8] And none of those watching crowds could have known that Ann Boleyn, decked in splendour, would in due course go down the same Fleet Street for her moment of radiance in 1533, the year in which she was both bride and mother.

Alongside St Bride's churchyard wall Wolsey and Campeggio went. The unhappy Katherine, symbolically but apparently not deliberately, received them with a red skein around her neck, for she was at work with her maidens. The poignant scene followed and history was being made. To that same Palace, on Sunday afternoon, 8 November 1528, Henry summoned the Lord Mayor, the Aldermen and the Privy Council to tell them how, loving Katherine as he did, he was yet forced to put her away for the nation's good – a brilliant political manoeuvre.

Henry VIII was a pivot of English history whether for churchman, parliamentarian, naval officer, or for the nation as a whole. Enormously gifted, he lived

The Coronation procession of Anne Boleyn to Westminster Abbey (from a drawing by David Roberts in the Tyrrell Collection)

The Bridewell Palace

with delirious excitement, and much of his life centred in the Royal Palace of Bridewell, which lay just below St Bride's on the right bank of the Fleet – extending to the Thames, and including a Royal Wardrobe with its own royal bridge across the Fleet. According to Stow, the first building of any repute on this site was a tower or castle belonging to the king as far back as 1087.

> 'Mauritius, then Bishop of London, began the foundation of a new church, to which King William (the Conqueror) gave the choice stones from the castle yard, so as to enclose and form the precincts of the new church. The castle being thus dismantled, stood in the place where now standeth the house called Bridewell. But, notwithstanding the destruction of the said castle, the house remained large, so that kings of the realm long after were lodged there, and kept their courts.'[9]

About the year 1515, when Wolsey became Cardinal and Lord Chancellor, it seems that Henry VIII determined on its restoration. Then in 1522, wishing to

Thomas Wolsey

provide Charles V with impressive hospitality, he saw to it that the Palace was made habitable. It was in 1528 that Cardinals Wolsey and Campeggio went to Bridewell to discuss the matter of Queen Katherine.

Master Nicholas Ridley, Bishop of London and destined to be a Protestant martyr, appealed to the young King Edward VI for the conversion of Bridewell into a place of correction. In 1553, only two days before his death, Edward demoted it into a chameleon combination of prison, hospital and school.[10] The surrender of Bridewell as a royal palace was indeed a charitable act, but it was also common sense. In the first place, English monarchs have never chosen to live for long in their capital. But more cogent still, the capital had still failed to find an effective cure for the ancient stench of the Fleet. 'Universally death is in London, and most about the Temple and Fleet Street', wrote a Mr Hales in 1532; and 'The plague increases in London, especially about Fleet Street', wrote Sir Thomas Audley, Lord Keeper. When the Thames and the Fleet were completely frozen over in 1536, the relief to the nose must have been at least as great as the pleasure of skating.

Bridewell, in its early days, was primarily for those of evil habits. 'Great care was to be taken that vagrants not belonging to the City were to depart for their place of birth or last abode. If they returned in a roguish manner, they were to be whipped at a cart's tail. If any escaped from Bridewell, they were also to be whipped when caught, and, on a repetition of the offences, they were to have their ears boxed.' They were days when punishment was administered with a vicious enthusiasm. A woman in Bridewell, for example, found the punishment for a scolding was sixty stripes. One of the sights of London was to visit Bridewell to see the public flogging of a prostitute. And the place was certainly used for such instruments of torture as manacles which kept the victim's head almost touching his feet.

> 'He is a traitor!
> I'll manacle thy neck and feet together.'

says Prospero in *The Tempest*. Shakespeare could have been to see what went on in Bridewell, and called in on his way to the Globe theatre. Or, if tradition is right, he could have called in on the way to his duties as Reader for the Hand and Star press in Fleet Street.

At St Bride's nearby, the clergy knew in their own lives the startling times through which the nation was passing: for example, Nicholas Myles, Vicar 1507-29, whose end appears to be his only claim to fame. He is apparently the unfortunate subject of a terse note by Stow in his *Summary* dated 16 May 1529: 'A man was hanged in chains in Finsburie field for murdering doctor Miles'.

Why Nicholas Myles should have so suffered remains a mystery. It could not have been because he was a wealthy man worth a robber's while. He was, as far as stipend went, poorer than his predecessors, for in 1505 the Abbot and Convent of Westminster gained permission from William Wareham, Bishop of London, to appropriate the benefice and all its rights. Technically Westminster Abbey became the rector and the incumbents became vicars. Letters Patent granted by Henry VII and solemnly confirmed by Colet, who in that year became Dean of St Paul's, and one Peter de Ayala as Protonotary Apostolic acting for the Holy See, left the Abbey with a financial balance – for the rectorial tithes were worth

Bridewell squalor

£26 13*s.* 4*d.* a year while the stipend assigned to the vicar was £16. The documents state that the money thus gained was for the worship of God in the monastery, for the entertainment of its guests and for the general relief of its burdens. Four centuries later, in 1954, the City of London Churches Act denominated St Bride's a parish church and its incumbent once more became a rector.

Where Nicholas Myles lived is not known. Certainly it was not in St Bride's rectory, for the monks of Westminster turned the building to far more lucrative use. First they leased it to Sir Richard Empson, Henry VII's revenue officer. Empson had already acquired from the Knights Hospitallers their 'orchard and twelve gardens', and the rectory must have rounded off a nice little property with ground probably running down to the bank of the Thames. In 1508 he sublet the rectory to Thomas Lucy of Charlecot, Warwickshire, who married Empson's daughter, Elizabeth. (The magistrate before whom Shakespeare was brought for trespass in his deer park, the original of Justice Shallow, was their descendant.)

But the following year the new king, Henry VIII, had Empson executed, taking his estates. And on 9 October 1509, paying an oblique compliment to St Bride's,

facing Philip II of Spain and Mary of England

he gave the rectory lease to no less a personage than Cardinal Wolsey. It was from 'this poor house of mine at Bridewell' that Wolsey wrote to Thomas Lord Howard, the Lord High Admiral, telling him he had supplied anchors to the fleet and telling him to be 'sparing of the victuals'.

The dissolution of the monastery of Westminster in 1540 made small difference to St Bride's. Since the Abbot became the first Dean of the new cathedral (as it was at first designated), the appointment of the vicar was left with Westminster, where it still remains. The first nominee under the new regime was the able but ill-fated John Cardmaker, who for some reason also used the alias of Taylor. Taylor's ministry had started as a friar in Cambridge. On his appointment in 1543 he 'renounced the presumed jurisdiction and power of the Bishop of Rome'. To his St Bride's title he duly added those of Canon and Chancellor of Wells Cathedral and Reader in St Paul's Cathedral. His sermons, laced with acceptable anti-Roman fire, won wide approval. And he showed his Protestant passion by stripping St Bride's of its five chantries and dissolving its Gild of St Mary, leaving the King's Visitors to remove the ornaments.

'Cardmaker', says the London Survey Committee's monograph on St Bride's, 'seems to have found the work of spoliation a congenial task, and he was among the purchasers of some of the vestments (as was Berthelet the King's Printer). From this time, Puritan views gained strength in the congregation and controversy became more popular than ceremonial.'[11]

Some of the large sums of money realised in the sale of these treasures went to the repair of the church and some to charity.

Cardmaker (who married a widow) was a man of his day, but his misfortune was that his day changed too quickly. With Mary back on the throne his prospects darkened. Disguised as a merchant he tried to escape overseas, but was

Wolsey surrenders the Great Seal

ETANNIS REGNO PH
LIPPI ET MARIE DEI GRA
REGIS & REGINE A H F VRIVS
G ET H FIDEI DEFEN SO
ARCHIDVCV AV DV B M ZBR
COVNTV H F ET QVASTI CQVINTO

caught and committed to the Fleet Prison. The Queen's mercy was offered to him if he would recant what she deemed his heresies. Cardmaker, after playing for time, stoutly refused. He was convicted. His body was added to the Smithfield fires and his name to Foxe's *Book of Martyrs*. They were perilous days for a man with convictions in either direction. Within little more than a decade Bishops Gardiner, Hooper and Bonner saw the inside of the Fleet Prison and attained martyrs' crowns. Cardmaker was not the only St Bride's parson to suffer martyrdom. John Bradford followed in his footsteps, after arrest on a Sunday afternoon in his lodgings under the sign of the Spread Eagle (now 184 Fleet Street), and transfer to the Tower. Cardmaker's predecessor, William Saxey, had also died a violent death, in prison for an offence under the Six Articles Act, by which, in 1539, Henry VIII tried to prevent the spread of Reformation beliefs and practices.

It was in the same year as Cardmaker's martyrdom that a printer's death was honoured more than a parson's – perhaps in response to the injunction in his will (which left 20*s*. to St Bride's): 'Myne funeralles to be done in such wise as for my degree shall be thought mete'. Thomas Berthelet, King's Printer from 1529 to 1547, was among the greatest of his craft; and his fellows acknowledged it in a memorial service different in style but similar in intention to those conducted at St Bride's today. Berthelet's shop was at the sign of the Lucretia Romana in Fleet Street, and it was under his shopfront stall that, on 7 December 1536 John de Serrate, Chamberlain to the French Ambassador, hid when a posse of Englishmen attacked the Frenchman's retinue. Serrate was lucky. He suffered only a dagger cut in the sleeve. A colleague of his was left dead in St Bride's churchyard. Berthelet's wishes about his own funeral were fully honoured and in his parish church,

> '. . . was buried Master Berthelet, Esquire and printer to King Henry; and was buried with pennon and with cote-amour and four dozens of escutcheons and two white branches and four gilt candlesticks, and many priests and clerks and many mourners and all the crafts of printers, booksellers and all stationers.'[12]

Berthelet, who paid £212 10*s*. 0*d*. into the King's treasury for his properties, was the printer of the first complete edition of William Lily's Latin Grammar (1540), used by St Paul's, Eton, and most of the public schools well into the nineteenth century.

Garish funerals were regarded as a symbol of status, as is shown by the following quotation from the diary of Henry Machyn, a merchant tailor who specialised in furnishing funerals,

> 'The first day of September (1562) was bered in the parryche of Sant Brydes in Fletstrett, Master Hulsun, screvener of London and Master Heywood's depute, and one of the masturs of Brydwell; and ther wher all the masturs of Brydwell with gren stayffes in their handes, and the children of the hospetell at ys berehyng; and ther was mony mornars in blake, and Master Crowley dyd pryche; and ther was grett ryngyng as ever was hard.'[13]

It seems that there were few visible differences between a funeral in 1555 and one in 1562. Yet, in the eyes of the State at least, England's religion had changed radically. Berthelet was buried during Mary's fanatical but unsuccessful attempt

The St Andrew Undershaft Memorial to John Stowe

to re-unite England with Rome. Master Hulsun's rites would have been consistent with the Act of Uniformity and its appended Prayer Book passed in 1559, shortly after Elizabeth had reached the throne.

It was during Mary's reign that St Bride's had one of its many physical changes – a new rood screen. To quote John Stow (who took time off from tailoring to become London's most famous historian):

> 'The partition betwixt the olde worke and the new, sometime prepared as a screne to be set up in the hall of the Duke of Somerset's house at Strand, was bought for eight score pound and set up in the yeare 1557 . . . One wilfull bodie began to spoyle and breake the same in the year 1596, but was by the High Commissioner forced to make it up againe, and so it resteth.'[14]

It probably continued to rest until either removed by the Puritans, or destroyed by the Great Fire of London in 1666.

Publicly branded a bastard when she was sixteen, emotionally thwarted, spiritually at variance with the England of the time, politically given to Continental entanglements which her insular people deplored, Mary had no wish for freedom of speech. Her device for press control was an interesting one. She issued a Charter to the Stationers' Company and gave its liverymen a monopoly over all print – though, printers being ingenious and enterprising, the monopoly was never really effective.

The first mention of a stationer occurs in the thirteenth century. By 1357 there was a craft gild in London to which scriveners (those who copied books) and limners (those who illustrated them) belonged. But not until 1557 did the Stationers' Company gain the Charter whereby only its freemen could exercise the art of printing without royal permission. It was then that they began a Register in which were recorded all books printed by their members. Such recording gave the printer an exclusive copyright and made 'Entered at Stationers' Hall' a mystical phrase, which carried weight until the Copyright Act of 1911 deprived the Company of its privilege. The Master and Wardens were also empowered to seize and burn all prohibited books and imprison offenders. The actual burning was done by the common executioner. Privileged visitors to today's Stationers' Hall, built in 1670 after the Fire, restored after World War II, and one of the finest Company halls in the City, are shown the garden where bonfires consumed the illicit printed word.

The Stationers' Company was one of Mary's few lasting foundations. By 1557 the fatal dropsy had set in. The Spanish Marriage in 1554 had upset her subjects. The Smithfield fires and their 300 victims had further decreased her popularity. Latimer, as he promised Ridley, had lit a candle such as should not be put out. Mary, frequently, so she thought, pregnant but never a mother, could not provide the heir she wanted. England was ready for Elizabeth and an international destiny.

5. New Thoughts and the New World

St Bride's entered the history of the New World in 1587, two years after Sir Walter Raleigh had discovered Virginia. Roanoke Island was the bridgehead but, famous as the name has become in American history, this first attempt at settlement ultimately failed. None the less the early colonists, led by John White (who had purchased a licence from Raleigh) made some progress, for on 13 August 1585 they recorded the baptism of an Indian. 'Our Savage Manteo, by the commandment of Sir Walter Raleigh, was christened Roanoke and was called Lord thereof.' Five days later came the baptism of the first American child of English descent. Named Virginia (after the colony whose name was already honouring the Virgin Queen), she was a granddaughter of Governor John White and the child of Elenor and Ananias Dare. St Bride's comes into the story since Elenor and Ananias were fairly certainly married in the church before crossing the Atlantic to produce the first white Anglo-American.

The 1580s were dangerous times. The Spanish Armada was being got ready, and to sustain supplies to the infant colony proved impossible. By 1590, when ships finally arrived, it had disappeared. Virginia was to be re-born with the foundation of Jamestown in 1607, and the connection with St Bride's continued because, in 1619, the governors of Bridewell Hospital were asked to send one hundred boys and girls 'to help populate Virginia'. They proved so successful that, three years later, another hundred were requested and sent for the same purpose. On coming of age they were awarded grants of land, and many became citizens of standing. By the arrival of the Pilgrim Fathers, who included a distinguished St Bride's parishioner, Virginia had already set up its own local government.

These were burgeoning years for England, and Fleet Street was in the middle of them. The half-glimpses which flit between Ludgate Circus and Temple Bar are tantalising. 1596, for example. Raleigh had already been arrested and temporarily reprieved for his love for Elizabeth Throgmorton whom he eventually married. Elizabeth and Essex were deeply involved with each other. And in that year, Edmund Spenser published the second of the three instalments of *The Faerie Queene*. He was at Essex's house near Temple Bar writing *Prothalamion*, a 'sponsal verse' professing to celebrate the double marriage of the daughters of the Earl of Worcester, but surely not unmindful of some of the gossip which was going on. Perhaps printers pondered these things as they smoked the new-fangled tobacco pipes of silver or clay which Raleigh had introduced, and which James I was going to deplore. Their apprentices made do with walnut shells fitted with straw.

The vigour and flamboyance of the Elizabethans coloured death as well as life – to judge by this account of a St Bride's funeral.

> 'The XX day of February (1563) was bered at sant Brydes in Fletestrett master Denham Sqwyre, and the chyrche ther was mad rayled and hangyd with blake and armes, and he was cared to the chyrch, a-for him a mornar bayring a pennon of armes, and after cam a harold of armes bayryng ys cott armur, and then cam the corse with a palle of blake velvett with armes on yt and iiij of ys men bare hym; and then the mornars, the cheyffe was ser Recherd Sakfeld [Sackville] and XX mornars; and the dene of Westmynster mad the sermon.'[1]

It must have been expensive. As far as the church was concerned the regular tariff was:

> 'For those buried in a coffin 3*s*. 4*d*.
> Those without a coffin 3*s*.
> For 'pitts and knells' – digging the grave and tolling the bell – 8*d*.

Half a century later these fees had doubled. But funerals were a bargain at plague times, when there was no charge for interment.

Despite the imminence of death, life prospered – notably in the arts, and characteristically expressed in drama, a democratic entertainment that drew courtiers and apprentices alike to the great inn yards. The Mitre, The Cock (Tennyson was to eulogise 'the plump head waiter at the Cock, to which I most resort' in *Will Waterproof*), the Bolt-in-Tun, the King's Head, the Devil, The Horn, and other inns round Fleet Street were packed to applaud Dick Tarleton as he rocked the audience with his jests. Was Yorick born as Shakespeare watched Tarleton's pranks and listened to his 'happy unhappy answers'? Was Tarleton introduced to Queen Elizabeth by the Earl of Leicester before he died in 1588 in dissipated poverty, the archetype of the tears behind a clown's grease paint? Those who stood in the Belle Sauvage Inn (named after Pocahontas) in the parish of St Bride asked no such questions. They were lost in laughter, not ashamed to appear groundlings.

When Elizabeth became Queen there were no theatres and few public buildings other than churches and taverns. Drama was seen in public open-air pageants or in the miracle plays before the altar. The first English comedy, *Ralph Roister Doister*, had been written by Nicholas Udall (1505-56) in Mary's day but not printed until Elizabeth's – and the author got into trouble at Eton, where he was headmaster, and was sent to the Marshalsea prison for his labours. Thomas Tusser, agricultural writer and poet, claimed he was flogged by Udall 'for fault

Sir Walter Raleigh.

above An Indian Chief.
Water-colour by John White
engraved by De Bry.
© *British Museum*

right The village of Secoton.
Water-colour by John White
engraved by De Bry.
© *British Museum*

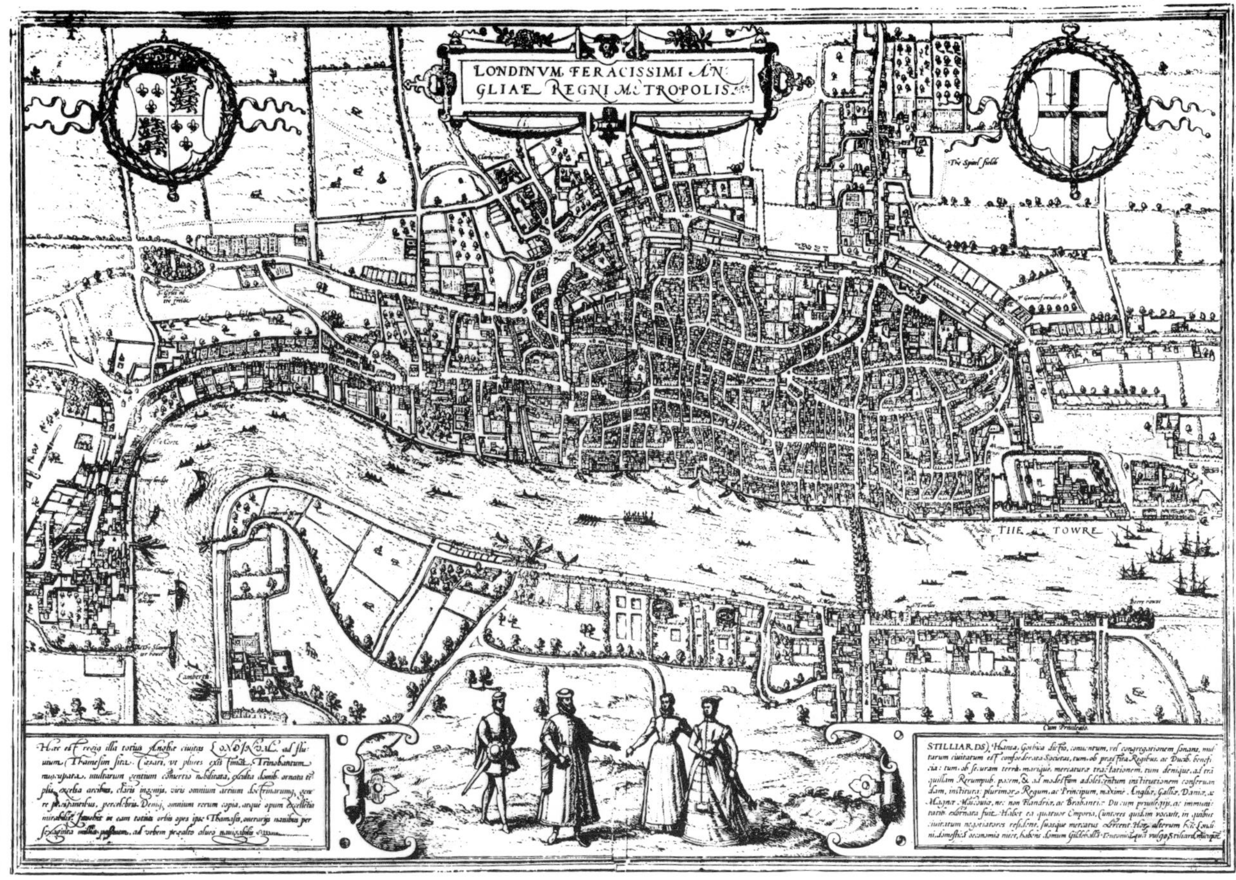

Map of London attributed to Hoefnagel about 1558

but small or none at all'. *Ralph Roister Doister's* successor, *Gammer Gurton's Needle*, published in 1575 and attributed to Bishop Still, is chiefly remembered for its good drinking songs. Tragedy, too, had its first raw beginnings at this time. In 1561 the Inner Temple Hall had seen *Gorboduc* which Thomas Sackville of Salisbury House had a hand in writing. His collaborator, Thomas Norton, also a student of the Temple, was also translating Calvin's *Institutes*, and helping Sternhold and Hopkins in their version of the Psalms published in 1562.

Gorboduc, hardly drama but rather a narration in blank verse, allowed no action on the stage. This was to wait for *Tancred and Gismond* by a parson, Robert Wilmot, a play based on a Boccaccio plot and performed at the Temple in 1568, when Elizabeth came to Fleet Street to see it. Six years later James Burbage, father of Shakespeare's famous associate, became one of the Earl of Leicester's players and within two years he had built England's first theatre. By 1596 he had built one in Blackfriars, and by 1598 the Globe had arisen at Bankside.

Put thus, it sounds simple. But the early impresarios had much to contend with. There was the objection of the Church to anything done during service times. There was the fear—and a very real one—of what would happen if crowds

The Bear Garden (left) and the Globe Theatre from the Venetian Map, 1629

should gather when the plague was abroad. The City was even more hostile to the theatre than the State, and it took a letter from the Privy Council to the Lord Mayor to obtain his even then grudging permission – which was why Burbage built his first theatre at Shoreditch, just outside the City's jurisdiction but near enough to attract its residents. 'And thither ran the people, thick and threefold', as a preacher of the time lamented.

The outlets for Christopher Marlowe, Ben Jonson, George Peele, Robert Greene, Thomas Kyd, John Lyly and Thomas Nashe were growing. Trade was good in the seventies and eighties, and tourists, backbone of the theatre trade then as now, were flocking into London, which boasted seventeen theatres by the time Paris had two.

In 1586 Shakespeare arrived in London – and found it 'the quick forge and working-house of thought'. Whatever the much-argued reason for his coming, it may safely be said that he would not have been Shakespeare without London. Fleet Street in particular, would have provided him with a wealth of human material. During the law terms it would be crowded with country gentlemen up at the Temple to finish their education, before settling down to manage their estates. The knight or the squire, his whole family with him, would gawp at the diversions of the metropolis. They would be easy targets for wayside entertainers, for the alluring tavern and for the cheats and knaves who were ready for 'coney catching' the gullible.

They would cross Fleet Dyke as Jonson saw it (though he was not 'rare' in having such a view):

'All was to them the same; they were to pass
And so they did, from Styx to Acheron,
The ever-boiling flood, whose banks upon
Yon Fleet Lane furies and hot cooks do dwell,
That with still-scalding streams make the place hell;
The sinks run grease, and hair of meazled hogs,
The heads, houghs, entrails, and the hides of dogs
For, to say truth, what scullion is so nasty
To put skin and offals in a pasty?'[2]

Elizabethan London did not lack books, especially of the 'how to' variety. The reader could learn how to garden, to do accounts, to play musical instruments, to navigate; or he could read potted classics and histories and religion. And if he could not afford books, there were broadsheets with their sensations or ballad-sheets with their woodcuts.

It is hard to exaggerate the importance of the ballad. Where subsequent generations have cast their propaganda and teaching into more prosaic forms such as pamphlets, the Elizabethan seemed naturally to turn to verse. The ballad both expressed and helped to form popular opinion. It would be sung in private houses, in taverns, at fairs, anywhere it could find a listener. It might be religious, hortatory, moralising or immoral, topical, instructive, amatory, scandalous, or fall under any heading of sacred or profane. The clergy of the day seemed already aware of General Booth's dictum, for they seized upon words and tunes which had become popular and adapted them to their own purposes. The market-place and the altar were close.

One category of literature, however, had relatively few titles. Playwrights were convinced that to print their plays was to cut down a potential audience. The only occasions when plays were rushed to printers was in a year, such as 1594, when plague closed the theatre and authors had to find some other way of making a living (an average play, it seems, brought its author about £6, so a playwright could not save much for a rainy day).

Shakespeare had little thought of putting his plays into print. Once written, they were the property of the company which played them. In any case, they were written not as literature but as vehicles for actors to attract audiences. The first of his works thought worthy of print was the narrative poem *Venus and Adonis*, duly licensed by Archbishop Whitgift and one of the Wardens of the Stationers' Company, and entered at Stationers' Hall in 1593 – for the usual fee of 6*d*. The printer and publisher of *Venus and Adonis* was a boyhood friend. Richard Field, the same age as Shakespeare, born at Stratford, had gone to London at the age of 15 to become a printer. By the time he was 25, Field had married his master's widow and taken over the business. Thus Shakespeare had at least one printer friend, but it is doubtful whether he esteemed the rest of them highly. In *Henry VI Part II* he makes Jack Cade charge Lord Say that, among other things, 'Thou hast most traitorously corrupted the youth of the realm in erecting a grammar school: and whereas, before, our forefathers had not other books but the score and the tally, thou hast caused printing to be used; and, contrary to the king, his crown and dignity, thou hast built a papermill.' On the other hand, later in his career he lets Mopsa tell the Clown in *The Winter's Tale*, 'I love a ballad in print, a-life, for then we are sure they are true'.

Despite all attempts at control, printing seemed a free-for-all and printers soon found that Shakespeare's plays would sell. If they could not secure the proper text, then they published the nearest approximation they could find. Worse still they would even get hold of plays by other, very inferior, men and suggest on the title page that they had come from Shakespeare's hand. The First Folio edition, the complete record of all his plays and memorial of Shakespeare's fellow actors to him, did not appear in print until seven years after his death. And it cost £1 a copy.

It must have been galling, for example, to see William Fisher 'at the sign of the White Hart, in Fleetestreete' selling the quarto edition of *A Midsommer night's dreame* in 1600 or the new play called *The Tragicall Historie of Hamlet, Prince of Denmark* in 1604. Shakespeare would have often walked up and down Fleet Street. He must regularly have crossed the river from the nearby bank – on a 1*d.* boat 'charmingly upholstered' and 'with embroidered cushions laid across the seats' to and from the Globe, at least until 1608 when he became part-lessee of

facing William Shakespeare, engraved by R. A. Artlett from the Chandos portrait

below left Francis Beaumont

below right John Fletcher

Ben Jonson

the Blackfriars theatre and spent much of his time there. In 1613 he bought a house in Blackfriars (for £140 from a musician named Henry Walker), apparently as an investment rather than for his own use.

Blackfriars – a Liberty, not a fully integrated part of the City – was already on the way to becoming the artistic centre of London (Van Dyck chose this spot to live). Its theatre had a snob value since it had a roof, and the wealthy would pay three times as much to go there as to the Globe. Its music and its more elaborate productions compensated for the high average admission price of eighteen pence. And its 500-seat capacity was deplored by local residents since playgoers' coaches jammed their streets, despite an open yard in front 'to turne coaches in'. It was at Blackfriars that professional actresses first appeared on the stage – in 1629.

Before a producer dared allow women act, the theatre had to be strongly entrenched in popular favour. No small contribution to this end was made by Francis Beaumont (whose father was a prominent member of the Inner Temple and who himself studied in the Middle Temple) and John Fletcher (son of a Bishop of London). Whether working separately or in their fruitful decade of partnership (1606-16), they were held in esteem. Indeed, Dryden says that Beaumont 'was so accurate a judge of plays that Ben Jonson, while he lived submitted all his writings to his censure, and 'tis thought used his judgement in correcting, if not contriving, all his plots'.

It was an age rich in dramatists, even though they had to compete with bear-

left Thomas Sackville. © *National Portrait Gallery*

right Richard of Lovelace

gardens, and London was their centre. John Webster, son of a London tailor and himself a freeman of the Merchant Taylors' Company, Thomas Dekker, also born in London, Thomas Heywood, George Chapman (translator of Homer), Thomas Middleton – the list grows and the area between Blackfriars and Whitefriars saw them all. By 1608, Whitefriars had its own theatre. Although one of its lessees was the Poet Laureate, Michael Drayton (at a rent of £50 a year on a lease to run for the odd period of six years, eight months and twenty days), it did not do too well. Very soon the lease was forfeited to the Sackvilles for failure to pay the rent, and by 1616 a survey could say:

> 'It hath little or no furniture for a playhouse, saving an old tattered curtin, some decayed benches, and a few worn out properties and pieces of Arras for hangings to the stage and tire house. The raine hath made its way in, and if it be not repaired, it must soon be plucked down or it will fall.'

Names associated with this theatre include Ben Jonson (who with his 'mounting belly' and his 'rocky face' could hardly have been a prepossessing stage presence when he played in his own *Epicoene* there), Beaumont and Fletcher, Chapman, Marston and Field. In 1629 came another playhouse on the Sackville land – probably on what is now the south side of Salisbury Square – called the Salisbury Court Theatre, where Lovelace's works were performed. By 1649 it had disappeared, razed to the ground by Roundhead soldiers: by which time it could have served no purpose, for in 1648 Parliament directed that all theatres ('Devils' chaples') should be dismantled, all actors of plays publicly whipped and each person found present at a stage performance fined five shillings. By 5 April 1660, in anticipation of the Restoration, Salisbury Court Theatre was rebuilt. In his Diary Pepys mentions many visits to the play there during 1661, and where he saw Betterton, whom he judged 'the best actor in the world'. In 1666 the Great Fire repeated the destruction which Roundheads had achieved in 1649.

But we go ahead of our story. As these dramatists strolled about Fleet Street, there were parsons in St Bride's and some of them deserve mention.

Henry Holland (1594-1603) had no doubt that it was the vicar's business to be concerned about everything that went on around him, including witchcraft. His best-seller was *A Treatise against Witchcraft: or A dialogue wherein the greatest doubts concerning that sinne are briefly answered . . . Hereunto is also added a short Discourse, concerning the most certain meanes ordained of God, to discover, expell and to confound all the satanicall inventions of Witchcraft and Sorceries*.

Holland was obviously concerned about spiritual evil, and its physical counterpart no less. In 1593 he published *Spiritual Preservations against the Pestilence* and, mindful perhaps of the Fleet Ditch (then too silted to deserve the name of river), he dedicated his opus to the Lord Mayor, Sherriffs and Aldermen. Holland's effort however did little immediate good: in 1594 the plague was bad enough to close the theatres.

Another St Bride's vicar with good cause to hate the plague – his wife died of it in 1625 – was James Palmer, whose ministry lasted from 1616 to 1645. One of his extra-parochial assignments was to preach before both Houses of Parliament on their monthly days of humiliation. He seems however to have been insuffi-

Monument of James Palmer in St Margaret's Church, Westminster, in 1939, subsequently damaged during World War II. © *National Monuments Record*

ciently puritan for the Puritans, for in 1642 the House of Commons ordered him to welcome to his pulpit twice a week one Simon Ash, noted as a dissenting minister. Palmer's ending was sad. His parishioners also judged him a poor Puritan, so they forced his resignation, lacking 2½ years' salary; but permitted him the use of his room over the church porch. On his death in 1660 he was honoured with a memorial in St Margaret's, Westminster. The plague that had killed Mistress Palmer was endemic in London, and modern man cannot be surprised at the fact. Not only was it customary for the remains of food to be scraped from plates on to the rush-strewn floor, and for father, mother and child to urinate and defecate in a corner: but they were urged to do so, for thus did they create the middens which were a source of saltpetre, essential for gunpowder. In 1601 a debate in the House of Commons angrily accused the saltpetremen of abusing their right to enter any building to dig up these middens, and equally angrily defended them since 'the kingdom is not so well placed for powder as it should be'. Until 1634 it remained illegal for floors of houses to be tiled or paved.

It was during Elizabeth's reign that Fleet Street lost its connection with the Bishops of Salisbury – though Salisbury Square remains today as a reminder – and gained a new one with the Sackville family. Sir Richard Sackville, one of the Queen's favourites, was given the mansion at the sign of the Hanging Sword, formerly the residence of Bishop John Jewel. Member of an ancient family, and cousin to Anne Boleyn, Elizabeth's mother, Sackville became owner of the largest dwelling house in the City of London with land stretching down to the river and

Frost Fair 1683–4.
© *London Museum*

Model of London Bridge about 1600. © *London Museum*

including some of its wharves, twenty-eight shops and tenements in and about Fleet Street, four shops in St Bride's churchyard and another forty-five houses round about. For this Sackville paid £641 5*s.* 10½*d.* and Sackville House started its career as the home of the Earls and Dukes of Dorset, a centre of culture and statecraft. It is little wonder that to the less respectful the name Sackville became 'Fill-sack'. The family could well afford the Farringdon Street burial ground which they gave to St Bride's in 1610, on condition there should be no more interments to offend their eyes on the south side of the church near their home. The name Sackville is frequent in English history. It was Sir Thomas Sackville who officially informed Mary Queen of Scots of her death sentence (and did so in such a gracious way that she gave him five figures carved in wood of the procession to Calvary: it is still a proud possession of Knole Chapel). It was he who presided over the state trial of the Earl of Essex, an event held in Sackville House which must have brought the best people to Fleet Street. It was the same Sackville who with Sir Robert Cecil proclaimed James I King of England.

Fleet Street was more than a haunt for the rich. It was the whole range of humanity, rich and poor, living cheek by jowl in a stuffy dark, cobbled way with overhanging houses almost meeting in the centre. Until c. 1614, no footpath separated the pedestrian from the carts and carriages. The street had its nobility and diplomats, including the French ambassador who lived here in 1580, and it had its notorious Ram Alley, 'perhaps the most pestilent court in London'. The street was much in Elizabeth's mind when she enacted her Poor Law burdening parishes with the care of beggars; and it was the place where she contemplated meeting the Duke of Alençon to discuss her rumoured marriage. Fleet Street was the place of gain to hard-working printers and merchants and tradesmen (and

Gunpowder Plot

their apprentices loudly calling their wares), while its environs were the place of pleasure for the theatre or concert-goer. It was the place too where national processions flowed majestically – in contrast to its river, so filth-burdened that it hardly flowed at all. Elizabethan Fleet Street was thus a noisy, exuberant, place by day. At night when the gates of Temple Bar were shut (it was only 1753 that the Commons enacted that a postern should be left open), it was generally silent – the darkness broken only by the few guttering candles required by law to stand outside the houses of the better-off citizens.

Such was the forum handed by Elizabeth to James I who, being a literary man (especially on the subject of royal authority) must have had a special feeling for this corner of his kingdom. James I was a determined author. Among his titles is one with particular relevance today: *A Counterblaste to Tobacco* was published in 1604, the year in which he called the Hampton Court Conference that yielded the 'Authorised Version' of the Bible, mainstay of so many printers ever since.

The year before, several conspirators, among them Guy Fawkes, had taken their last journey along Fleet Street to a scaffold at the west end of St Paul's.

A sufferer from James's dislike of smoking was Timothy Howe who seems to have kept one of the first tobacco shops. In 1618 he and a neighbour were indicted 'for keeping their tobacco shops open all night and fyers in the same without any chimney, and uttering hott water and selling ale without licence, to the great disquietude, terror and annoyance of that neighbourhood.' In 1630 they were 'presented' once again, this time for annoying the judges of Serjeants Inn 'with the stench and smell of their tobacco'.

One permanent mark which 'the wisest fool in Christendom', as Henry IV of France is supposed to have called James, left in Fleet Street is Prince Henry's Room. Now the upper storey of No. 17, it was built in 1611 as the Council Chamber of Henry, Prince of Wales, probably on the spot where John Stow's *Chronicles* were published.[3] Henry did not enjoy his room for long. In 1612 he died of typhoid, though men darkly hinted at poison.

Had Henry lived, English history might have been different, and passions about Spaniards and Roman Catholics gentler. Fleet Street was the scene of riots on this account in 1618 and in 1629. It was from his lodging in Fleet Lane that John Felton, buying a knife as he left the City, set out in 1628 to murder George Villiers, Duke of Buckingham. His mother and his sister also lodged in Fleet Street at the house of Owen Hughes, a haberdasher. Felton had conceived the idea in the Windmill tavern in Shoe Lane. Immediately after his arrest in Ports-

left Henry Purcell by J. Closterman © *National Portrait Gallery*

right Izaak Walton by Jacob Huysman © *National Portrait Gallery*

mouth, Felton told his interrogators that he was to be prayed for in St Bride's. In due course, he died at Tyburn. Another but more honoured death was that of James Kinnon whose memorial tablet in the pre-Fire St Bride's recorded him as 'a citizen and Cannoniere and a souldier, died aged 67 by overheating his bloud in preparing of forty Chambers at the entertainment of the Prince in the Artillery Garden'.

Fleet Street was a hectic place. But that did not stop people spending holidays there. Named with Henry Purcell, William Byrd, Orlando Gibbons and Thomas Morley as among the most illustrious of the composers who enriched the music of England and its Church, Thomas Weelkes was organist of Chichester Cathedral. In 1623 he came to stay with his friend Henry Drinkworth in Salisbury Square. He died during the visit and was buried in St Bride's. On the tercentenary of his death the English Madrigal Societies set up a memorial tablet in the church.

Perhaps, as in so many generations, it was the literary company which attracted Weelkes. About that time Michael Drayton lived at the corner of Fetter Lane. A few doors away lived Izaak Walton, 'milliner-sempster or dealer in shorts' by trade, but known to succeeding ages for his hobby. *The Compleat Angler* was written ten years after Walton, stout Royalist and churchman, had left a Civil War-torn city for rural peace (though he had also found good fishing in the Thames). The book came back to Fleet Street to be published by Richard Marriott of St Dunstan's Churchyard. It cost 1*s.* 6*d.* bound in sheepskin. Marriott's name also appeared on the title page of *Paradise Lost* (price 3*s.*). Among the biographies written by Walton was one of George Herbert, one of

Izaak Walton's House, from the *Mirror*, Saturday February 23, 1828

Sir Francis Drake.

John Donne who was Dean of St Paul's 1621-1631, and one of Richard Hooker who had been Master of the Temple. Nearby, too, in Shoe Lane, lived John Florio who died in 1625. His Italian-English Dictionary and translation of Montaigne's *Essays* left their mark on English literature. Richard Lovelace ('Stone walls do not a prison make, nor iron bars a cage'), whose life seemed so well favoured until the Puritans gave him the experience behind those famous lines, was buried in the west end of St Bride's Church. Later Thomas Flatman, poet and painter of miniatures, was one of the first to be buried in the St Bride's of Christopher Wren.

As influential as any local resident (his house for a time was in Fetter Lane) was Thomas Hobbes (1588-1679), whose premature birth was supposed to be due to

his mother's fright at the Armada. This man who 'in the sphere of mental science effected a breach with scholasticism similar to that instituted by Copernicus in astronomy, Galileo in physics and Harvey in physiology' had a chequered existence. His argument that it is the people who in effect rule and they, by contract, transfer their right to the Crown, satisfied neither those who believed in the divine right of kings nor those who did not believe in kings at all. He suffered in consequence. Scared of the power of the Parliamentarians, he fled to France and lived there for eleven years. In 1651 the publication of *Leviathan* made him unwelcome at Charles' exiled court. He returned to England, made his peace with the Commonwealth and was allowed to return to Fetter Lane where he continued a long friendship with William Harvey, expounder of the circulation of the blood. There too he 'took pains to find a church where he could receive the Sacrament according to the Anglican rites'. The St Bride's of the time, alas, failed him. But, since Hobbes acquired so great, though mistaken, a reputation as an atheist, perhaps St Bride's can be forgiven if it did not try very hard to meet his wishes.

Thomas Hobbes by J. Michael Wright. © *National Portrait Gallery*

Of the many streams which have coalesced to make the river of American history, two stand out. The first of them, the colonial stream and Virginia Dare, we have already noticed. The other is even better known – the Pilgrim Fathers and New England. That any one church should have played a fundamental part in helping both streams flow is surely worthy of note.

On 4 November 1594 Edward Winslow, yeoman farmer and salter of St Peter's Manor, Droitwich, was married in St Bride's Church to Magdalene Ollyver whose family were probably printers. On 18 October 1595 the first of their five sons was born in Droitwich and was named Edward after his father. On leaving the King's School, Worcester, at the age of 15½ he started farming. Two years later he rode horseback to London and on 19 August 1613 he was apprenticed to John Beale, citizen and stationer of London. The Ent ry Book of Stationers' Hall records the fact. There was nothing more natural than that Winslow, a printer and the son of parents married at St Bride's should himself attend here regularly. Thus he came under the influence of its vicars, Nathaniel Giffard, 1603-16, and James Palmer, 1616-45. Both of them, as it happened, were highly sympathetic to the view of Continental Protestants. Winslow began to find himself drawn towards the Separatists. By 1617, he was allowed to break his apprenticeship and throw in his lot with the group at Leyden in Holland who had accepted exile as the price of religious freedom (from the middle of the sixteenth century to the end of the seventeenth, the Netherlands exercised great influence on printing, especially in type-design and type-founding). As one of their printers, Winslow was responsible for some of the books smuggled into England in wine casks. But Holland – indeed all Europe – proved too cramping, particularly when in 1619 James I persuaded the Dutch authorities to seize the Leyden press. A new world was calling. In July 1620 the Pilgrim Fathers sailed from Delfthaven for England. The following September, the *Mayflower* left Plymouth with 102 people on board. It took them 66 days at an average speed of 1½ miles an hour to reach New Plymouth. A great storm broke the *Mayflower's* mast and it was the screw of a printing press which made possible the first aid which enabled the ship to sail on.

The Pilgrim Fathers arrived. They drew up their *Compact* – 'the first American Constitution'. They made friends with the Indians. They founded New England. Winslow's name appears at the centre of affairs throughout. Three times he

October anno 1594

10 Mr William Kettle and Mrs Judith Layston were maried the xth daye
14 Mr John Summet and Elizabeth Yeomans were maried the xiiij daye
20 Henry Neelson and Maryon Graveson were maried the xxth daye
27 Richard Stubbins and Barbara Sampford were maried the xxvij daye
28 William Page and Johan Gysbye were maryed the xxviij daye

November anno 1594

3 John Merideth and Ann Rogers were maried the iijd daye
4 Edward Winslowe and Magdalene Ollyver were maried the iiijth daye
21 John Stapleton and Ursly Wyett were maried the xxj daye
21 Thomas West and Ellen ffrancklin were maried the same daye
24 Henry Hawes and Susan Bothum were maried the xxiiij daye
25 James Williams and Christian Bras were maried the xxv daye

December anno 1594

15 Robert Upton and Johan Center were maried the xv daye
16 Christofer Yerdlye and Easter Leonardes were maried the xvj daye

The Marriage Register entry for Edward Winslow and Magdalene Ollyver

became Governor of Plymouth, Massachusetts. Several times he visited England on behalf of the Colony – 'America's first ambassador'. He was a skilled diplomat and had a wide knowledge of law and local government. He was accused by Archbishop Laud of dubious church teaching and of marrying colonists. He gracefully answered each charge – by pointing out that if clergy had been available people would not have to rely on laymen for moral exhortations or civil magistrates for marriages. But Laud remained unconvinced and had Winslow, during one of his ambassadorial visits, flung into the Fleet Prison. Released after seventeen weeks, he returned to New England to serve another term as Governor. In due course he attracted the attention of Cromwell who gave him Government employment at £300 a year. The Commonwealth eventually made him Chief Commissioner of the 1655 naval expedition to the Caribbean at a salary of £1000 a year. He died during the capture of Jamaica from Spain that same year.

A democrat in revolt against rule by squire and parson, indisposed to the doctrine of the divine right of kings, champion of the freedom of the press, ready to throw away a comfortable career for the sake of adventure, convinced that men must be free to worship as they will and travel where they choose, Winslow was a man worthy of Fleet Street and deserved his commemoration on the side of the reredos at St Bride's. He appears never to have been hostile to the Church as such. He accepted the Thirty-nine Articles and the institution of episcopacy, but since he rejected prelacy, the twentieth century can understand his feelings. His devotion to the Christian Faith is amply proved by his part in founding The Society for the Propagation of the Gospel in New England in 1649. And the colony may be described as the first English effort to set up overseas for the sake of godliness and not for the sake of gain.

The Pilgrim Fathers went to America to seek freedom. That is a sentence which calls up images of an ogre in ecclesiastical vestments smelling of an Inquisition

Governor Edward Winslow

and brandishing the *Index Librorum Prohibitorum*. This is a book about Fleet Street as well as its church and censorship must have a place in its pages – even though to do so must do violence to our historical scheme.

Within a century of Gutenberg's invention, control of the printed word had become the universal practice of both secular and church authorities throughout Europe. The Church had been the mother of print. It also tried to become its gaoler.

Printing was born in Mainz. So was censorship, a form of control exercised as much by the State as by the Church. In 1485 Archbishop Berthold von Hennenbert (1484-1504) persuaded the town council of Frankfurt to set up machinery for prohibiting what were deemed theologically dangerous publications. When the Archbishop appealed to the secular arm, he was unleashing a power greater than he imagined. The horror of the State about sedition, real or imagined, was to prove much more effective than the dislike of the Church for heresy. And the prince was to become a more ruthless silencer than the prelate. The first appearance of the general *Index* was in 1559 – ironically it banned the works of several cardinals.

In England, proclamations against 'naughty printed books' began in 1529, and by 1538 all books were required to be licensed by the Privy Council or other royal nominees before being printed. Edward VI condemned popish books of prayer and theology in 1547 and 1549. Mary reversed the process and went further by restricting imported books unless they had been specially approved. We have already seen why the Stationers' Company received a charter in 1557, together with exclusive rights of publication which proved impossible to enforce. Elizabeth had barely reached the throne before she issued Injunctions – though even she was not able to stop a steady stream of illicit publications. In 1586, in a further effort to impose control, the Star Chamber was introduced to ensure that no printing was permitted outside London other than by the privileged presses of Oxford and Cambridge. Even in London new printing houses were prohibited until the existing number had been reduced to a figure deemed adequate by the Archbishop of Canterbury and the Bishop of London. This figure was fixed at 22 in 1586, at 23 in 1637, and 20 in 1662, at which level it remained until 1695. In 1588 the insouciant 'Martin Marprelate' began his exuberant anti-episcopal pamphlets, 'the best prose satires of the Elizabethan age': the probable author was Job Throckmorton. In 1599 an edict directed that no further satires or epigrams should be printed.

One of the last and worst measures of the Star Chamber came in 1637. But what the king had taught, a commoner could practise, and in 1643 the Long Parliament issued a decree insisting on a licence before printing. It was this that stimulated Milton to write his *Areopagitica*, the great plea for freedom to publish. For him the distinction between banning bad books and permitting good ones was entirely false, for 'it is but a fugitive and cloistered virtue that never sallies out and sees her adversary'. In any case, the attempt to keep out evil doctrine by licensing is like 'the exploit of that gallant man who thought to pound up the crows by shutting his park gate'.

Yet, superb irony, in 1651-2 Milton accepted office as a licenser.

One result was to apply a tremendous stimulus to the Dutch printing trade where, though a nominal policy of censorship existed, the general atmosphere was much more liberal. Another was to increase both prices and sales of books.

Contemporary painting of the Fire of London. © *London Museum*

St Bride's from the Thames engraved by Matthews from a drawing by J. P. Neale, 1815

facing Sir Christopher Wren by G. Kneller. © *National Portrait Gallery*

CHR: WREN.
Surveyor General of
Royal Buildings ·
died the 25. of Feb. 1723. aged 91.

Jacob Tonson by G. Kneller. © *National Portrait Gallery*

facing John Milton. Artist unknown. © *National Portrait Gallery*

John Milton

Thus when Hobbes' *Leviathan* was prohibited, Samuel Pepys at once went out and bought a copy secondhand for 30*s*. The original price was 8*s*. As early as 1656 an Amsterdam publisher was trying to have one of his books banned because its slow sales needed a stimulus. The circulation of news distribution added a new complication, and the various media were subjected to the same restrictions. A fleeting sheet, however, was more difficult to penalise than a permanent book.

The advent of the Restoration meant little to the printer in terms of freedom. In 1662 a Licensing Act was passed to suppress anything scandalous to Church or Government. In 1685, the Act was confirmed. In 1694, renewal was refused thanks to the arguments of John Locke, whose *Essay Concerning Human Understanding* had been written in Dorset Court (1689). In 1697 the situation improved when offending printers became subject to the processes of ordinary law. Thus the licensing system came to a final end in England. Its demise was due to the conviction that it was ineffective, not because the authorities were converted to the virtues of free speech. But Macaulay was being over-optimistic when he said: 'English literature was emancipated, and emancipated for ever, from the control

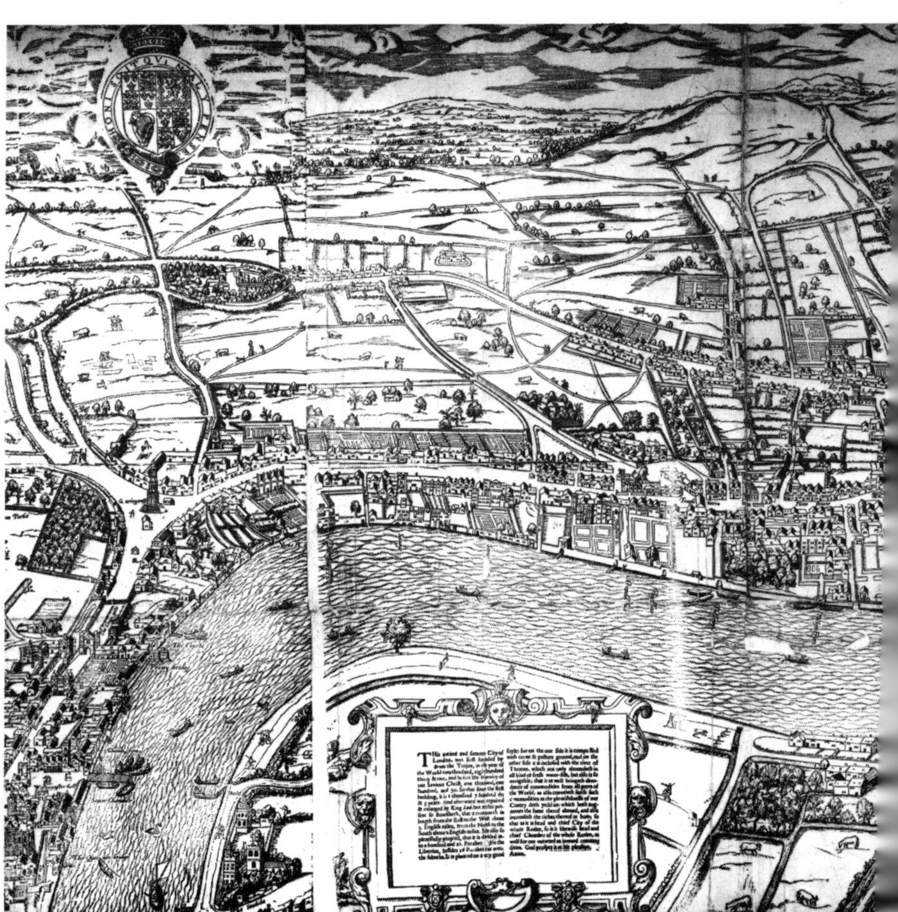

Known as the Agas Map, *c.* 1563. © *Guildhall Library*

of the government'. The authorities still had means to persecute offenders. The solicitor to the Treasury was charged with the duty of suppressing libellous matter and his definition of the term was wide indeed. After all 'libel' had started its life meaning merely a little book! And the punishment was severe. Daniel Defoe knew the inside of a prison for his ecclesiastical pamphlets in 1703. John Matthews was hanged for high treason in 1719, in consequence of his pamphlet which said that James III was the rightful King of England.

The *Freeholders' Journal* and the *True Briton* were suppressed in 1723 and 1724. At the same time the Stamp Act of 1712 (not abolished until 1855) burdened every periodical with a duty of ½*d.* for every half sheet. Throughout the first three-quarters of the eighteenth century Parliament fought to keep its debates out of print. There were the notorious examples of Wilkes and his *North Briton* (he was responsible for the abolition of 'general warrants' for the arrest of un-named 'authors, printers and publishers'), of Thomas Paine and his *Rights of Man* (1791-2), and of William Cobbett, who in 1810 was sentenced to two years in prison and a fine of £1000 for denouncing flogging in the army.

Censorship was more strictly exercised by the State than by the Church, for it

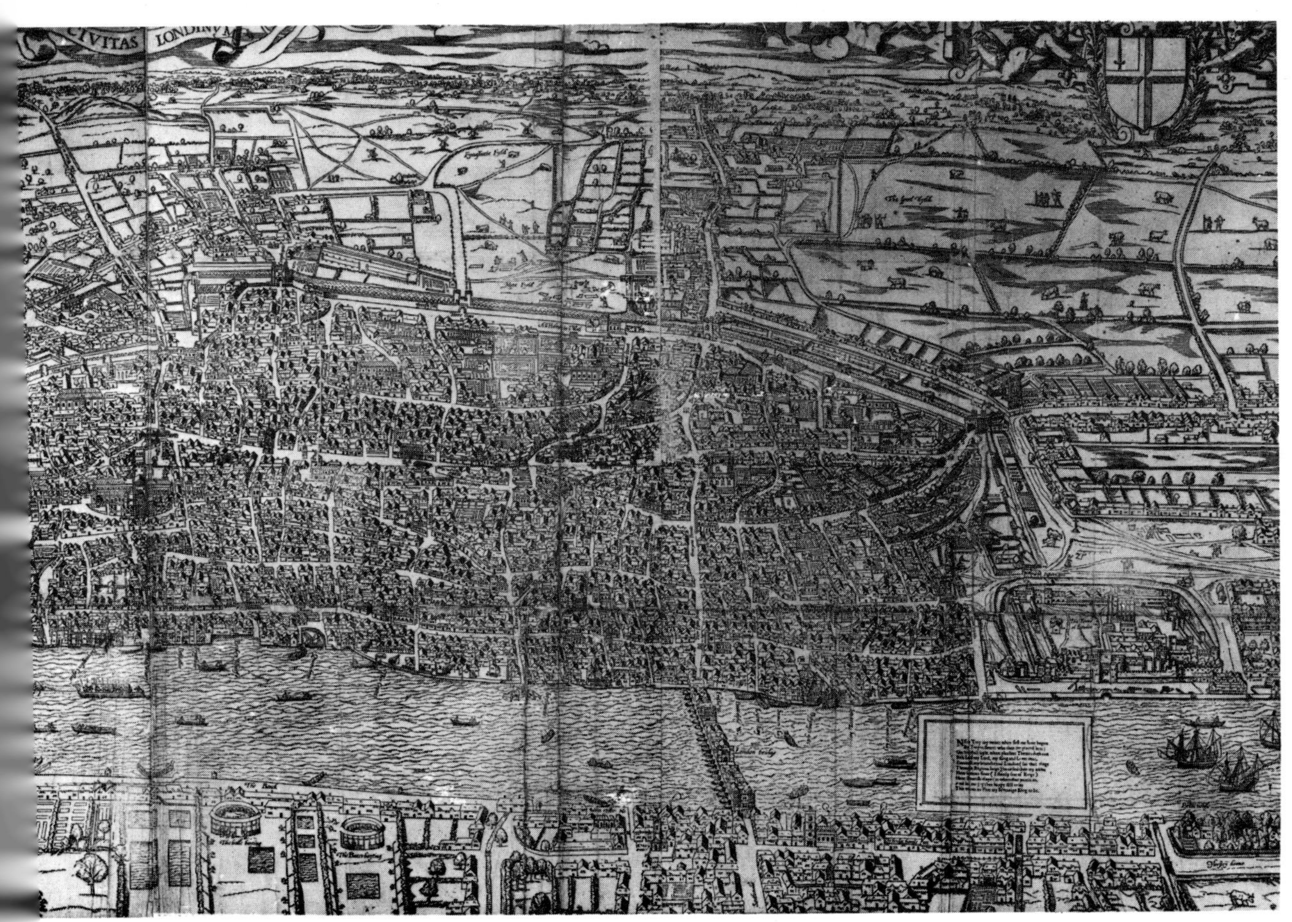

was concerned with thoughts dangerous to authority, rather than to individuals. Thus sedition and heresy were promptly dealt with while sexual obscenity was usually left in peace. Censorship existed not to save souls but to safeguard the State and the formal religion which supported it.

Areopagitica, published in 1644, is a key document in the story. Perhaps its message was formulating in Milton's mind during the time when he lived in St Bride's Churchyard. He may well have seen the sort of punishment handed out to those who erred in print. They included removal of ears, slit noses and face branding, and the operation was done publicly (no wonder Hobbes was scared). Milton was still a youngish man and he lodged with one Russell, a tailor. The site of the house has been an open space since 1824, when the buildings were burned down and public subscription made it possible to buy the land and thus make St Bride's church visible to Fleet Street.

Milton was a difficult man to live with. It seems that, when they were living under St Bride's shadow, his first wife, Mary Powell, temporarily left him (she had been only seventeen when they were married). Aubrey's *Lives* says:

> 'His first wife was brought up and lived where there was a great deal of money and merriment, dancing etc., and when she came to live with her husband at Mr Russell's in St Bride's Churchyard she found it very solitary; no company came to her, oftentimes she heard her Nephews beaten and cry: this life was irksome to her so she left and went to her Parents.'[4]

Mary Powell's parents were Royalists. It was an improbable marriage. She and Milton lived together only a short time at first. After she had gone, he wrote his notorious pamphlets on 'the doctrine and discipline of divorce'. She came back to him in 1645, but died in 1652 leaving three daughters. Milton subsequently contracted two further marriages.

Again we are reminded, Fleet Street was a place of ordinary domesticities, as well as a magnet for those who had something to tell the world. Poor Mary Milton discovered something which by today has become a social problem: you can be very lonely in the midst of a crowd.

An effigy of Virginia Dare in St Bride's Church by Marjorie Meggitt, 1957

6. Commonwealth and Restoration

In 1944, an unfortunate date since so much more about St Bride's early history was soon to be discovered, the London Survey Committee published a lavish book about the church.[1] It contains, as such books always do, a list of incumbents. One section clearly antedates today's ecumenical atmosphere. Before 1507, the incumbents were known as Rectors. From 1507 until 1645 they were Vicars. Then comes a striking category, 'Nonconformist Intruders'. By 1663 Vicars have been restored, and so it remained until the 1950s when the Rectory was restored.

'Nonconformist Intruders'. The mid-seventeenth century St Bride's, like every other Anglican church, saw a greater temporary break in its continuity than at any other period in its history. Milton remarked that 'New Presbyter is but old Priest writ large'. He was commenting on the capacity of any group of men to assert themselves as soon as they achieve power. It was not that the Puritans were better or worse than other men, more religious or less religious. They were not. But they were determined to practise a form of Christianity, alien to the broad stream of the Church of England as it always had been before and as it still is. The direction was set by the *Solemn League and Covenant* in 1643, of which one of the explicit provisions was to extirpate episcopacy. In 1644 the Book of Common Prayer was declared illegal and replaced with the *Directory of Public Worship*.

It was inevitable that St Bride's should be involved in these events, even if other parishes were able to escape, for Fleet Street was home to two stern anti-monarchists, Colonel Pride and Praise-God Barebones.

Thomas Pride, significantly, is not given any birth date in the reference books. He was a Fleet Street foundling, brought up by the parish of St Bride's. He began his working life as a drayman and progressed to become a brewer. The Civil War was still young when be became a colonel. After making his mark at the battle of Preston, he had a hand in the military occupation of London and in 1645 'purged' Parliament by standing at its door and excluding those who had failed to gain his approval. The remnant of the House of Commons was persuaded to see things *facing* Oliver Cromwell

the Roundhead way and brought the king to trial. Pride was among Charles's judges, and had somehow managed to gain a coat-of-arms by the time he signed the royal death warrant. He died before the Restoration.

Praise-God Barbon, Barebone or Barebones was a Fleet Street leatherseller who used his house, *The Lock and Key*, as a meeting place for a congregation to which he preached with great effect. In 1641, this house was stormed by a mob. In 1653 after the expulsion of the Rump, Cromwell called him, as a member for London, to the assembly of nominees which thus derisively gained the name of Barebones Parliament. This gathering asked Cromwell (who had a daughter called Bridget) to become king. The Lord Protector found that as a result he was 'more troubled with the fool than with the knave'. At the Restoration Barebones was consigned to the Tower, but was eventually released on bail and died obscurely.

The day when a monarch was executed might well have seemed the end of an era in England, and the beginning of a new and decisively republican period. But the anti-monarchists had gone too far. G. M. Trevelyan has described the execution as 'a crime against England even more than against Charles'. 'The regicides little realised that in cutting off Charles's head they were cutting their own throats

The execution of Charles I

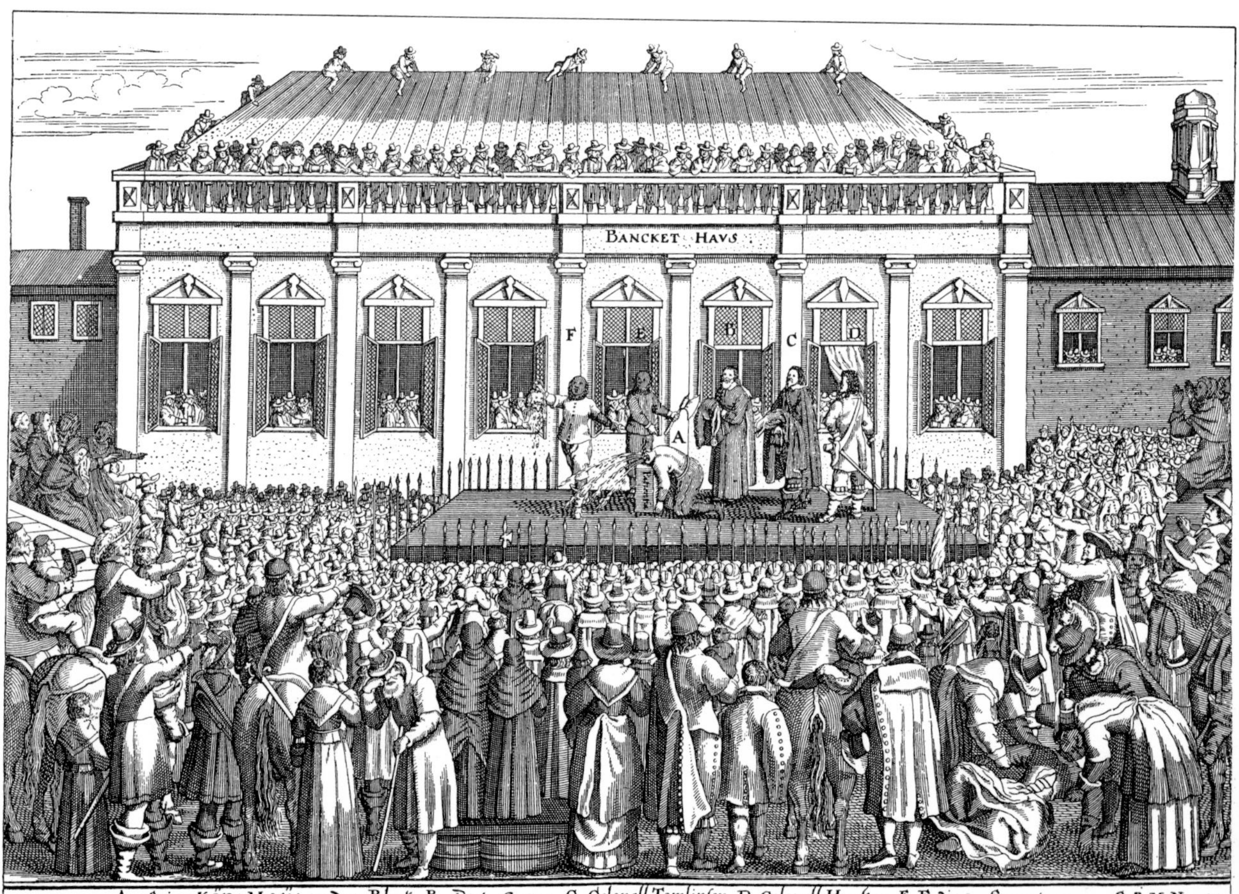

. . . With Charles's death the fate of Puritanism was sealed and the Church's future ensured', says Bishop Moorman.[2] They had lost the sympathy of the country.

There followed a decade as confused as any in England's religious history. In 1650 the government issued an order insisting that everyone attend a place where religious exercises of some sort were held. This did not work, and in 1654, Cromwell, aiming at some measure of toleration, announced the *Instrument of Government* which allowed people to worship as they wished 'provided this liberty be not extended to popery or prelacy'. Cromwell probably spoke truly when he said he did not want to meddle with any man's conscience, none the less he was a politician. To countenance popery was to open the door to Continental influence which sought to restore the monarchy. And prelacy, if it did not mean popery, meant Anglicanism which was no less keen to do the same thing.

Not all Anglicans were in agreement. About 60 per cent of the clergy were ready to conform to the new regime. But there were also those who were ready to endure deprivation and persecution rather than surrender. It was they who kept Charles II in the *via media* between Rome and Geneva.

So religious confusion grew. Anglicans and a few papists remained. Presbyterians, Congregationalists, Baptists and Quakers grew in numbers. And human nature, as ever, demonstrated its oddities; the Adamites, for example, who wished to return to the days of man's innocency and worshipped in the nude: the Diggers whose doctrine required them to dig up other people's land and give it to the poor: the Ranters who insisted on uninhibited inner experience: the Muggletonians who insisted that during the Incarnation Elijah was the governor of

Playing cards as satires on the Puritans

The industrious 'Prentice performing the duty of a Christian from Hogarth's *Industry and Idleness* series

heaven, and were convinced that matter was eternal and reason was evil. England had become a theological zoo.

Meanwhile the ordinary Englishman was puzzled. He was denied the Sacraments. He was forbidden a religious service at his marriage. His Church lost its treasures and its cheerful appearance. He was not allowed a bishop – and there *were* bishops who were true fathers-in-God and whose loss would be felt. He was not allowed to observe Christmas. And his amusements were severely curtailed – there would have been no Shakespeare had Puritanism gained control less than a single lifetime earlier.

All of this hit the Englishman the harder because he had been accustomed to a lusty, hard-swearing, hard-drinking (drunkenness was the acknowledged national fault), ribald and roistering existence. It may have provided grounds for a doctrine of human depravity, but it did not condition a nation for accepting its consequences. The last thing Englishmen wanted was a Lord Protector; but having got one, they began to long for the legality of a monarch in their national lives, for the orderliness of a bishop in their religious lives, and a holiday from Puritan restrictions in their spare time. What they had instead speaks for itself:[3]

1642	Recd of Mr. Bellamy for having Company in his yard drinking on the Saboth daie	9*s*. 0*d*.
1645	Recd of some younge men that were taken att Mrs. Hicks her garden in Sermon time on the Lord's Day	6*s*. 0*d*.
1653	Recd of a man for swearing Tenn Groats but being poore I gave him one shilling againe	2*s*. 4*d*.

Hamsted Mills
Hamsted
the Water house
S Brides
The Eall Schipes
THAM
The Bear Gardn
Visscher Delineavit

In the year 1655 Mr Thomas Mee, Constable of St Bride's parish, reached a fine pitch of enthusiasm for safeguarding the morals of others:

> June 12th Recd of Mr. Mee for a ffine of a porter in Beards Alley for Swearing 2*s*. 6*d*.
> July 8th Recd of Mr. Mee a forfeiture for carryinge a pair of shoes on the Sabboth Day 1*s*. 0*d*.

The general cost of living must have risen considerably, but so did the costs of the authorities. The Puritans may have felt they had removed visible evidence of such Catholic superstitions as an orderly service, but there were other things beyond them, e.g. witchcraft. In November 1656 it cost St Bride's churchwardens 2*s*. as payment to the Lord Mayor's officer 'for warnings about the supposed bewitched Maide'. A month later 'the Lord Mayor's younge man and the Carver' were awarded the same amount for information about 'the supposed bewitched people'. And quite a large sum was spent in 'looking about the parish for papists'. One parishioner of St Bride's showed he had no truck with such behaviour for he paid 13*s*. 4*d*. for 'a Flesh Lycence in Lent'.

Meanwhile St Bride's had its 'Nonconformist Intruders'. One was still in its pulpit when General Monk lodged near the Conduit in Fleet Street, and laid his plans for the return of King Charles. James Palmer, mentioned in the last chapter and who became vicar in 1616, was indeed no intruder, but he inclined to Nonconformity. For example, in 1637 he omitted the prayer for bishops and clergy, and sometimes he wore neither surplice nor gown. By 1637 the authorities decided to rebuke him publicly for his Puritan-inspired irregularities. Yet he did not go far enough to satisfy the Puritans, for in 1642 – as explained – he had to share his pulpit with Simon Ash. By 1645 the Vestry of St Bride's, like the rest of the City, was solidly behind Parliament. By then too the Dean and Chapter of Westminster had been temporarily deprived of their right of appointment, and the Vestry, appointed by the parishioners, firmly told Palmer he was no longer required. On 9 October 1645 a Vestry minute recorded:

> 'that Palmer desired the parishe to helpe him to £40 that was due to him from the Dean and Chapter of Westminster for two yeares and a halfe sallary, and then he would go alonge with suche of the parishioners as should be appointed to the Committee of Ministers, and that he might part lovingly and fairely he would relate his infirmities to the Committee. That hee was ancient, his voice failed him, his hands shooke, and hee could not write and doe as he hath done, and much more to this purpose; and if they thought fitt he would resign his place to any suche minister as the parish should think fit to make the choice of . . . but if in case that were done, he desired he might have the use of his roome over the Church porch where his books and things are, for this winter time, until he can provide himself elsewhere.'

Palmer was then 61, a good age in those days. He was allowed his room in the tower for a year, and the money he saved he gave away. His dismissal was shabby treatment. However, he bore no grudge, and spent the rest of his life doing charitable work, not least for the widows of parsons who had lost their parishes

facing Engraving after Visscher, early seventeenth century. © *Guildhall Library*

A Puritan

The Register in which Samuel Pepys' baptism was entered

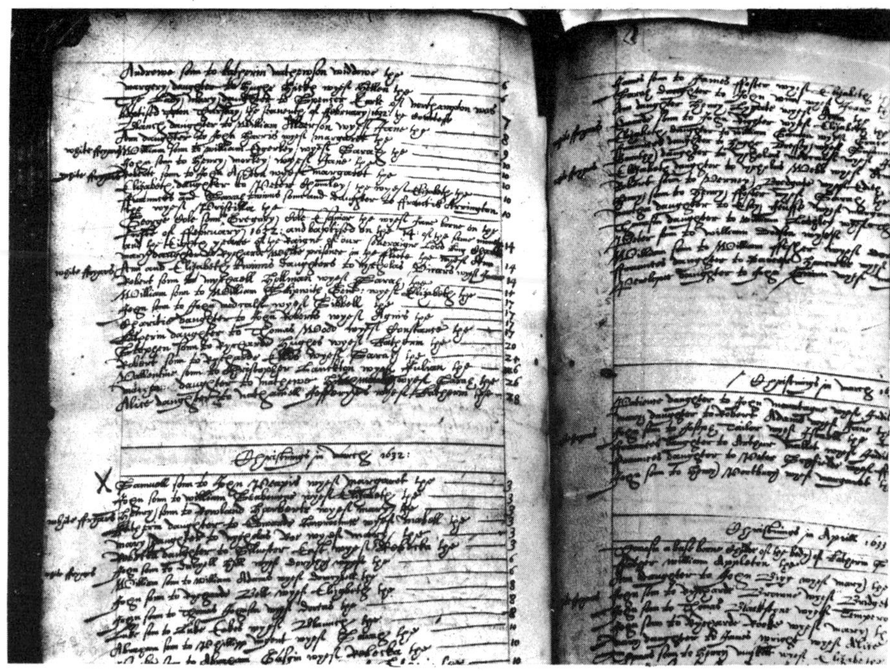

below Detail of above

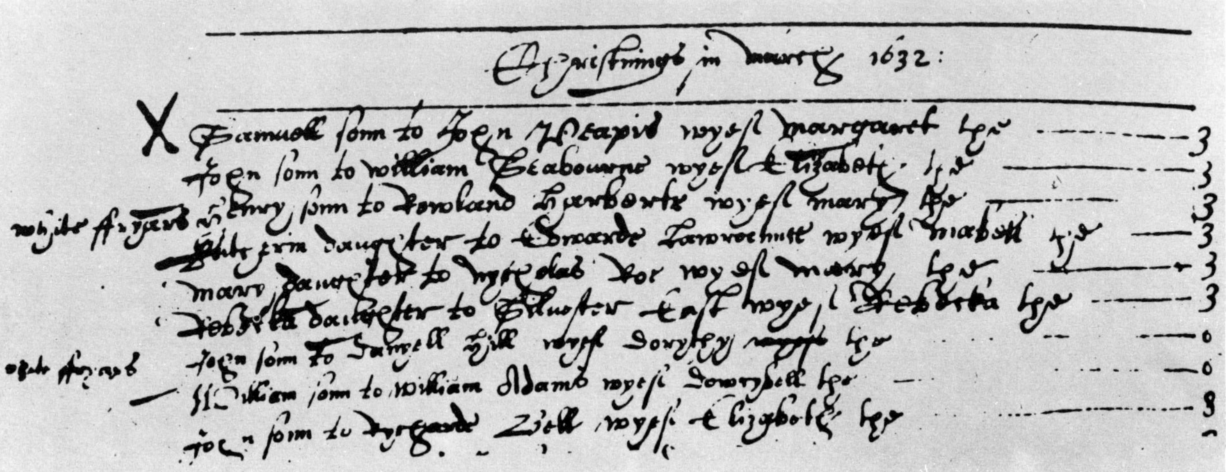

on grounds similar to his. He built houses for the poor of St Bride's alongside the Fleet Ditch and almshouses at Westminster; and up to the time of his death at the age of 75 gave 'a comfortable sermon' once a week in St Margaret's, Westminster.

There were plenty of major events during James Palmer's incumbency, but one minor one was of more than domestic interest. On 3 March 1633, John Pepys, tailor of Fleet Street and Margaret his wife carried their fifth baby son the twenty yards or so from their home to St Bride's to be christened Samuel. He was then eight days old. Between 1 August 1627 and 5 November 1640 nine Pepys children were christened in St Bride's – and in the nine entries there are five different ways of spelling Pepes, Peapes, Peapis, Pepys and Peepes. But this is a relatively modest number. In Hoare's Bank records, where Pepys was a customer, there are no fewer than twelve different spellings, enough to confuse a computer. In St Bride's burial register there was yet another way – Mr Thomas Pepyes. This was the diarist's brother who died in 1664, and Samuel makes it clear that he was willing to pay another 20s. in order to have him buried not in the churchyard but 'in the church in the middle aisle, as near as I can to my mother's pew'. The Diary throws an interesting light on the craft of the sexton:

> 'To church, and the gravemaker chose a place for my brother to lie in, just under my mother's pew. But to see how a man's bones are at the mercy of such a fellow, that for sixpence he would, as his own words were, "I will jostle them together, but I will make room for him" speaking of the fulness of the middle aisle, where he was to lie; and that he would, for my father's sake, do my brother, that is dead, all the civility he can.'

'For my father's sake'. Pepys senior was a citizen of some importance. After all, he had a cousin who became an earl. He figured in a document which says that Alice Ramsay had given £50 to provide sea coals for the poor of St Bride's. And his fellows bore him sufficient esteem to confer upon him the office of Public

Engraving after Visscher, early seventeenth century. © *Guildhall Library*

Scavenger, an honour he appreciated so little that he paid a fine to St Bride's Vestry to discharge himself of the duty – despite the fact that the Scavenger was an appointed officer of some importance. The dirty work was left to the 'rakers'. To gain more light for his house, John Pepys was allowed to move the churchyard wall two yards farther away. This appears to be the reason why, nearly three centuries later, the Press Association was able to build its headquarters so close to the church.

Had Pepys been born a few years later, he would not have been christened in St Bride's. Indeed, if the Government had had its way, he would not have been christened at all. And whether the ceremony would have been performed secretly depended very much on which 'intruder' was in charge at St Bride's at the time. Orderliness and consistency were at a discount. People might have been able to tolerate a church with whitewashed walls and not too carefully painted scripture texts in place of the ancient beauty, if they had known from incumbent to incumbent what they were supposed to believe.

Thomas Coleman, who succeeded James Palmer in 1645, was a learned Hebrew scholar (he became known as Rabbi Coleman), a Grand Covenanter, a member of the Assembly of Divines. His tenure lasted only four months. John Dicks who followed him (with a brief interlude by a Mr O'Neale) lasted only a few months before his previous congregation in Dover lured him back. There followed a series of brief appointments until 1651 when Fleet Street gained another connection with Stratford-upon-Avon, Samuel Fisher, son of a shoemaker, born there in 1617. Educated at Oxford, he became Lecturer of St Bride's in 1651. The Puritan Lecturer was a preacher without a pastoral responsibility, an activity which in some ways resembled that of the mediaeval friar. It eventually became a regular appointment at St Bride's and was held in 1691 by Dr Francis Atterbury, a Tory High Churchman, who later became Bishop of Rochester and Dean of Westminster. The lectureship was an office of some honour, and Atterbury had many rivals for it. Thackeray thought otherwise; for in *Esmond* he says that Atterbury...

> 'had reached no great church dignity as yet but was only preacher at St Bride's, drawing all the town thither by his eloquent sermons . . . Our good messanger found the good priest already at his books at five o'clock in the morning'.

Thackeray may have been influenced by the fact that Atterbury ended his life in 1732 an exile. Imprisoned in 1720 for alleged complicity in a Stuart plot, he left the country three years later, and threw in his lot with the Jacobites in France. Perhaps he was able to give hints on how to treat the English to Voltaire, who came here 1726-1729 to raise a subscription for his *Henriade*. He was probably introduced to Fleet Street by Pope and he met Congreve in the Temple. Another distinguished Lecturer at St Bride's, in c. 1647, was Thomas Fuller, widely known for ability and wit, and best remembered for his *Worthies of England*. He is said to have had such a memory that, after walking once from Temple Bar to the Royal Exchange, he could recall the tradesman's name over every door.

In 1652 Samuel Fisher exchanged the office of Lecturer for that of incumbent. The records suggest that one significant event in his time was the celebration of the Sacrament.

Both the last and the longest-lasting 'intruder' was John Herring who served for eight years. In 1662 he was unable to accept the Act of Uniformity on grounds

Francis Atterbury

Landing of Charles II at Dover by Chapman

of conscience, and so departed. In his Diary, Pepys referred to his last sermon in Fleet Street, not at St Bride's but at nearby St Dunstan's. Pepys had heard Herring preach two years before (on 22 January 1660, the year in which he tasted tea for the first time) and had thought it 'a lazy poor sermon'; but he evidently found reason for his appreciation of Herring to grow in the next two years. St Bride's Vestry, too, esteemed him enough to take a special collection all over the parish 'to be given to him to help in his necessity'. The same day as Herring preached his last sermon, Pepys spent the afternoon in St Bride's 'and there heard one Carpenter, an old man, who they say hath been a Jesuit priest, and is come over to us; but he preaches very well'.

On 9 June 1660, the Churchwardens' Accounts record that they 'Paid Mr. Audley for drawing the King's Armes to hang in ye Church. £7 0*s*. 0*d*.' Charles II had entered London only eleven days before. The Churchwardens must have been eager to please him or to see the end of the Commonwealth – or perhaps both. The night before Charles returned, he slept in the City and was the last monarch to do so. On 5 July 'Paid the ringers when the King dined in the Cittie 2*s*. 6*d*.' was added to the Churchwardens' reckonings.

Restoration England had begun. Long live the king. Let joy be unconfined. The tightened spring was released. Nowhere was its recoil more felt than in Alsatia, Fleet Street's epitome of vice and squalor with a name derived from the no-man's-land border between France and Belgium where no law had power. Alsatia was the final corruption of the mediaeval idea of the sanctuary afforded by a holy place.

In days when the monarch was a tyrant and the law a means of savage revenge, the ordinary man needed some last desperate refuge, if only to give himself time to crave pardon before being summarily executed. Such refuges grew up around religious buildings, and the area south of Fleet Street between St Bride's and the Temple, being largely occupied by the Carmelite monastery, provided a natural haven. Until Henry VIII a man who sought sanctuary was usually banished abroad. It was then realised that such involuntary exiles could only too easily share English secrets with those from whom the English would hide them. They therefore had to be allowed to stay at home.

The dissolution of the Whitefriars monastery in 1538 led to the abandonment of many persons who had depended on its charity. They, remembering ancient rights of sanctuary, stayed on the spot and from this pustule the baccilli multiplied. Alsatia was born, providing the raw material for Shadwell's *Squire of Alsatia*, Walter Scott's *Fortunes of Nigel*, and Kathleen Winsor's *Forever Amber*. Alsatia was the sump to which the lowest elements of society sank. It was, in

The Restoration Banquet at Whitehall

MARY FRITH, *alias* MAL *or* MOLL CUTPURSE,

fact, the underbelly of an age which could use one of its main City thoroughfares, Fleet Street, as a place for erecting gibbets, hanging men and letting their putrefying corpses swing for days to foul the air. If the Lord Mayor could countenance that, what could the outlaw do? Alsatia provided the answer, and blazoned the fact in dens with names like 'The Bucket of Blood'.

Alsatia flourished illegally. No law founded or regulated it. A document in the Lansdowne MS suggests it had some sort of codification in the reign of Elizabeth, whereby in return for freedom from City rules, laws, ordinances, and taxation, the denizens promised to attend St Paul's, appoint their own officers, arrest any rogues found in their precincts, look after their own poor and maintain, in winter time, 'lanthornes and lights' – all subject to the elastic phrase 'as hitherto hath been accustomed'. Alsatia just happened. In 1608 James I bestowed a charter on the City confirming the ancient rights, privileges and immunities of its citizens. Alsatians, if they bothered to read it, merely interpreted it in their own way. They accepted no liability for taxes. They accepted no responsibility for cleaning their ordure-piled alleys. Having a myriad entries and exits from their disorderly bolt-holes, they mocked any authority which tried to apprehend them. They were a complete community – including their own dissipated parsons who had to be dug out of a bawdyhouse or brandy shop when wanted. They were a remarkable exercise in human bestiality and fit material for Hogarth who drew them.

Not until William III and 1697 was the freedom of Alsatia diminished, but it

The Fleet Prison in Hogarth's *Rake's Progress* series

left John Dryden, drawn by T. Unwins, engraved by E. Smith

right William Davenant, Poet Laureate

took two further Acts of Parliament under George I and George II to extinguish it. Daniel Defoe found Alsatia both a useful place of refuge and the ideal source of material for *Moll Flanders*. Geographically Flanders and the original Alsatia are close. London's Alsatia and St Bride's were practically contiguous. This may be the reason why on 10 August 1659 'Moll Cutpurse', the notorious Mary Frith, thief, fortune-teller and forger, was buried in St Bride's churchyard. Middleton and Dekker helped to keep her memory alive in *The Roaring Girle*.

The Alsatians, it seems, were beyond the control even of the Puritans. The same could not be said of those more amiable vagabonds, the actors. In 1648 Parliament directed that all theatres should be dismantled, that anyone found acting, even in private, should be publicly whipped and anyone found watching actors should be fined 5*s*. For a dozen years England had no theatre. Then on 5 April 1660, still twenty days before Charles II landed at Dover, William Beeston made a contract for the rebuilding of the Salisbury Court Theatre at a cost of £329. It seems to have been one of Pepys' favourites in 1661, and he went there as often as three times in one week.

Within a stone's throw was the Whitefriars Theatre, which eclipsed all others in London, 1671-82. Nearer the river was the Dorset Garden Theatre designed by Sir Christopher Wren and, judging by illustrations, reminiscent of his designs for St Bride's Church. Dryden wrote many pieces for it, while the playwrights, Davenant, Betterton, Wycherley, Shadwell and the egregious Mrs Aphra Behn all

left William Wycherley

right Thomas Shadwell, Poet Laureate, engraved by Yates

contributed. Likewise all Otway's plays, except the last, were first produced there. Otway was much praised by William Hazlitt (who lived at 3 Bouverie Street and used to hold his levées in a coffee house off Chancery Lane) and Walter Scott. His debt-laden misery and unrequited passion for Mrs Barry, stage creator of all his tragic queens, found their focus between Fleet Street and the river. He died, dissipated and despairing, in a nearby tavern aged only 33.

It was at the Dorset Garden Theatre that men of the day showed their conviction that Shakespeare, dead only half a century, was archaic and needed updating. Perhaps they were influenced by Pepys, who thought *A Midsummer Night's Dream* 'the most insipid, ridiculous play' he ever saw. Thus Dryden produced his version of *Troilus and Cressida*, Shadwell of *Timon of Athens*, Davenant of *Macbeth*, while Mrs Behn turned *The Tempest* into an opera.

> 'She was the first woman in England to live by her pen. She aimed at writing like a man, and finding a licentious stage, she accepted it. The startling indecency of her comedies has no other explanation, for her own life was blameless. And she was ingenuous, too; when outcry was raised against her grossness, she "wondered at the impudence of any of her sex who would pretend to an opinion in such a matter".'[4]

She was buried in Westminster Abbey.

left Aphra Behn, drawn by T. Unwins, engraved by J. Fittler

right Thomas Otway, engraved by Rivers

In 1674 Wren rebuilt the theatre in Drury Lane. Dryden in his Epilogue for the reopening suggested why Dorset Garden had declined in favour:

> 'Our house relieves the ladies from the frights
> Of ill-paved streets, and long dark winter nights.'

Dryden, of course, was out to promote the interest of Drury Lane, but fashion was on the move, and many of the 'best people' were settling west of Temple Bar. Why should people come to Fleet Street where Alsatia was still a reality? By 1699 the Dorset Garden stage was a place for wrestlers and weight-lifters. When there was a move to rehabilitate the theatre in 1703, the City Fathers showed they still hated the stage by calling for 'some effectual course to be taken to prevent the youth of the city from resorting to the playhouse'. The theatre was pulled down in 1720, and since 1855 its site has been occupied by the City of London School.

By contrast, it can be said that scientific institutions owed much to Fleet Street at this time, replacing Nell Gwyn with persons of different distinction.

The Royal Society, which concerns itself with the whole field of knowledge, derived from the Philosophical Society founded in 1645. It received its Charter in 1665, and included in its Council such names as Robert Boyle, theologian and scientist, the precocious Abraham Cowley (who was born in Fleet Street), Dryden,

facing The Duke's Theatre, Dorset Garden

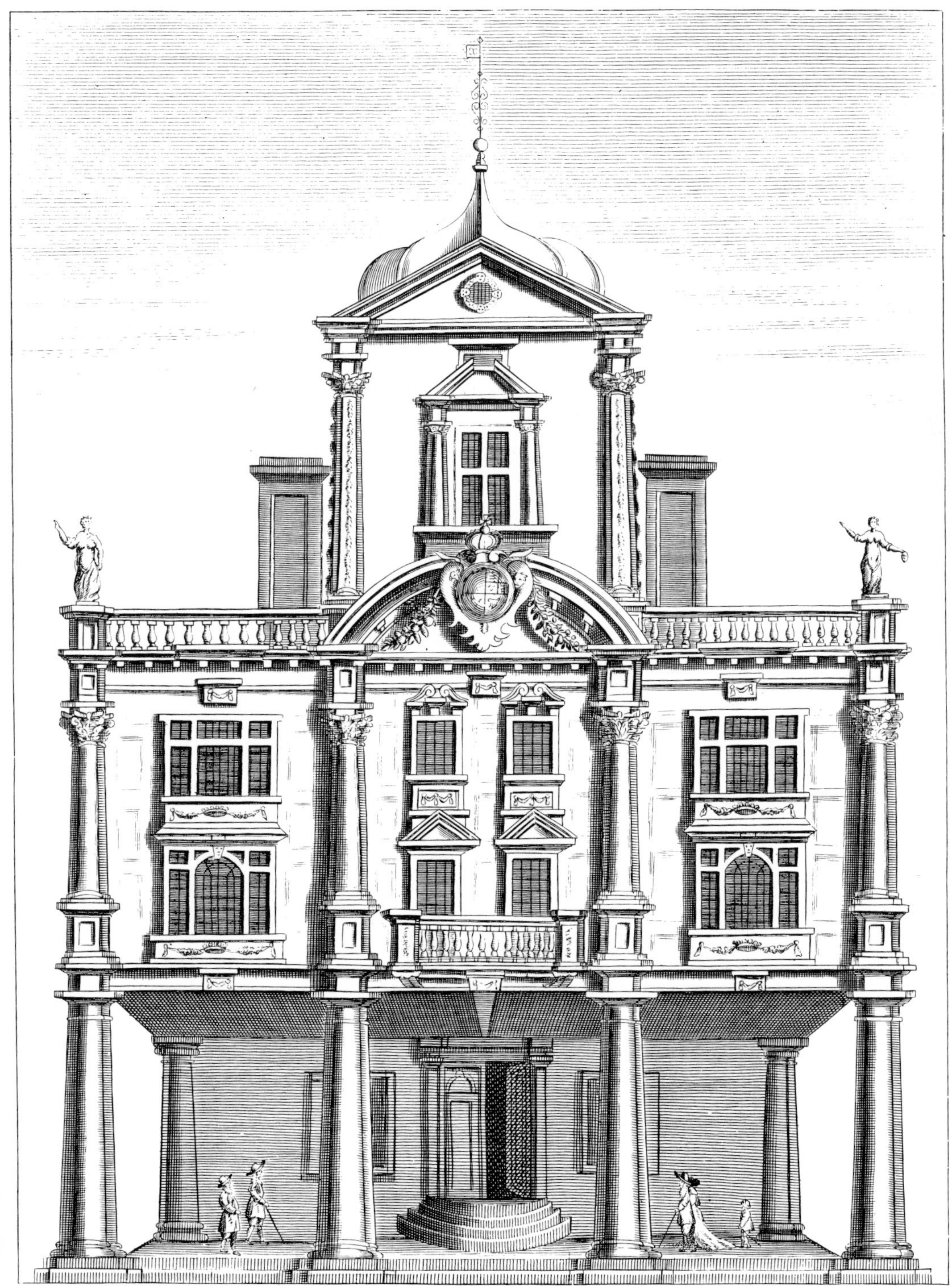

left John Evelyn by R. Nanteuil. © *National Portrait Gallery*

right John Aubrey engraved by T. Cook

Waller, Evelyn, Ashmole (who lived in Middle Temple Lane and assured Pepys that 'frogs and many insects do fall from the sky fully formed'), Aubrey and Thomas Spratt. For a long time, 1710-1782, its headquarters were in Crane Court off Fleet Street in a house once owned by Dr Edward Browne, son of Sir Thomas Browne, author of *Religio Medici*. Members met customarily at the Mitre for their dinner. The move to Crane Court, bought for £1,450, was conducted by Newton in a most imperious manner.

Other learned organisations, associated with Crane Court, include the Society of Arts (1754-74) and the Society of Antiquaries which met to dine at the Mitre in 1739. Coleridge gave his lectures on Shakespeare there in 1819-20.

In 1665 the Great Plague savaged London from June to September. Daniel Defoe described it in *A Journal of the Plague Year* published in 1722. 'A rather cunning work of art, a confidence trick of the imagination', Anthony Burgess calls it in his Introduction to the Penguin edition, for Defoe was only five at the time. Yet it is a brilliant – and factual – account which, though based on records and not on personal experience, has all the authority of an eye-witness. 1665 was not however London's first plague year in the seventeenth century. James I was crowned during an epidemic in 1603 with an estimated death toll of 30,000. There was another in 1625 when he died. Outbreaks followed in 1636-7 and, worst of all, in 1640, which lasted six years. Some authorities regard the Plague as endemic on English soil from the time of the Black Death. Carried by the fleas which lived in rats, it was characterised by the enlargement of the 'bubos', the lymphatic gland (hence 'bubonic') followed by headache, chill, back pains, fast pulse and breathing, high fever, restlessness, and finally vomiting and delirium.[5]

For the individual sufferer it was physical agony combined with mental hopelessness. For his immediate family it was a death sentence as well as economic loss. For the community at large it was a seemingly unmanageable, unpredictable, ruthless destroyer. The killer took about three days, and then the last gasp and the plague pit. The whole machinery devised by a Lord Mayor whirred frantically on. The Examiner, the Watchmen, the Searchers, the Chirurgeons, the Nurse-keepers, the Rakers, the Lay-stall emptiers. And the whole phalanx of camp-followers. The beggars, the thieves, the destitute who, certain they were to die,

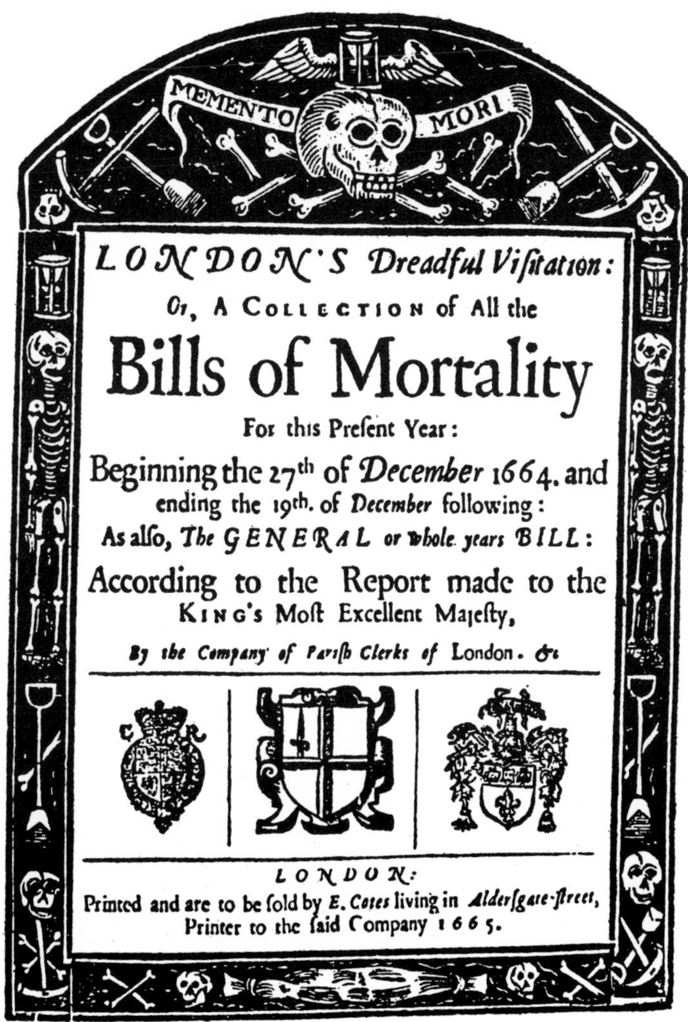

LONDON'S Dreadful Viſitation:

Or, A COLLECTION of All the

Bills of Mortality

For this Preſent Year:

Beginning the 27th of *December* 1664. and
ending the 19th. of *December* following:

As alſo, *The GENERAL or whole years BILL*:

According to the Report made to the
KING's Moſt Excellent Majeſty,

By the Company of Pariſh Clerks of London. &c.

LONDON:
Printed and are to be ſold by *E. Cotes* living in *Alderſgate-ſtreet*,
Printer to the ſaid Company 1665.

'The Body of Annabel carried to the Dead Cart.' From Ainsworth's *Old St Paul's*, engraved by J. Franklin

'The Plague Pit.' Same source

filched some last pleasure from a corpse before they were themselves cadavers. The moral horrors of Alsatia seem more forgivable when one remembers they happened in an age conditioned to the physical horrors of the Plague and the mental horror of being helpless before it.

The first knell of the Great Plague of 1665 was tolled at the western approaches to the City and then made its relentless way eastward. Fleet Street, ancient line of communication, was one of its highways. And St Bride's parish, crammed with residents and workers, bounded by its mephitic ditch suffered horribly. Whereas in normal times the parish could expect fewer than ten deaths in any week, the Plague pushed them up to a peak of 238 at the end of a summer when the weather had been hot, dry and cloudless, and the drought had made even elementary cleanliness difficult. That sentence has to be qualified: 238 deaths so far as the parish clerk knew. An identified and notified case of plague was best avoided. In many cases the body was taken out of the house at night and thrown on to the death cart, with a bribe to the carter. Nobody was able to keep a strict check on the number of bodies cast into the stinking death pits. Even that was preferable to being locked for forty days in a house, where plague had struck and was probably still striking.

Statistics, in any case, were dependent on a chancy system. Each parish clerk made his weekly returns to the Company of Parish Clerks which compiled the weekly Bills of Mortality. But parish clerks were dependent on searchers who for a miserable few pence would enter a death house and bring back their testimony. It was a job few people wanted, so it was usually thrust on old paupers, frequently women, who would otherwise have been a charge on the parish. For a shilling or so a searcher was ready to swear there had been no death, or that a purulent corpse had died as the result of an accident. The watchmen set to guard an infected house and to keep captive its inhabitants, perhaps until all were dead, also had their price and, in a matter of life and death, frightened people were ready to offer it. St Bride's vestrymen, upon whom fell the responsibility of fighting the horror in their parish, worked hard and they were not inexperienced or inept. But terror of the unknown makes a man willing to flaunt the known.

So the Plague mounted. First week in August, 66 deaths, second week, 90, third week 119, fourth week 152, first week in September, 219. The bearers of the dead were busy – and a source of danger. The halberds (the arms kept by each parish under statute) were cleared out of their storehouse in the churchyard, and the bearers (wages 12*s*. a week) given lodging there. Soon the neighbours complained that the bearers' washing hung out in the churchyard was offensive. Their quarters were railed off. The death rate still rose. 43 in this one parish in a single day – 11 September – and the City had 131 parishes. In all it seems that about 80 masters and men of the printing trade succumbed.

So the death carts rumbled until, as Pepys remarked to Lady Carteret:

> 'the nights, though much lengthened, are grown too short to conceal the burials of those who died the day before, people being thereby constrained to borrow daylight for that service. Little noise heard day or night but the tolling of bells'.

And door after door was chalked with a cross and the plea 'Lord have mercy upon us'.

The Royal Court left the capital. Parliament rose and ran. The lawyers left the Temple. The wealthy left their banks and their counting houses. Watermen left the river. Printers left their presses. And many clergy left their parishes – but not the vicar of St Bride's. Week by week, page by page, the Rev. Richard Peirson sorrowfully but neatly signed his name in the swollen burial register. Henry Clarke, senior churchwarden, became a victim. William Clarke succeeded him, both as churchwarden and as corpse.

'So', says Defoe,

> 'the plague defied all medicines; the very physicians were seized with it, with their preservatives in their mouths; and men went about prescribing to others and telling them what to do till the tokens were upon them, and they dropped down dead, destroyed by that very enemy they directed others to oppose.'

Then the rains came. The Lord Mayor directed fires to be lit in the streets to cleanse the pestilent air. The rains put them out. The Plague diminished, flared up again, and finally subsided. Richard Peirson went back to ten funerals a week or less. Indeed, to quote the Register for one red-letter week, 'John Child was sworne parishe Clerke of St Bride's ys 9 day of May, 1666, in which weeke not one dyed'.

Woodcuts of the Great Plague in a broadsheet 1655–6. 1. A 'searcher of the dead' in a bedroom. 2. Dog-killers at work. 3 and 4. The exodus from London by river and road. 5 and 6. Bodies being taken for burial. 7. Mass burial. 8. Mourners defying the prohibition on crowds. 9. Eventually the rich return.

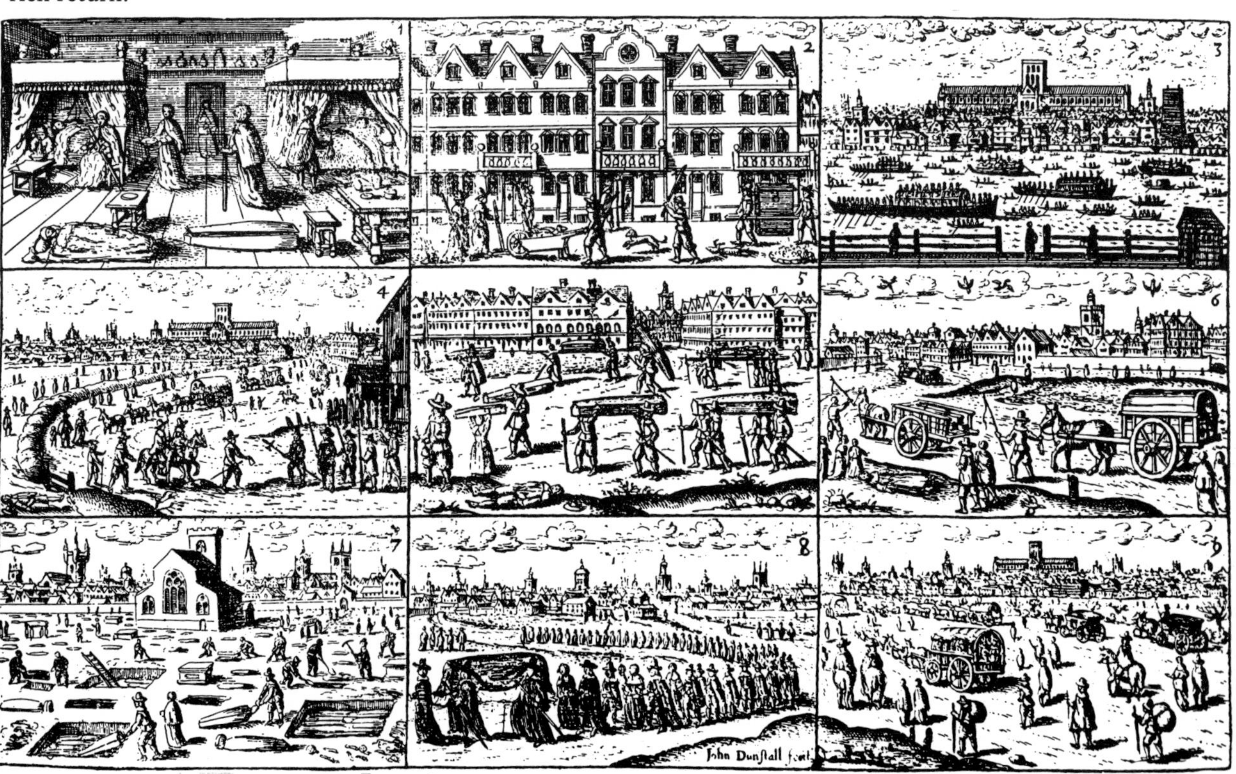

Escaping the Plague

Plagues were expensive. The parish – which was the civil as well as the ecclesiastical authority – had to find the cash disbursed on all the extra bearers, gravediggers and the other supernumeraries of death. An elementary justice suggested that the deceased pay for their own harsh obsequies, and so there arose the gruesome trade of the 'brokers of the dead'. Few survivors claimed the effects of dead persons; thus they became the property of the parish. The brokers hazarded the infected dwellings, took the contents, and sold them. This sombre harvest yielded only a part of what was needed. The Poor Rate was increased. A special Pest Rate was levied. The wealthy who had escaped sent donations – the Countess of Dorset £2, for example. The City Cash made contributions totalling £140 'for the visited' in the parish. There was one collection in Bristol, and the Bishop of London made another. In all, St Bride's spent £581 from all sources in little over half a year, total deaths being estimated at 2,111. The total for the City was 68,500.

Within a few months an insignificant baker's shop in Pudding Lane caught fire. It was the start of another catastrophe. 'There is no such fire of any great city on record, unless it is the burning of Rome under Nero', said Sir Walter Besant over two centuries later. Hitler destroyed only a quarter of the City's buildings. In 1666 five-sixths vanished. In narrow streets, where timber-framed houses looked like pot-bellied aldermen whispering Guildhall secrets, there was little to be done. Although the City had been issuing ordinances about fires and fire-fighting since the thirteenth century, the only equipment consisted of overgrown garden syringes which had to be dipped in buckets, and firehooks for pulling buildings down. A few parishes had acquired fire-engines – mere water-tanks on wheels with squirts attached. Fuller, in his *Worthies*, mentions two: St Bride's and St James, Clerkenwell. But St Bride's, it appears, had not obeyed the injunction to keep the machine 'scoured, oyled and trimmed' for an emergency. At all events, the church was totally destroyed and there is no reference anywhere to the fire-engine being used. All the Churchwardens managed to salve from the debris, apart from the registers, was some fused bell-metal – thus preserving something of the twelfth century curfew bell for a resurrected life.

Few took the conflagration seriously until it was too late. Samuel Pepys was roused by a maidservant to see the great sight. He looked at it, wondered, and went back to bed. In the event, however, he did more than most towards ending the fire. He soon realised its gravity ('a most horrid malicious bloody flame') and also realised that the City authorities were not succeeding in fighting it. So he persuaded the king to take the responsibility – and act. Charles II rode from place to place with a satchel of money hiring casual labour. A contemporary letter in the London Museum tells of the King and the Duke of York 'handling the water in bucketts when they stood up to the ancles in water'.

Four days the blaze lasted. And a city which had taken fourteen centuries to grow was no more. 13,000 houses disappeared and with them 87 churches, St Paul's Cathedral, the Royal Exchange, the Guildhall and 44 City Company halls. The City was more ravaged by fire in three days than by Hitler in three years. 100,000 inhabitants – of whom 'but only eight dead' – had nowhere to go. Rebuilding had to be rapid. Samuel Rolle, later Chaplain to the king, was one who in many sermons urged haste 'I know of no secular design . . . of greater importance, and that to thousands of families, than is the rebuilding of London'. People needed homes. A great commercial centre needed place to work. There was not time to wait for perfect plans to be developed by Mr Wren or anyone

London's burning. Painted by J. de Loutherbourg, engraved by A. H. Payne

Fire engine made by John Keeling of Blackfriars. From a print of 1678

else. An almost bankrupt City had to depend largely on a tax on sea coal entering its port to find the money for rebuilding – the tax continued until 1889.

When the parish clerk of St Bride's came to make a permanent record of the fire, he decided that the proper place to enter the details was the burial register. St Bride's had suffered as seriously as any part of London. Evelyn, on fire duty in Fetter Lane, was an eye-witness.

> 'All Fleete Streete, the Old Bailey, Ludgate Hill . . . now flaming and most of it reduced to ashes; the stones of St Paul's flow like grenados . . . Ye melting lead running downe the streetes in a streame, and the very pavements glowing with fiery rednesse, so as no horse nor man was able to tread on them, and the demolition had stopp'd all the passage, so that no help could be applied. The eastern wind still more impetuously drove the flames forward. Nothing but ye Almighty power of God was able to stop them, for vaine was ye help of man.'[6]

Paul Boston, the new vicar of St Bride's, was particularly unlucky, for he had arrived only two weeks before. He never had a church to serve, for Wren's foundations were only being laid when he departed. Nor did he have many resident parishioners. For long after the fire, burials never exceeded four or five a month; most were poor people. The rich ratepayers did not return quickly, and it was a royal appeal for fire-victims which yielded in all some £690 for the relief of 'those that lived in St Bride's parish, some in shedds or vaults'. In his will Paul Boston left £10 to those distressed by the fire, as well as £10 for the poor, and £50 for communion plate. The silver gilt vessels bought with that money are still prized parish possessions.

One of the men driven from Fleet Street by fire was James Shirley, a favourite dramatist of Charles I and his circle. During the royalist eclipse he had lived quietly in Whitefriars making a grudging living as a schoolmaster. With the Restoration he resumed his trade as a playwright, but as his pieces lacked licentiousness, he never regained success. He contrived to live however in Fleet Street, near Serjeants' Inn, until his house was burned down, and thereafter moved outside the City's bounds. He and his wife died on the same day shortly after.

Living near Shirley and also burned out was the versatile John Ógilby, who began his career as a dancer. He became a 'sworn viewer', a surveyor, and as such produced his famous map of London, being appointed 'King's cosmographer and geographic printer', and financing his printing by lotteries. He translated Virgil and Homer, for which he was denigrated by Dryden in *MacFlecknoe* and pilloried by Pope in *The Dunciad*, a satire on the booksellers. The fire cost him his house in Kings Head Court, Shoe Lane, together with £3000 worth of printing plant and stock which, added to losses he had sustained by the death of customers in the Plague, left him bankrupt. He was buried in Wren's then unfinished St Bride's Church in 1676.

William Lilly was a paradoxical victim of London's fire, though he does not

The square tower of medieval St Bride's is visible over the bridge

left John Ogilby. Drawn by J. Thurston, engraved by W. C. Edwards

right James Shirley. Drawn by J. Thurston, engraved by W. H. Worthington

seem to have lost any visible assets through it. Lilly was the Prime Prognosticator of his day, the seventeenth century Old Moore. He started publishing his annual almanack in 1644, and it continued until his death in 1681. The most renowned astrologer of his age, he learned the arcane methods from one Rhys Evans (there were still Celts hereabouts) in Gunpowder Alley, Shoe Lane. In 1644 rumours began to fly that he had prophesied a mighty blaze. So incensed was he by these rumours that he bought space in the 9 April 1665 issue of *The Perfect Diurnal* and delivered himself of an impassioned advertisement. Any suggestions that he had predicted a fire, he said, were 'untruths forged by ungodly men and women to disturb the quiet people of the City, to amaze the nation, and to cast aspersions and scandals on me'.

The Great Fire came after all in the following year, and he must have kicked himself for not letting a lucky prophecy stand. Who started the conflagration? Some attributed it to the Roman Catholics. 'Here, by permission of ye heaven, hell broke loose upon this Protestant city from the malicious hearts of barbarous Papists . . .' said the inscription affixed to 25 Pudding Lane in 1681, and happily removed in 1830. On the other hand the Dutch, smarting from the flames the English had applied to their fishing boats, attributed the fire to a much greater authority and saw it as God's vengeance on a wicked enemy. *The London Gazette* (No. 85, 3-10 September 1666), however, blamed neither Roman Catholics, the Dutch, nor even the French; 'the whole was the effect of an unhappy chance'.

John Ogilby's *Britannia*, Vol. I, London, 1675 (the first English road atlas). Engraved title-page by W. Hollar after Francis Barlow. © *British Museum*

7. Wren's St Bride's

In the year 1671, Newton finished constructing his reflecting telescope, Milton published *Paradise Regained* and *Samson Agonistes*, Wycherley published *Love in a Wood*, Dryden was Poet Laureate and Royal Historiographer, and the churchwardens of St Bride's took Mr Christopher Wren (not yet knighted, but already Surveyor-General and Principal Architect for rebuilding the City) and Mr Robert Hook (City Surveyor) out to dinner at the Globe Tavern in Fleet Street at a cost of £2 17*s*. 0*d*. Their purpose was not difficult to divine – they needed a new church. A year later, they tried again: 'Jan. 22. Spent at Mr. Hodersall's giveing the doctor Wren a treate 6*s*. 6*d*.' Their persistence was rewarded, since St Bride's was one of the first post-Fire churches to be opened for worship. This was appropriate for, to quote old citizen Rugge in his *Diurnal*, 'The first brick laid after the Fire was in Fleet Street, a house of a plumer to cast his work in, only one room.'

But to imply that a good dinner was solely responsible for lubricating Wren's attention is unfair. Here was a man already distinguished for his talents. Son of a Dean of Windsor, nephew of a bishop, the young Wren became a pupil of the fearsome Dr Busby at Westminster School, at the same time as Dryden and Locke. Thence to his father's home at Bletchington where his very able brother-in-law, William Holder, taught him geometry and arithmetic. At 17 he went to Oxford where his brilliance flourished (Newton in his *Principia* applauded it), and where at the age of 23 he became professor of astronomy. Soon after he was appointed Deputy-Surveyor of the King's Works. Some insist that Wren's greatness lay in science and engineering. No one can deny his ability in these matters. At the same time anyone who has, for example, read one of his letters to his first wife, Faith, before their marriage, will know that he was also a poet, a creator.

His affianced had dropped her watch in the sea and had asked the best man she knew to put it right. The note which accompanied its return must have been more acceptable than the watch:

'Madam – the artificer having never before mett with a drowned Watch,

left Isaac Newton by Vanderbank engraved by E. Scriven

right Newton's original reflecting telescope. © *Science Museum*

like an ignorant physician has been soe long about the cure that he hath made me very unquiet that your commands should be soe long deferred; however, I have sent the Watch at last and envie the felicity of it, that it should be soe neer your side, and soe often enjoy your Eye, and be consulted by you how your Time shall passe while you employ your Hand in your excellent Workes.

'But have a care for it, for I put such a Spell into it that every Beating of the Ballance will tell you 'tis the Pulse of my Heart which labours as much to serve you, and More Trewly than the Watch; for the Watch, I believe, will sometimes lie, and sometimes perhaps be idle and unwilling to goe, having received soe much injury by being drenched in that briny Bath, that I despair it should ever be a Trew Servant to you more.

'But as for me (unless you drown me too in my Teares) you may be confident that I shall never cease to be – your most affectionate humble servant, Christopher Wren.'

The artist and the scientist had met in one man, and the Great Fire of London enabled him to display his genius.

For nearly five years St Bride's had stood desolate. Part of the mediaeval tower remained upright, but its calcined stones neither had nor offered security. St

Christopher Wren by Edward Pierce. © *Ashmolean Museum*

The black stratum of charcoal, found below the steeple, marks the level of the Great Fire

Dunstan's up the road had escaped, so had the Temple Church and St Clement Danes, so the congregation did not lack a place for public worship. Yet such is the loyalty of a man for his own sanctuary that, before long, St Bride's churchyard, like many another in the City, was adorned with a 'tabernacle', a temporary structure. The word was a reminder that while the Israelites had wandered forty years in the wilderness, God had been content to live, nomad-like, in a portable shrine. There was a reasonable theology in this. God would surely be content to put up with temporary accommodation until men had had a chance of attending to urgent needs for homes and places of work.[1]

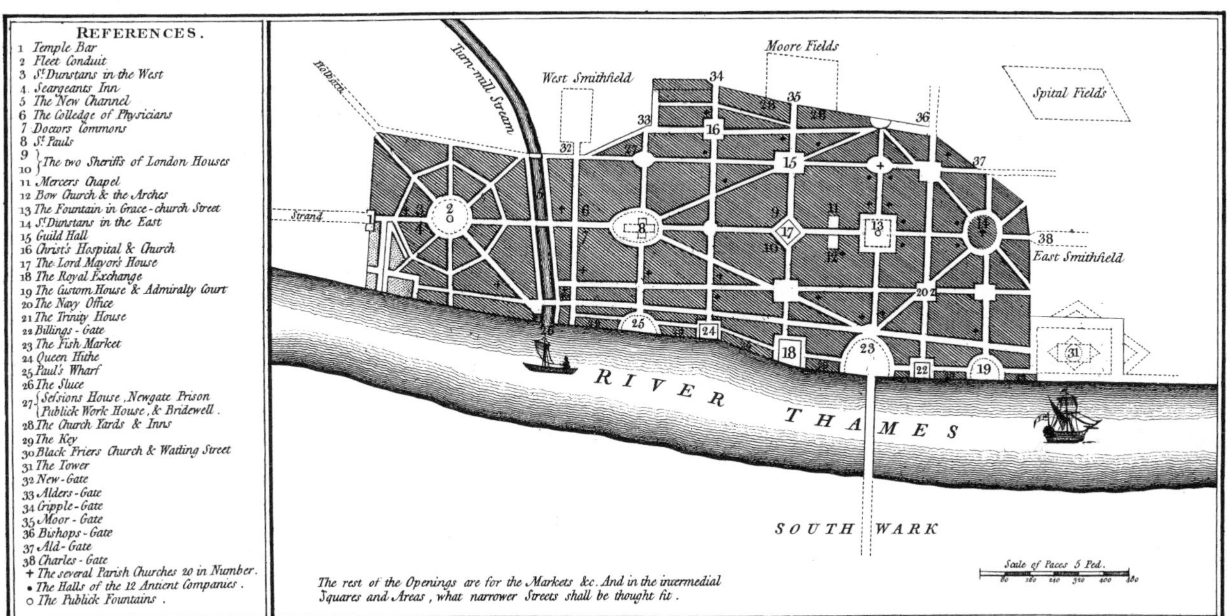

Plans for rebuilding the City after the Fire of London by Evelyn *(top)* and Wren *(below)*

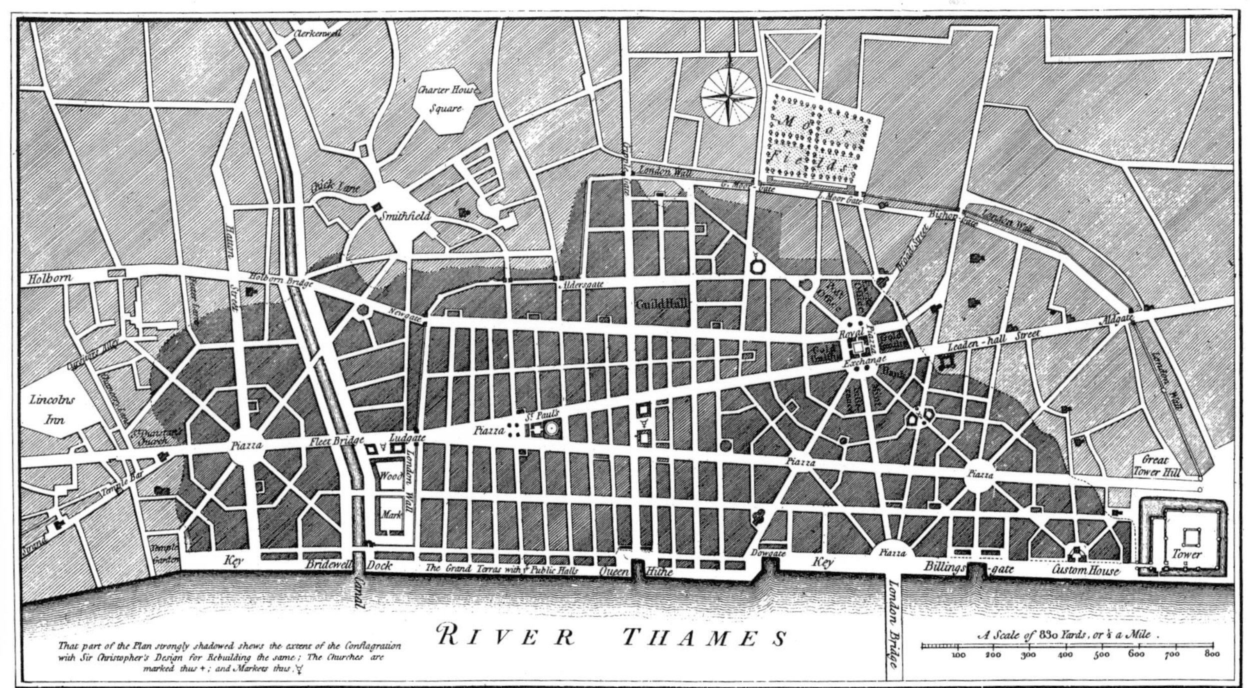

So Fleet Street was rebuilt and the urgency of the rebuilding was greater than elsewhere in the City. Less than a week after the rains came and the fire ceased, Sir Gerald Moore and other Fleet Street property owners had sought leave, under Charles II's Royal Proclamation, to start work. The leave was granted and Fleet Street was the first main thoroughfare to be substantially remade.

There was a further cause for delay before church rebuilding began. How many of its ancient phalanx of churches did the City really need? Wren said that 39 were enough to replace the 87 destroyed. Had Wren had his way, there can be little doubt that the Church throughout England would have benefited, for much of the resources of men and money invested in the very over-churched square mile would have been released for areas of new population. The conurbations generated by the future Industrial Revolution might have gained more parsons and more equipment, if the City of London had not been too greedy in this respect. It was not that Wren, a parson's son, wanted to see London de-churched. He wanted to be rational i.e. to amalgamate two or three small parishes, or to give a new parish one magnificent church, and so reduce the problem of staffing, heating, lighting, and maintaining all the others.

But Londoners are curious about their churches. They insist on having a quantity of buildings, even if only to stay away from them. Local loyalties, not unmixed with local jealousies, the long association of some City Company with a particular building, the difficulties of alienating some fund or some privilege traditionally held by a particular church, these were only some of the considerations. Authority yielded. In 1670 – within months of William Penn having written his learned dissertation on Christian self-sacrifice, *No Cross, Nor Crown* – the Additional Building Act directed 51 churches, each individually named, to be rebuilt.

Within four years of the Fire, Wren had prepared plans for the first ten churches, St Bride's among them. These plans were revolutionary, for the classical style of church architecture had barely been seen before in Britain. The change was due to several causes – social, technical, and religious. For mediaeval man the theological emphasis was on God as a remote mystery, to be offered the sacrifice of the Mass by a priest standing far off at the east end of the church, remote from the congregation and using a remote language. Hence Gothic architecture with its arches, aspiring to celestial heights and its long quires, and its separation of chancel (the priest's part) and nave (the people's part). But now the age of reason had dawned. Like other buildings, a church had to echo an appeal to the mind. Instead of having two compartments, it was now designed as a single space where priest and people worshipped together, with emphasis on the pulpit rather than on the altar. A building might still be vast – like St Paul's – but somehow it had to be amenable to reason. Salisbury Cathedral spire points to infinity. St Paul's dome is finite, enclosing heaven with earth. It is the ancient tension between the immanent and the transcendent in man's concept of God.

Wren made his plans. The congregation of St Bride's were still rebuilding their own homes, offices and shops; but they exerted themselves for their church too and, with the aid of the Bishop of London, they sought help wherever it could be found. Within a month they raised £500, the sum required by the Guildhall as a deposit when a City church started rebuilding, a remarkable effort at a time when most of those parishioners had lost homes and businesses in the Fire. St Bride's has never lacked loyal and enthusiastic friends.

One of Wren's first ideas for St Bride's steeple. This design is now carved in oak on the font cover

pages 146 *and* 147
John Clayton's drawings provide the best source for contrasting the pre-1940 St Bride's and its present successor, particularly in respect to the galleries and interior furnishings

NORTH ELEVATION
0 5 10 20 30 40
TRANSVERSE SECTION
EAST ELEVATION
LONGITUDINAL SECTION

All the financial problems, however, were far from over. Much of the cost of the new building had to come from the Coal Dues voted by Parliament. These yielded 1*s.* per ton on all the coal brought into London. This rate proved inadequate, and in 1670 it was raised to 3*s.* per ton. Even then, much depended on private enterprise. A loan of £500 was raised on security of part of the parish land. House-to-house collections were made both for gifts and interest-free loans; and £260 was advanced under this latter category by Sir William Playter, Chamberlain of the City.

Even so, money was always tight, and there were times when work had to be held up because the funds had run out. Amazingly, London was rebuilt during and in spite of a financial blizzard. In 1667 the Dutch had annihilated the British Fleet in the Medway. Shipping into the City – and the trade and money it brought – was limping. The king was making financial demands, which would not have been popular even if the reasons had been convincing. A few years later he introduced the 'stop on the Exchequer' – a moratorium – and men who were wealthy one day headed for a debtor's gaol the next. Viner went bankrupt for £500,000, Backwell for £300,000. Meanwhile Charles was annoying both Parliament and the City by his dalliance with the hated French, while his war on Holland was further dislocating trade. About this time, the Earl of Shaftesbury formed the Green Ribbon Club in Chancery Lane, the origin of the Whig Party. Rumours flew. Documents alleged to have been found in a meal tub suggested that London was to be burned again, while the Titus Oates plot convinced every good Protestant that the Papists were planning to kill the king and replace him with his quisling brother. The magistrate concerned, Sir Edmundsbury Godfrey, was found murdered in a ditch. The trained bands were called up. The City gates were closed. The king prorogued Parliament, and suppressed the City's Charter. Hardly the best time for raising money to build churches, yet the money was raised; and subsequent generations have idly accepted an illusion of wealthy and leisurely merchants making vast tax-free fortunes in a gracious age, and leisurely beautifying a serene though busy City.

Joshua Marshall, a parishioner living in Fetter Lane, was the main contractor for St Bride's. His first job was to clear the site at a cost of £150. St Bride's made a wise choice in Marshall as the subsequent history of his workmanship was to prove. He, like his father before him, was Master Mason to Charles II, an office that carried a miserable salary (12*d.* a day) but magnificent perquisites. Marshall was already engaged in several important works and to him (also with Wren as architect) we owe Temple Bar and the Monument. Marshall kept strict records. His bill amounted to £8,964, four-fifths of the cost of the entire building less the steeple. In the Rawlinson MS in the Bodleian Library, Oxford, we can read the names of the master painters, carpenters, joiners, plumbers, smiths and glaziers who sub-contracted for him, together with the sums they were paid. One assistant was the young Nicholas Hawksmoor, subsequently a famous architect in his own right.

Digging the foundations cost £90, representing many man-hours at the then unskilled labourer's rate of 1*s.* 6*d.* for a ten-hour day as against a mason or stonecarver's 2*s.* 6*d.* – 3*s.* 6*d.* As in most Wren churches, the main material was Portland stone (the same company supplied the stone for the post-Hitler church) with small quantities of Reigate stone and Kentish ashlar. Small sums were also included in the accounts for re-working stone from the burned church.

Wren's outer walls, top left, indicate how he built over remains of earlier churches

The work went well. By September 1672, within a year of starting, the walls had reached the upper part of the cornice, the great east window was approaching full height, the tower was high enough to contain eighteen steps, and only £3,270 had been spent. Perhaps it was because the management was shrewd enough to keep its workmen near the site. Alongside St Bride's churchyard is 'The Old Bell Tavern', believed to be on the spot where 'The Swan' anciently stood. A tradition honoured in Fleet Street and illuminated in its bar says 'This house was built by Sir Christopher Wren about 1670 as a hostel for his workmen then busy on the re-erection of St Bride's church'.

By 1674 the masons had finished the structural work on the main body of the church – apart from the tower which at that stage was left unfinished and jagged. Four years later it was squared off and sealed with a temporary wooden cover until the erection of the steeple in 1701-3. In 1674 John Longland, the carpenter, was covering in the roof (with a great sheet of lead at 17*s.* 6*d.* per cwt., totalling £846) and finishing the ceiling. George Drew and Stephen Leaver were doing the ironwork, William Cleeve the joinery. John Cole and Charles Atherton were responsible for the plumbing. Robert Streeter, sergeant-painter to Charles II and who painted the ceiling of the Sheldonian Theatre at Oxford, did the painting with Edward Bird; while, most improbably, the glazing was the work of a woman, Hannah Brace, who was paid £72.

The whole work, including the tower but excluding the steeple, cost £11,430 5*s.* 11*d.* and came next only to St Lawrence Jewry (£11,870) and Christ Church, Newgate (£11,788) in the cost of all Wren City churches. St Mary le Bow cost only £8,071, but later increased by £7,388 for the steeple. The account for St

Bride's steeple does not appear to have survived, but Wren's comment 'good material and good work' sounds like an apology for a heavy bill. The Vestry seemed to agree about the quality, for they gave the workmen a gratuity of fifty guineas. Time and violence have justified their judgement. That steeple withstood a war as well as two strikes by lightning.

Edward Hatton's *New View of London*, published in 1708, gave a detailed description of the church:

> 'It is a strong pleasant well-built Church and very regular all the Apertures etc., on one side answering exactly to those on the other. And the Roof is elevated on Pillars and Arches with Entablements of the *Tuscan* Order: the groynings of which Arches are neatly carved, having a Rose between two large moulded Pattens, on the Key-stone of each Arch a Seraph, and in the middle between them a Shield, with Compartments and Imposts finely done.
>
> 'It is wainscotted round the Oak about 8 foot high, having spacious Galleries on the North, South and West sides, with curious Fronts of deep Bolection-work, as is the pulpit, being carved and finniered; which are also right Wainscot.
>
> 'The inner Doorcases are five, two on the North and two on the South sides of the Composite order; and a very spacious one toward the West having folding Doors, and adorn'd with Pilasters, Entablature and Parabolically arched Pediment of the Ionick Order all of Wainscot, and at the same West end of the Church is likewise a large strong outer

Another example of how Wren utilised what he found

The South Prospect of the City of London, 1710.
© *Guildhall Library*

Doorcase, of the Ionick Order (as the other outer Doorcases are) over which are these words under a Seraph *"Domus Dei"*. And the Church is well pew'd.

'The Altar-piece is beautiful and magnificent. The lower part consists of 6 carved columns (painted Flakestone colour) with Entablature and circular Pediment, of the *Corinthian* Order, embellish'd with Lamps, Cherubims, Etc. all gilt with Gold. Above a circular Pediment, are the Queen's Arms finely carved, gilt and painted, with the Supporters. Under the pediment, the words in 1 *Cor.* c.10.v.16. The inter-columns are the Commandments; and here is also the Lord's Prayer and Creed. Over the former, the words of *Matth*.6.v.8 and over the latter, 2 *Tim*.1.13 all well done in Black upon Gold. The upper part is painted, and consists of 6 Columns (3 on each side of a handsome arched 5-light window, adorned with a neat scarlet-silk Curtain edged with Gold Fringe) with their Architrave, Friese and Cornish finely done (white and vein'd) in strong Perspective. In the front of which are the Pourtraictures of *Moses*, with the Two Tables in his Hands, and *Aaron* in his Priest's Habit; over the Window 'tis painted Nebulous and above the Clouds appears (from within a large Crimson Velvet Festoon painted Curtain), a Celestial Choir, or a Representation of the Church Triumphant, in the Vision and Presence of a Glory in the shape of a Dove, all finely painted, the Enrichments are gilt with Gold, and the whole is enclosed or fenced in with Rail and Bannister, and the Floor within that paved with black and white marble.'

By 1675 – the year in which Wren was beginning work on St Paul's Cathedral – St Bride's was ready for worship, and was formally opened on 19 December. (272 years later, the anniversary of the day would be marked by the opening of the post-Hitler church.)

The great event took place on a Sunday and Dr Dove, golden-tongued Vicar of

St Bride's, had prepared his best sermon for the occasion. The Lord Mayor (Joseph Sheldon) came. So did many of the Aldermen and Common Council members, all appropriately attired. The church was packed and it is probable that Pepys honoured his father's memory and his birthplace by being present.

But much remained to be done. The galleries, for example, were still incomplete. Three weeks before the opening Dr Dove was sending out an urgent call for a Great Bible and service books. The requisite vestments were lacking. The painting of the Ten Commandments (in black on gold) had still to be done. The material for pews and benches was still being discussed. And Sir Jeremiah Whichcote had to be pressed to supply the pulpit cushion and cloth he had promised. Sir Jeremiah had become Warden of the Fleet Prison by purchasing the office under the Commonwealth, but had gained his baronetcy by helping the king in exile. When the Prison was burned down in the Fire, Sir Jeremy had first sheltered the prisoners at his house in Lambeth and then rebuilt the prison on its old site.

For 35 years St Bride's had only one bell, hung in the middle aisle next to the unfinished tower. The mediaeval church had had a peal of eight or nine bells. They had rung for Henry VIII, Elizabeth I, Mary, James I, and Cromwell. They had proclaimed royal occasions and Parliament's victories. But for forty years and more there had been silence. Finally an appeal for new bells was launched in 1706, and four years later Abraham Rudhall of Gloucester was asked to tender for ten bells (which in due course became twelve). Rudhall secured the contract – subject to the tunefulness of his work satisfying the organist of Westminster Abbey. In 1711 the ring was ready. They ranged from 26 cwt. to 5½ cwt., and

The Fleet River joins the Thames, by Samuel Scott, *c.* 1760. © *Guildhall Library*

The Fleet Prison engraved by F. W. Fairholt

Wren's steeple was to carry nearly 6 tons of reverberating metal. Nine of Rudhall's bells remained to crash down under Hitler's bombs.

St Bride's bells, so the records show, attracted valiant teams of ringers. Among them the Society of College Youths, which surprisingly included a Lord Chief Justice and Rear Admiral Sir Francis Geary. It is said that all who rang on one famous occasion were men of substance who left the church in their own carriages. Perhaps they were attracted by the organ no less than the bells. This was the creation of that doyen of organ-builders, Renatus Harris, a parishioner of St Bride's with his workshop in Wine Office Court. He completed his task, 1485 pipes, all metal apart from about 24, in 1695 and his son gilded the pipes in 1728. It was rebuilt in 1886 and again in 1920. Hitler ended its life.

About this time Fleet Street seems to have played the part of Harley Street. One of the foremost physicians of his day was Dr Jasper Needham. He was John Evelyn's personal medical attendant and on 4 November 1679 Evelyn wrote: 'In the evening went to the funeral of my pious, dear and ancient learned friend, Dr Jasper Needham, who was buried in St Bride's Church.' Needham had been a regular worshipper and benefactor of St Bride's. Seven years later came the burial of 'James Molins, Master of Chirurgery and Dr. of Physick: Servant to their Majesties King Charles the 2d and King James the 2d.'

Fleet Street housed bankers too, notably Hoare's, Gosling's and Child's. W. G. Bell records some interesting names connected with Child's Bank under the sign of 'Ye Marigold':

> 'What would not a collector of autographs give for the signatures on their drafts? Oliver Cromwell was among the customers; and King William the Third and his Consort kept money at Child's. These scraps of paper, stained with time, recall men and women who have made English history – John Churchill, Duke of Marlborough, and his strong-willed Duchess; Dryden, Poet Laureate; the Earl of Chesterfield, whose witty *Letters* are now more talked about than read; Lady Mary Wortly Montagu; the Earl of Oxford, originator of the South Sea Bubble; Lady Rachael Russell, widow of that Lord William Russell who was "a lover of constitutional liberty," as runs the simple record at the spot where he

North side of St Bride's engraved by W. H. Toms, 1736

was beheaded in Lincoln's Inn Fields; Blackstone, of the *Commentaries*; Lord Keeper North; Edward Harley, Earl of Oxford and founder of the Harleian Library; Hyde, Earl of Rochester, and a host besides. The room over the gate of Temple Bar, which the bank occupied as a store-room until its demolition, was stuffed with old ledgers containing these and other accounts.

Fair and frail, too, were some of those who banked with Child's. Charles the Second's mistresses supported the house, which still preserves the debit and credit of Mistress Eleanor Gwynne, and of Barbara Villiers, Countess of Cleveland. Poor Nell Gwynne! She was no scholar, and could only write her mark, "E.G." in great sprawling letters on her drafts. Living extravagantly, she died in 1687 a debtor to Child's to the tune of £6,900. Of this sum her ennobled son, the Duke of St. Alban's, paid off £2,300, plate was accepted by Child's to the value of £3,791, and the bankers were accommodating with respect to the balance, allowing it to stand at five per cent interest. Titus Oates's signature is endorsed on a cheque of the Duke of Bolton. The rascal wrote a good firm hand.

The ducal houses seem almost without exception to have banked at Child's; indeed, an index of the firm's accounts would constitute a fairly representative list of the British peerage.'[2]

Child's Bank is held to be the original of Dicken's 'Tellsons', in *The Tale of Two Cities*.

'Tellson's Bank, by Temple Bar, was an oldfashioned place even in the year 1780. It was very small, very dark, very ugly, very incommodious. Everyone of the partners would have disinherited his son on the question of rebuilding Tellsons. Thus it came to pass that Tellsons was the triumphant perfection of inconvenience. After bursting open a door of idiotic obstinacy with a weak rattle in its throat, you fell into Tellsons, down two steps, and came to your senses in a miserable little shop, with two little counters, where the oldest of men made your cheque shake as if the wind rustled it, while they examined the signature by the dingiest of windows, which were always under a shower bath of mud from Fleet Street, and which were made the dingier by their own iron bars and the shadow of Temple Bar.'

Child's Bank goes back to 1676. Almost contemporary is Hoare's, founded in 1677 in Cheapside, which set up in Fleet Street thirteen years later. Hoare's is now the only surviving private deposit bank to remain unamalgamated. With two exceptions only, all the partners since its foundation have been direct descendants of the founder. Few families have given greater public service to the City of London. Three partners have been Lord Mayor.

By 1682 the Churchwardens of St Bride's were again in touch with Wren, this time about the building of the steeple. They also sought the Lord Mayor's blessing. In 1696 they waited upon Wren again; but not until 6 October 1701 was the first stone laid on the tower. The accounts include an item of 10*s.* for drinks for the workmen to toast the occasion. It took exactly two years to complete construction, which must have been soundly done, for almost immediately the steeple succeeded in weathering the violent storm of 1703.

Child's Banking House and Temple Bar, drawing by Findley, 1855

During these years, 1689-1710, the vicar of St Bride's was Peter Birch, Doctor of Divinity, a Presbyterian who conformed, but succeeded none the less in irritating authority. For example, he got into trouble with the Royal family by choosing as his text on the Princess's birthday 'Sufficient unto the day is the evil thereof'. Birch became a Prebendary of Westminster and Chaplain to the House of Commons, whose members found several occasions to protest at his sermons. He was also involved in a lawsuit, which he lost, over the living of St James, Westminster. He was three times married, the first wife being a daughter of Edmund Waller the poet, the second the widow of Francis Millington possessed of a fortune of £20,000, and the third Sibyl, daughter of Humphrey Wyrley. He was buried in Westminster Abbey in 1710.

Wren did his work brilliantly. With his genius for relating a building to its surroundings and, as in this case, enabling it to overcome them, he made St Bride's church a simple structure on the outside but exquisite inside. He then liberally bestowed his creative imagination and engineering ability on the tower and steeple, together 226 feet high. St Bride's is Wren's tallest steeple. St Mary-le-Bow's is two feet less, and the Monument 24 feet less. St Bride's rises literally above its circumstances, and is a jewel among them. Given a site hidden by a jostling throng of shops and houses, Wren raised the steeple to reign over its surroundings and he created an interior which according to the Historical Monuments Commission 'is generally considered one of Wren's most successful designs'. A vast number of words have been written about the steeple. We will content ourselves with quoting the most quoted of all, those of W. E. Henley in *The Song of the Sword*:

> 'The while the fanciful, formal finicking charm
> Of Bride's, that madrigal in stone,
> Grows flushed and warm
> And beauteous with a beauty not its own.'

The new St Bride's soon attracted two noteworthy associations. The first was the annual service of the Society of St Cecilia for which Purcell wrote music. The choir was augmented and an orchestra added. The service included an anthem and a sermon on the subject of cathedral music, after which the members of the Society walked to Stationers' Hall for some more music followed by a banquet. It was for the St Cecilia Festival of 1697 that Dryden wrote his *Alexander's Feast* which, forty years later, was given a musical setting by Handel when he first came to London in 1711. The Society paid Dryden £40 for his ode, which, so he said, was more than he expected. One Fleet Street habitué missing from the Festival was John Aubrey, who spent much time in the streets and alleys around St Bride's picking up gossip to give spice to his *Lives*. He died in 1711.

Another annual event was the Spital (the word means 'hospital') Sermon which the Lord Mayor and his retinue attended in full splendour. This sermon was first mentioned in 1415 when it was preached from a special pulpit in the churchyard of St Mary Spital. It came to St Bride's in 1686 and remained until 1798.

Both occasions attracted large congregations and Ned Ward, tavern-keeper, doggerel-contriver and contributor to the *London Spy*, in his *Dancing School* (1700) wrote of a room 'being crammed as full of company as St Bride's church upon the singing of a spittle psalm at Easter or an anthem on Cecilia's day'.

On 2 April 1662 (when the sermon was not in St Bride's) Pepys noted:

Fleet Street, looking west, 1790

> 'Mr. Moore came to me, and he and I walked to the Spittle an hour or two before my Lord Mayor and the blewcoat boys come, which at last they did, and a fine sight of charity it is indeed. We got places, and stayed to hear a sermon; but, it being a Presbyterian one, it was so long that after above an hour of it we went away, and I homed and dined; then my wife and I went by water to the opera.'

The date is significant: four clear months before the ejection of the Nonconforming ministers. Seven years later, however, Pepys had another unhappy experience on Spital day when he 'heard a piece of a dull sermon'. But he felt compensated by the fact that he enjoyed seeing the Lord Mayor and Aldermen and 'their wives also went in their coaches; and indeed the sight was mighty pleasing'. Pepys was unfortunate but he could have fared worse. A Dr Barrow, for example, preached a Spittal sermon lasting $3\frac{1}{2}$ hours. Probably the most notorious of all Spittal preachers was Dr Dodd whose moment came in 1769. His career terminated by hanging at Tyburn for forgery. Despite the advocacy of Dr

Samuel Johnson and an enormous public petition, George III resisted all pleas for clemency.

John Fell. © *Bodleian Library*

Finally Dr John Fell (1625-86)[3] enters the story on two grounds. He is known to have received St Bride's vicar, Peter Birch, at Christ Church, Oxford; but more importantly it was largely due to him that England owed a leap forward in her book trade about the time St Bride's steeple was being built. First Dean of Christ Church, then Vice-Chancellor of the University, then Bishop of Oxford, Fell had a passion for type and was able to bring about an English reformation. From abroad he brought the best matrices and punches he could find. He joined with others in providing finance, and in 1667 added a type-foundry to the Oxford University Press. Year by year he and his friends arranged the special publication of some classical author; and from this action the reputation of the Oxford University Press as a fine as well as a trustworthy printer began its illustrious progress. Reliability was indeed much needed.

> 'It is characteristic of the low quality of the English book-work in this period that even the text of the Scriptures was affected by the prevailing carelessness. Notorious examples are the Judas Bible of 1611, in which Matt.XXVI.36 had Judas instead of Jesus, the Wicked Bible of 1632 ('Thou shalt commit adultery'), the printer's Bible of 1702 ('Printers have persecuted me' Psalm CXIX. 161) and the Vinegar Bible of 1717 ('Parable of the Vinegar' Luke XX).'[4]

The stimulus given by Dr Fell, the lapsing of the Licensing Act in 1695, and the passing of the Copyright Act in 1709,[5] all contributed to advances in the presentation and marketing of books – and thus to the encouraging of literature. Printing firms began to multiply in the provinces, but London remained the centre, and in this respect Fleet Street remained the centre of London.[6]

A Fell typeface

ABCDEFGHIJ
KLMNOPQRST
UVWXYZ Æ.,

The pre-war interior of St Bride's. The only item of furnishing remaining to today is the medieval brass eagle lectern

facing The pulpit in 1935. (There is no pulpit in the present church)

The font destroyed during the war. It was a memorial to Henry Hothersall, proprietor of the Globe Tavern at which the Churchwardens dined Christopher Wren. The font, in white-veined marble, cost £2 9s 10d, 2s 10d more than the Wren dinner

8. Print, Parsons, and Prison

When printing began in England, all the processes of production were combined into a single business. Thus Caxton printed, published and sold his books himself. In due course the cell began to split. Printing on the one hand, and publishing and bookselling on the other, became separate enterprises – a process well under way by the seventeenth century, and one that yielded some notable personalities in and around Fleet Street.

Jacob Tonson (1656-1736) – 'gentleman usher to the muses', Wycherley called him – set up shop in Fleet Street in 1678. He was the publisher of Otway, Addison, Steele, Pope, and Rowe, as well as of his own famous *Miscellany*; but it was his connection with Dryden which earned him immortality (though he said he made more from *Paradise Lost* than from any other poem). In 1679 he published Dryden's *Troilus and Cressida*. Apparently he was slow in paying. Dryden loosed a verbal fusillade:

'With leering looks, bull-faced and freckled fair,
With two left legs and Judas-coloured hair
And frowzy pores that taint the ambient air.'

Nor was Dryden exhausted by the exercise. 'Tell the dog that he who wrote those lines can write more', he told the messenger who carried them. But Tonson was too competent a publisher to be readily replaced. So the stormy relationship went on. By the time Dryden had finished translations of the eighth book of the Aeneid, he could demand payment in advance. And Dryden was too good a seller for a publisher to throw him away. So for twenty years Tonson put up with poetic spleen. Perhaps it was because he realised that an author – though usually the least able to profit from his work – could call the tune, once he commanded the public. Dryden, commercially speaking, was before his time. Stow's *Survey of London* had earned him £3 and forty free copies. Shakespeare had thought little of book profits. John Milton was paid only £10 for *Paradise Lost*, though a

Thomas Chatterton, painted by W. B. Morris, engraved by W. Ridgway

left Joseph Addison engraved by J. Chapman

right Richard Steele by W. Holl

further £8 subsequently went to his widow. Dryden, on the other hand, made £1200 for his translation of Virgil, while within a few years Pope was to make £5000 out of the *Iliad*. The public had learned to follow an author's tune, and occasionally the piper asked and got his price. Tonson was shrewd enough not only to make concessions and gain authors, but also to die worth £40,000 He exerted great influence. He did much to create the climate of opinion which ensured the passage of the first Copyright Act in 1709, thus putting the emphasis directly on the protection of literary property, instead of indirectly on printing. Tonson, says Steinberg, 'The first publisher to give his firm a profile of its own . . . did as much for the Augustan age as Cotta did for German classicism a century later'.[1] He was also presiding genius and secretary of the Kit-Cat Club, which met in Shire Lane near Temple Bar and subsequently at his house. Kneller painted his portrait.

A man very different in character was Edmund Curll who added, at least temporarily, a word to the English language. 'Curllicism' stood for publishing in bad taste and Curll explored most avenues in this respect – breaches of privileges and pornography, for example. His efforts landed him in the pillory, earned him a damnation in *The Dunciad* and the description: 'a contemptible wretch in a thousand ways: he is odious in his person, scandalous in his fame: more beastly, insufferable books have been published by this one offender than in thirty years before by all the nation.'[2]

facing John Milton aged 62 engraved by G. Vertue

JOANNES MILTON
Ætatis LXII 1670.
Τὸν περὶ Μοῦσ' ἐφίλησε,
δίδου δ' ἀγαθόν τε κακόν τε·
Ὀφθαλμῶν μὲν ἄμερσε,
δίδου δ' ἡδεῖαν ἀοιδήν.
G. Vertue Sculp.

Another Fleet Street publisher, Jacob Robinson, secured his place in history in a manner he neither expected nor relished, when one day he showed a customer a critical review of *A Treatise of Human Nature*. David Hume, anonymous author of the work, showed little philosophic calm. Indeed, the incident

> 'so highly provoked our young philosopher that he flew into a violent rage to demand satisfaction of Jacob Robinson the publisher, whom he kept at bay, during the paroxysm of his anger, at his sword's point, trembling behind the counter, lest a period should be put to the life of a sober critic by a raving philosopher.'[3]

The printed word has always been capable of rousing emotions, and printed periodicals have always had their particular emotional atmosphere – urgency. No doubt even the earliest printers felt the need to issue their editions as quickly as possible, if only to anticipate a rival and safeguard their sales. By this time there had developed a whole area of printing where speed was of the essence, for the newspaper and periodical producer had to justify his claim to regularity. That meant fitting distribution to coaching schedules – long before and hardly comparable with the demands of aeroplane take-offs and now the hectic immediacy of television – yet urgency was the common factor.

The English are among the world's greatest newspaper readers. Apparently they were notoriously news-hungry even before newspapers were invented. 'You in England expect newes with everie happie winde', wrote a French correspondent before the sixteenth century reached its close. 'Although excellent eaters the English would, I think, go without breakfast or supper rather than neglect their morning or evening paper,' added a German, J. H. Campe, in 1801.

Immediacy has always been the mark of news. What is accounted the first English news-book has as its title *Hereafter ensue the trew encountre of Batayle lately don betwene England and Scotlande. In which batayle the Scottsshe kynge was slayne*. It was the story, seemingly an eye witness account, of Flodden Field and was in print almost before the spilled blood had soaked through the soil. It consisted of four leaves and it managed to have an appropriate woodcut for its title-page. Its resourceful midwife was William Faques (Fawkes) and the year was 1513. There were others to follow. Soon men learned that a publication of this kind could contain a miscellany of items and that the public would count on regularity of appearance and get their money ready. By 1621 Thomas Archer was apparently printing his 'corantos' in London (though none have survived), and in the same year Nathaniel Butter, freeman of the Stationers' Company, was producing his 'Corante, or, newes from Italy, Germany, Hungarie, Spaine and France'. He published seven in that year and these are the oldest English periodical newsbooks extant. In 1622 Nathaniel Butter began his *Weekeley Newes* which lasted for some years, though it did not appear as frequently as its title implies. Most of the contents concerned the Continent, for the Crown forbade the printing of English news of any importance. The Star Chamber decree of 1632 also prohibited the publication of foreign news, so the printing of newsbooks in England lapsed until 1638. In that year Butter and Bourne were given a 21-year licence to print newsbooks, in return for an annual payment of £10 towards the repair of St Paul's. In due course their partnership was dissolved. Bourne turned to book publishing and made a fortune. Butter continued with periodicals, landed

St Bride's Avenue, Fleet Street, drawn by Thomas H. Shepherd, engraved by J. Tingle, published 1829 by James & Co., Temple of the Muses, Finsbury Square

St Paul's and St Bride's from the Thames, by E. A. Gruning, architect, *c.* 1850

PARIS AND THE CONTINENT
LONDON
CHATHAM
AND
DOVER RAILY

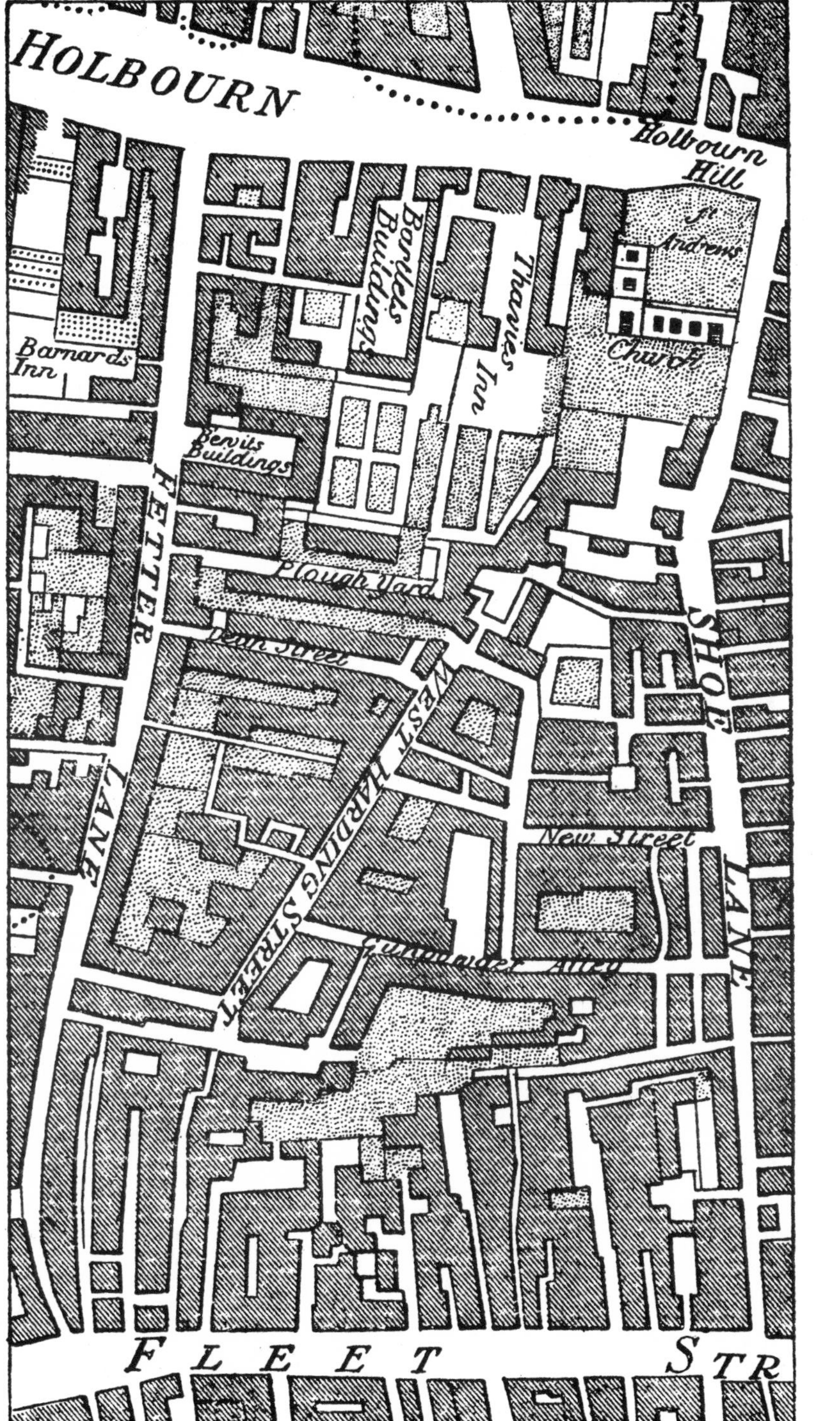

facing Samuel Johnson by Joshua Reynolds. © *National Portrait Gallery*

New Street Square and its neighbourhood, 1772, from Maitland's *History of London*

174

in the Fleet Prison for debt, and eventually had to be buried at the cost of the Stationers' Company. The Continentals had been ahead of the English in this respect. They did not have to depend on ships for news from other countries, while the Dutch merchant network provided a ready-made army of correspondents. But what the Continentals invented the British were quick to adopt and improve. In the words of Folke Dahl of Sweden, they 'were miles ahead of almost all their continental colleagues'.[4]

Daniel Defoe engraved by J. Thomson

Steinberg says:

> 'There are especially two features which have remained a distinguishing mark of English news-sheets. There are the easy and friendly terms prevailing between editors and readers, which started in the 1620s by editors taking readers into their confidence and led to the readers putting their confidence in "letters to the editor"; and there is the skilful layout of news-sheets, which "gave evidence of a truly journalistic inventive genius" in compelling the prospective reader's attention.'[5]

It has been estimated that, between 1640 and 1660, some three hundred separate news publications appeared, stimulated by the abolition of the Star Chamber and the need of both sides in the Civil War to obtain a hearing. The pressure gradually transformed the newsbooks into a form approximating to a newspaper. The favourite title at the time was *Mercurius*, followed by *Intelligencer*, *Scout*, *Spy* and *Post*.

The first English newspaper which has lasted to the present day came out, most improbably, in November 1665 in Oxford (but only because the Court had fled from the Plague in London). Called the *Oxford Gazette* and subsequently the *London Gazette*, it would not now, however, be recognised as a newspaper but as a record of official appointments, notices of bankruptcies and, in wartime, of the official casualty lists. Probably deriving its name from the Italian coin which was the cost of the first *gazetta*, it must be the only newspaper title which has enriched the English language with a verb. This *London Gazette*, so Pepys said, was 'very pretty, full of newes, and no folly in it'. With the Court Imprimatur, the *Gazette* had unrivalled sources of information – notably the foreign embassies.

The revolution which was to produce Northcliffe had begun. The man-in-the-street, no less than the man-in-the-coffee-house and the cultured scholar, began to learn that he too could enjoy regular access to information and reading matter that titillated his imagination. It was in the same year, 1665, that the first 'magazine' appeared. Sponsored by the Royal Society and entitled *Philosophical Transactions*, it could hardly have imagined itself forerunner of *Playboy* or the comics.

> 'By the early years of the eighteenth century, the periodical press, newspapers as well as magazines, had become an established institution, and from decade to decade gained new strength. The provinces, too, were beginning to have their own local papers, mostly bi-weekly at first.'[6]

Britain's first daily newspaper, the *Daily Courant*, made its bow at Fleet Bridge on 11 March 1702. In 1704 Defoe started his *Review*.

The periodical had been born and, contemporary with it, there grew the postal and coaching services. Editors and publishers learned not only to seek punctuality but also to use it as a sales promoter. Perhaps it was because it aimed too high – by claiming publication 'precisely as the Horse Guards strikes five' that *The Cabinet* (1792) did not last long. On the other hand, in 1804 *The Times* – which had begun life in 1785 as *The Daily Universal Register* and changed its name in 1788 – adorned its brow with a clock set between the open book of times past and the closed book of times to come, and implied publication at 6.06 a.m. daily. It has thundered ever since. The reason may lie not only in its editorial excellence but also in its customary readiness to adopt new methods. *The Times* of 29 November 1814 was the first issue to be printed on a power-driven machine, not a handpress. Almost within sound of that press Sheridan had fretted away nearly a year in a sponging house in 1813, while the young poet Coleridge had caught sight of a placard asking for 'smart lads for Light Dragoons' and had answered, for a brief space, his country's call. About the same time, Michael Faraday, the great scientist, was working in Salisbury Court.

But we go ahead of our story. The Fire of London over, the Warden of the Fleet rebuilt his prison. His was a hereditary office, so competence and integrity were not regarded as essential qualifications. The merchants and traders of

The last remains of the Fleet Prison

Fleet Parsons and Fleet Marriages

Restoration London had grounds for saying that the Warden not only cheated prisoners under his charge but also, for an appropriate consideration, allowed them to escape. Out of 1651 prisoners who entered his gates between 1696 and 1699, only 285 were legally discharged. Some died. Some bought their way out. The Fleet became a magnet and prisoners in other gaols found that by means of a *habeas corpus* they could get themselves transferred to it.

The prison population included a number of 'Fleet parsons' – men who had been ordained, but for debt or some other reason had lost their freedom. Such men prospered at the turn of the century, before and after. A marriage was worth 12*s*.–20*s*. Soon there were those who had never seen a bishop in their lives, but had invested in the appropriate outfit and were ready and willing to marry people, as their advertisements in shop windows made clear (the usual sign was a male and a female hand conjoined), without any awkward questions. In the four months beginning 19 October 1704, no fewer than 2975 such weddings took place. These nuptials, obviously, had little of the atmosphere of romance about

Sarah Malcolm by Hogarth. © *National Galleries of Scotland*

them. Girls were forced into wedlock to secure their fortunes, highly experienced bridegrooms were on hand to marry any woman who wanted thereby to escape her creditors or claim her child was born in wedlock. The register which every Fleet parson, bogus or otherwise, kept in his possession was liberally spattered with blank spaces in which, for an extra fee of course, a marriage could be back-dated. On at least one occasion the two parties to a marriage were believed to be women. But did that matter if the right to some property was secured?

E. C. Hawkins, vicar of St Bride's and father of Anthony Hope, wrote:

> 'Burn's Parish Registers, quoting the *Gentleman's Magazine* for February 1735, gives a lively picture of the scandals and abuses resulting from this lawlessness. Marriages were performed by swearing, drunken parsons. The streets were infested by touts and bullies pretending to be clerks and registrars, shouting: "Do you want a parson?", "Will you be married?", and coaxing or dragging anyone who seemed to be likely to be wheedled or forced into a marriage into some public or private house or even worse place, where the parson was ready in his canonicals and with his witnesses and his book. Signs were hung out over many houses, and notices appeared in the windows that marriages were performed within, and the scale of charges was appended. Publicans, of course, had an interest in the trade, as the married couples and their friends often had a carouse after the ceremony, and some landlords found it paid them to keep a parson on the premises. One of the most notorious of such houses was the "Hand and Pen", near the Fleet Ditch.'[7]

The Fleet prison was burned down by Gordon rioters in 1780 and rebuilt to last until it was abolished by Act of Parliament in 1842. Its story does little credit to Fleet Street. Yet the contemporaries of the Fleet parsons did not always find them intolerable. There was the Hon. Henry Fox, afterwards Lord Holland, for example, who eloped with Georgiana, daughter of the Duke of Richmond, and came to Fleet Street to make an honest woman of her – if that be the right phrase in such a situation.

Until 1753, the taking of a woman as wife before witnesses and acknowledging her position with a clergyman present to keep the register, was all that a Common Law marriage required. So a wedding in an ale-house (many of which had a 'kept' parson) was as binding as one in a cathedral. It was inevitable that parsons, who fell outside society and into the Fleet prison, should see this chance of making the price of a drink and do things their own way. After all, as Smollett said in *The Adventures of Peregrine Pickle*, this place of residence was a 'city detached from all communication with the neighbouring parts, regulated by its own laws, and furnished with peculiar conveniences for the use of the inhabitants'. It was a complete city with both grief and its own cosy humour – as Dickens implied when he sent Mr Pickwick there for refusing to pay Mrs Bardell's damages. Fleet Prison was a savage place, but it was set in a society capable of great savagery. There was, for example, the infamous Sarah Malcolm whose atrocious triple murder aroused attention even then. Hogarth painted her. Or Constantine Macgenius (even Dickens could not have invented that name) who savaged a woman – whom he believed to be a witch who had cast him under a spell. Or the horrible Mrs Brownrigg who whipped to death a parish apprentice girl.

But people and parsons in Fleet Street were not all bad in the eighteenth century, and St Bride's provides a charming and human conclusion to the period. It concerns William Rich (1755-1811), a Gloucester boy who walked to London to seek fame and fortune, and settled as apprentice to a master cook named Pritchard at 3 Ludgate Hill. William did well, married the boss's daughter Susannah, acquired the business and enhanced its repute. From Ludgate Hill St Bride's steeple was a familiar sight. Why not, thought William, design a wedding cake on the lines of its soaring tiers? The idea caught on and became the familiar 'bride cake', perhaps because William did not stint his customers. His cakes contained best French brandy 'even when it cost a guinea a bottle'. He also supplied venison for City banquets. William's brother John was an intimate friend of Jenner, pioneer of vaccination, and his children were among the first vaccinated by Jenner himself. Susannah's party dress may be seen in St Bride's crypts. She was buried with a sprig of rosemary ('that's for rememberance') on her bosom. And who would be jaundiced enough to want to forget her?

Richardson reading from the ms. of *Charles Grandison*, 'from a sketch made by one of the party at the time'

9. The Eighteenth Century

In 1703, the re-building of St Bride's – church and steeple – was finished at last. Queen Anne was on the throne. Marlborough was winning victories on the Continent. Addison was abroad, planning to spend his life as a diplomat, Swift and Steele were keeping printers busy. Pope was only fifteen but already disfigured by illness. Congreve had made enough money to stop writing. Vanbrugh was writing plays and building mansions. Grinling Gibbons was carving. Kneller was painting. Halley was making rules for comets, channel tides and lines of magnetic variation. Newton was discovering, Walpole had just become a Member of Parliament.

By contrast, on 31 July, alongside Temple Bar, Daniel Defoe was locked in the pillory. Head and hands held rigid in holes, condemned to ignominy by the Establishment, he was receiving, not eggs and other missiles but flowers and adulation from a throng of sympathisers. His *Hymn to the Pillory* published that morning was earning him money from eager purchasers around his curious throne.

'Tell them the men that placed him here
Are scandals to the times:
Are at a loss to find his guilt
And can't commit his crimes.'

were some of the words they read and remembered and quoted. It was in the same year he changed his name from Foe to Defoe.

Defoe had tried his hand at being a hosiery merchant. He had also sampled the army. In 1701 he had ventured into satirical journalism, and it was this that earned him the pillory and nearly six months in prison in 1703. The following year he started his newspaper, *The Review*, which came out three times a week and was practically a one-man job. It lasted ten years and it revealed Defoe as a brilliant reporter. After service as a secret agent and more activity as a pamph-

Daniel Defoe in the Stocks, painted by E. Crowe, engraved by J. C. Armytage

leteer, he published *Robinson Crusoe* in 1719; then followed five years of prolific writing, his output declining to his death in 1731.

The Review was preceded by London's first daily morning newspaper, the *Daily Courant*, in 1702, and succeeded by the *Tatler* first published by Steele in 1709. The latter sold for 1*d.* and appeared three times a week until replaced in 1711 by the *Spectator*, jointly produced by Steele and Addison. Their motive, 'to enliven morality with wit and to temper wit with morality', made them acceptable in the world of gracious living, inhabited by people living in Queen Anne houses and sitting on Queen Anne furniture; people who would ride in one of the 800 hackney coaches or 200 hirable sedan chairs available in London at that time, and who would read the papers over a cup of coffee or chocolate (at 15*s.* a pound), now rapidly growing in popularity or even, in the exclusive echelon, with a cup of tea, still ruinously high in price though well below the £3 a pound it had cost in 1666. Perhaps as they read, they pondered the possibilities of investment in the South Sea Company which, formed in 1711, was within a decade to become the South Sea Bubble. But neither the *Tatler* nor the *Spectator* would be read along with the other new drink, gin, with its baleful advertisement 'Drunk for a penny, dead drunk for twopence, straw free'.

Dramshops belonged to the dark side of Fleet Street, as did Alsatia and the Fleet marriages. The Fleet Ditch provided an appropriate atmosphere, but there had been a moment when the stench might have been modified and the waters improved. Wren had made plans for a Thames Quay. He would have cleared and canalised the Fleet as far as Holborn Bridge and thus given London both an amenity and some much needed river frontage. But short sight and vested interests prevented him. Later, in 1737, the building of the Mansion House involved the removal of a market. To create a new site for the dispossessed traders, the Corporation arched over the Fleet river from Ludgate Circus to Holborn, at a cost of £10,256 17*s.* 10½*d.* Nearly thirty years later, in 1765, when Blackfriars Bridge was built (after much violent argument in the Guildhall) the Fleet was covered in right down to the Thames. Londoners must have loved their cloacal Fleet, for it was the last river they enclosed. Not that it willingly stayed trapped. For example, when the Metropolitan Railway was being cut in 1860, it over-

Interior of the Fleet Ditch

George III, from the studio of A. Ramsay. © *National Portrait Gallery*

facing Benjamin Franklin, after J. S. Duplessu. © *National Portrait Gallery*

Sir William Staines, Lord Mayor of London and the contractor who repaired the steeple

flowed into the workings and it can still menace those who have to clean it out.

Five years before the submerging of the waters, occurred St Bride's fourth significant American episode – an incident to which an imaginative historian might at least partially trace 'the loss of the first British Empire'. Not that St Bride's had any deliberate hand in fomenting the American revolution – merely that its steeple accidentally became a point of contention between two eminent antagonists, George III and Benjamin Franklin.

George III had been on the throne nearly four years when, on 18 June 1764 (the year in which London streets were first numbered), there was a furious storm and lightning struck the stone obelisk which formed the crown of the steeple. The lightning ran down the iron spindle in the centre, causing an explosion. Stones were forced apart, some falling into the street, some into the church itself. One, weighing 72 lb, was hurled over the full length of the building and landed in the garret of a house in Bride Lane. An expert reported that, had gunpowder exploded, the effects would have been similar. In due course, Mr Staines the contractor, eventually Sir William Staines and Lord Mayor of London, rebuilt 85 feet of the steeple at a cost of £3000. In doing so he is said to have reduced the height of the obelisk by eight feet, thus bringing the total height of the steeple to 226 feet.[1]

From earliest days man had regarded lightning as an Act of God and accordingly had left protection against it in the hands of the deity. Lightning was certainly not unknown in the City. For example, in 1561 it had struck the spire of St Paul's and burned it down, all but gutting the whole cathedral. In due course avoidance of lightning damage became a public concern. Two theories existed about lightning conductors, and the experience of St Bride's in 1764 became the centre of controversy.

The Royal Society had appointed a committee of five to settle the best way of safeguarding buildings. Four of them called for lightning conductors with sharp points spread fanwise at their business ends. The fifth, an egregious Mr Wilson, insisted on blunt ends. It became a public issue, and a good healthy argument was therefore poisoned with politics, for the sharp points had been invented by Mr Benjamin Franklin, the wicked spokesman of the disaffected American colonists. Franklin had, indeed been given a medal by the Royal Society in 1753 and elected a Fellow because of the success of his 'experiment for drawing lightning from the clouds'. But subsequent political chicanery – the British public and its king decided – had ruined his judgment. Perhaps the fact that he had received a complimentary letter from Louis XV on his scientific acumen also had something to do with it. This was unjust because at that time Franklin's hope was to see America grow and develop *within* the British Empire. But Englishmen had their prejudices and the physical barrier of the Atlantic was allowed to become a rampart between kinsmen. Mr Franklin came from the wrong side of the water so whatever he said on any subject was necessarily wrong. Pointed lightning conductors became the symbol of people given to sharp practice. The true loyalist was a blunt knob.

Sharp ends or blunt? This, George III soon became convinced, was a matter which called for the attention of the best and most authoritative brains. So he personally entered the controversy. And did so, typically, so to speak, at the pointless end. First he told the Royal Society committee to reverse its majority decision. Their professional integrity made this impossible. Then he told Sir John

Pringle, President of the Royal Society and the King's Physician, to arrange things so that honest bluntness should prevail. 'Sire', said Sir John, 'I cannot reverse the laws and operations of nature.' 'Then', replied his monarch, compounding ignorance with offensiveness, 'you are not fit to be President of the Royal Society.' George showed what he thought of natural laws by placing blunt knobs on his palace. Probably he also changed his doctor.

The affair was eventually summed up by a friend of Franklin's:

'While you, great George, for knowledge hunt,
And sharp conductors change for blunt,
The nation's out of joint;
Franklin a wiser course pursues,
And all your thunder useless views,
By keeping to the point.'

Lightning struck St Bride's steeple again in 1803 but happily the physical damage was minimal, and this time it had no perceptible effect in terms of international relations.

But we cannot yet leave Franklin, described by one biographer as 'gifted by nature with a versatility of genius unexampled by any figure known to history, with the exception, perhaps, of Leonardo da Vinci'. That, maybe, is a little exaggerated. None the less few men have excelled him in his ability to handle every aspect of the printed word. He could conceive an idea and express it superbly. He could set up and machine his manuscript, and produce it as book or newspaper. Further, he could devise adequate promotion and distribution for it. Much of this knowledge he acquired in London. He was still a youth when he established 'the first sensational newspaper of America', the *New England Courant*, 1721. He then built the *Pennsylvania Gazette* into a great newspaper, which soon had the largest circulation in America. He created *Poor Richard's Almanack* which made him a fortune. He became Public Printer for Pennsylvania, and established America's first circulating library in 1744. He reprinted Richardson's *Pamela* as the first novel published in America. It has been said of him that nobody in the eighteenth century knew so well as he how to pull the wires of public opinion and make use of newspapers.

Benjamin Franklin was well known in Fleet Street. At one time a union was mooted between his family and that of one of the greatest of England's eighteenth century printers. William Strahan – who was printer and to some degree publisher to such men as Dr Johnson (he paid £100 for *Rasselas* and £150 for *A Journey to the Western Islands of Scotland*), the Wesley brothers, David Hume, and Gibbon (he printed *The Decline and Fall*) – was a close friend of Franklin. As early as 1750 the possibility of marriage between Strahan's son (then only a child) and Franklin's daughter Sally was being discussed. In 1760 the matter was seriously proposed and Franklin and his wife gave it serious consideration. Eventually Franklin rejected it on the grounds that he could not bear to have his daughter live so far away, nor could he contemplate moving to England. The hostilities between Britain and her colonies wrecked the Franklin-Strahan friendship for some years, especially when Strahan became a Member of Parliament, but by 1784 relations had been restored.

The House occupied by the Royal Society in Crane Court, Fleet Street

To American independence and 'the loss of the first British Empire', St Bride's

and a streak of lightning (which energised the quarrel between George III and Benjamin Franklin) may well have contributed, since personalities always play a large part in politics. Publishing – as the communication of ideas through print – was of primary importance, and American newspapers played a major role in forcing the breach. 'The Revolution' said John Adams, 'was effected before the war commenced. The Revolution was in the hearts and minds of the people.' The sword had relatively little to do once the pen had done its work. It was printer's ink which bound together the colonies which had once seemed thirteen separate nations. As Benjamin Franklin pointed out, the press could not only 'strike while the iron is hot' but also 'heat it continually by striking'.

The printing press that Winslow had transported on the Mayflower was soon joined by others. As early as 1638 journeymen were being lured from England – a seventeenth century brain drain. The first American newspaper came into being in 1704 in Boston, then America's largest city. When the lightning struck St Bride's the total from New Hampshire to Georgia had reached 23, all active. By

Samuel Richardson, painted by J. Highmore, 1750 (© *National Portrait Gallery*) and the title page of his most famous novel (© *British Museum*)

PAMELA;
OR,
VIRTUE Rewarded.
In a SERIES of
FAMILIAR LETTERS
From a Beautiful
Young DAMSEL to her PARENTS:
And afterwards,
In her EXALTED CONDITION,
BETWEEN
HER, and Persons of *Figure* and *Quality*,
UPON THE MOST
Important and Entertaining Subjects,
In GENTEEL LIFE.

Publish'd in order to cultivate the Principles of VIRTUE and RELIGION in the Minds of the YOUTH of BOTH SEXES.

VOL. IV.

LONDON:
Printed for S. RICHARDSON:
And Sold by C. RIVINGTON, in *St. Paul's Church-Yard*; And J. OSBORN, in *Pater-noster Row*.
M.DCC.XLII.

The remains of Samuel Richardson's coffin

1773, the year when to the burdens of the Sugar Act of 1764 and the Stamp Act was added the offence that led to the Boston Tea Party, there were 33. Only one of them could find a word to say for Britain. This was the property of 'Jemmy' Rivington, a lone Tory among a seaboard full of Whigs, who could slant even a social column to a political purpose – by pointing out, for example, that there 'was not a single Whig' at a fashionable wedding he reported. In due course the mob descended on him and he fled, only to return the moment he thought it possible to print again – although he had to flee again and return again and once more flee. Eventually in September 1777, he arrived in Manhattan with a glorious but by then virtually meaningless title, 'Printer to the King's Most Excellent Majesty'. The Independent pamphleteers had a glorious chance and they took it gladly. Governor William Livingston of New Jersey wrote 'If Rivington is taken, I must have one of his ears, Governor Clinton is entitled to the other and General Washington, if he pleases, may take his head.' Yet bulldog Rivington succeeded in living out the rest of his days in New York and died from natural causes.

Another link with Fleet Street was forged at the time by Samuel Richardson, 'father of the English novel', whose coffin, much crushed by wartime upheavals, is still to be seen in St Bride's crypt. When Charles Rivington, founder of the famous publishing house, died, two of his sons, John and James ('Jemmy'), were placed under the supervision of Richardson who remained trustee for James until he attained his majority. A third son, (also named Charles) was likewise articled to Richardson, and he subsequently succeeded to the printing business. Richardson must have esteemed James Rivington; he left him a mourning ring.

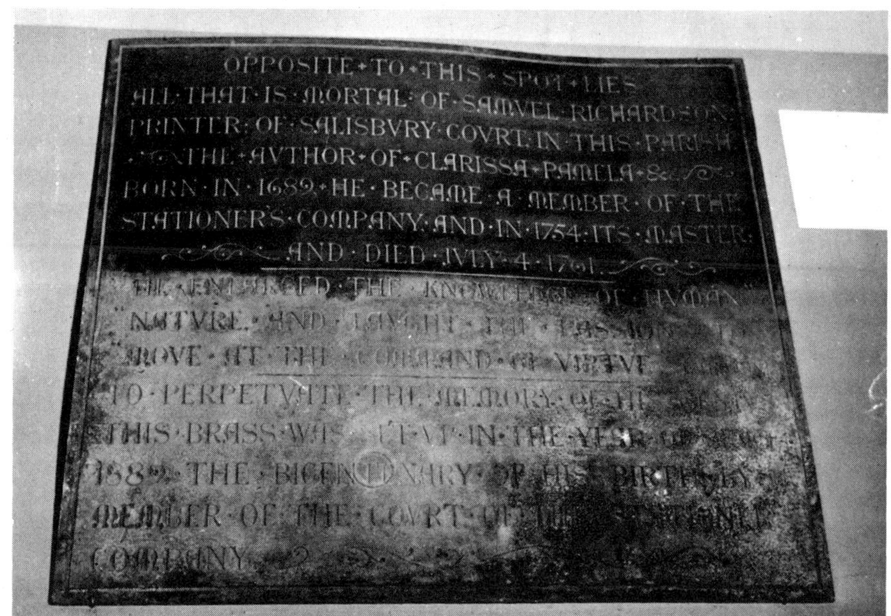

A bronze memorial tablet to Samuel Richardson in the crypt. 'He enlarged the knowledge of human nature and taught the passions to move at the command of virtue' (Johnson)

Samuel Richardson, 1689-1761, son of a joiner, had little formal education and was himself apprenticed to a printer. In due course he set up his own business and eventually had seven different premises alongside St Bride's. It was in his house in Salisbury Court, often visited by Johnson, that the Sage clashed with Hogarth who thought Johnson mad because he disliked George II. Richardson's repute as a printer was obviously high – he was printer to the House of Commons. But it is as a literary man that he attained European reputation in his own lifetime and maintained it afterwards. Madame de Staël came all the way from Paris to kneel down, in circumstances of high emotion, on Richardson's tombstone and kiss it and chant 'Je t'adore'.

It was Charles Rivington and his bookseller friend, Osborne, who in Richardson's words

> 'entreated me to write for them a little volume of letters, in a common style, on such subjects as might be of use to those country readers who were unable to indite for themselves. "Would it be any harm" said I, "in a piece you want to be written so low, if one should instruct them how they should think and act in common cases as well as indite?" They were the more urgent for me to begin the little volume for the hint ['little' was over-modest. It consisted of four volumes!] I set about it, and in the progress of writing two or three letters to instruct handsome girls who were obliged to go out to service, as we phrase it, how to avoid the snares that might be laid against their virtue, the above story occurred to me, and hence sprang Pamela.'

Thus was born what Saintsbury called 'the ancestress of all English novels', the book that Pope asserted would do more good than twenty sermons, about which a critic wrote that if all books were burned, the Bible and *Pamela* ought to be preserved, a book which went through five editions in the first year of its publication (1740), and which Lecky said 'probably contributed something to refine the tone of society', having 'a marked influence on subsequent writers of fiction.'

'Richardson's bust' says Bryan W. Downs, Master of Christ's College, Cambridge, 'should be set up over the door of every circulating library not only in this country but all over the world.' It was he who made honest women of people like Moll Flanders. He made the novel respectable and therefore acceptable to the middle class then growing in wealth, power and numbers.

Pamela, though seen through oceans of tears, was to be a progenitor of *Tess of the D'Urbevilles* and *Anna Karenina* and *Madame Bovary*. It was written by a printer under the shadow of St Bride's, as were *Pamela's* successors, *Clarissa Harlowe* (1747-8), which Macaulay claimed he knew almost by heart, and *Sir Charles Grandison* (1753-4).

In 1899 the Stationers Company, of which Richardson was Master in 1754, set up a tablet in St Bride's. It carried Samuel Johnson's tribute to the master of emotionalism and the manipulator of lovesickness, adulation, virtue and villainy: 'He enlarged the knowledge of human nature, and taught the passions to move at the command of virtue.' The tablet is still in the crypt and the tombstone on which Madame de Staël knelt was fortunately preserved and is now attached to the east wall of the church.

Richardson has at least one more claim to our attention. In 1757 he found work in his Salisbury Court office for a penurious, rejected ordinand and doctor manqué. His name was Oliver Goldsmith and his duties were those of reader and corrector of the press. Perhaps it was the drudgery of some of his work which

Fleet Street near Chancery Lane in 1790

left A house at the corner of Break-neck Stairs, Green Harbour Court, Old Bailey, where Oliver Goldsmith lived in 1758. Engraved by S. Rawle

right Oliver Goldsmith, from the Joshua Reynolds studio *c.* 1770. © *National Portrait Gallery*

made him feel he could do at least as well himself. A few years later, probably when living in Wine Office Court, a hundred yards from St Bride's, Goldsmith wrote *The Vicar of Wakefield*. How it secured publication was recorded by Boswell in what purport to be Johnson's own words:

'I received one morning a letter from poor Goldsmith that he was in great distress, and as it was not in his power to come to me, begging that I would come to him as soon as possible. I sent him a guinea and promised to come to him directly. I accordingly went as soon as I was dressed, and found that his landlady had arrested him for his rent, at which he was in a violent passion. I perceived that he had already changed my guinea, and had got a bottle of madeira and a glass before him. I put the cork in the bottle, desired he would be calm, and began to talk to him of the means by which he would be extricated. He then told me he had a novel ready for the press, which he produced to me. I looked into it and saw its merit. I told the landlady I should soon return; and having gone to a bookseller, sold it for sixty pounds. I brought Goldsmith the money, and he discharged his rent, not without rating his landlady in a high tone for having used him so ill.'

The landlady probably went downstairs wishing Mr Goldsmith would spend less on clothes and more on a roof over his head. Forster's *Life of Goldsmith* tells of his bills to Mr Filby the tailor. There was the 'Tyrian bloom satin-grain, and garter blue silk breeches' which cost £8 *2s. 7d.* There was the suit 'lined with silk and with gold buttons'. There were 'the purple silk small-clothes, a handsome scarlet requelaure buttoned close under the chin, and with all the importance derivable from a full-dress professional wig, a sword and a goldheaded cane.'

Perhaps the clumsy little figure with pockmarked face and stumpy legs needed a peacock's camouflage more than most. His admirers certainly forgave him any idiosyncrasy. On the day he died Burke burst into tears, and Reynolds did no painting.

The Swan of Lichfield has crept into the story almost by accident – yet can there ever be a greater personification of Fleet Street than Samuel Johnson? Like others in this street, he began with few advantages. He suffered from scrofula,

left James Boswell dressed as an Armed Corsican Chief, as he appeared at Shakespeare's Jubilee, Stratford on Avon, 1769. Painted S. Wale, engraved J. Miller

right Dr Johnson's house in Bolt Court, painted by Shepherd, engraved by S. Rawle

A Literary Party at Sir Joshua Reynolds'. Boswell, Garrick, Paoli, Burney, Warton and Goldsmith

and was brought to London at the age of three to be touched for the king's evil by Queen Anne. He had St Vitus' Dance, only one good eye and no money. He was an innate melancholic, and to all his real aches added a pronounced hypochondria. Yet his cheerfulness kept breaking in. Whenever a guest came he entertained lavishly and fed Hodge his cat on oysters. After an unsuccessful venture as a schoolmaster, he arrived in London in 1737 and worked for Edward Cave the printer, founder of *The Gentleman's Magazine*. He demonstrated the versatility of his pen, and overpowered Fleet Street for 38 years. He began, continued, and ended, a character – companionable, irascible, arrogant, humane. He was buried in Westminster Abbey, unfortunately before the day when a television camera would have made him the best-known man within the range of its reception. He was a convivial romantic and every generation must thank Boswell for recording him. Goldsmith, Burke, Reynolds, Garrick (whom he taught in Staffordshire), Beauclerk, Burney, Langton, Hawksworth, Hawkins, Hogarth, Mrs Siddons – were the members of his circle less scintillating, the list would become tedious. Yet, one more must be mentioned.

'In 1784, a youth may have been seen at Johnson's door with Barber, Johnson's black servant. It was Isaac D'Israeli leaving a poem for the doctor's consideration. When he called again, he was told that Johnson was too ill to see him and on December 13th 1784, the great lexicographer had ceased to breathe.'[2]

On 31 July 1817 another and more famous D'Israeli, Benjamin, was baptised at the age of twelve in St Andrew's Church, Holborn, now in the parish of St Bride's.

Johnson compiled his immortal Dictionary at his home in Gough Square within a hundred yards of St Bride's, and had it printed by Strahan in New Street Square ('I dismiss it with frigid tranquility, having little to fear or hope from censure or from praise'). Its definitions revealed the man.

> '*Pirate:* a sea robber, any robber; particularly a bookseller who seizes the copies of other men; *Oats:* a grain which in England is generally given to horses, but in Scotland supports the people; *Lexicographer:* a writer of dictionaries, a harmless drudge; *Patron:* commonly a wretch who supports with insolence and is paid with flattery.'

Johnson's honesty and devotion to freedom were personified by another no less famous contemporary, on the fringe of his circle.

The title page and a detail of the contents from Johnson's Dictionary

A

DICTIONARY

OF THE

ENGLISH LANGUAGE:

IN WHICH

The WORDS are deduced from their ORIGINALS,

AND

ILLUSTRATED in their DIFFERENT SIGNIFICATIONS

BY

EXAMPLES from the beſt WRITERS.

TO WHICH ARE PREFIXED,

A HISTORY of the LANGUAGE,

AND

AN ENGLISH GRAMMAR.

BY SAMUEL JOHNSON, A.M.

IN TWO VOLUMES.

VOL. I.

Cum tabulis animum cenſoris ſumet honeſti:
Audebit quæcunque parum ſplendoris habebunt,
Et ſine pondere erunt, et honore indigna ferentur,
Verba movere loco; quamvis invita recedant,
Et verſentur adhuc intra penetralia Veſtæ:
Obſcurata diu populo bonus eruet, atque
Proferet in lucem ſpecioſa vocabula rerum,
Quæ priſcis memorata Catonibus atque Cethegis,
Nunc ſitus informis premit et deſerta vetuſtas. HOR.

LONDON,

Printed by W. STRAHAN,

For J. and P. KNAPTON; T. and T. LONGMAN; C. HITCH and L. HAWES; A. MILLAR; and R. and J. DODSLEY.

MDCCLV.

In Kent they brew with one half *oatmalt*, and the other half barleymalt. *Mortimer's H ſb.*

OA'TMEAL. *n. ſ.* [*oat* and *meal.*] Flower made by grinding oats.

Oatmeal and butter, outwardly applied, dry the ſcab on the head. *Arbuthnot on Aliment.*

Our neighbours tell me oft, in joking talk,
Of aſhes, leather, *oatmeal*, bran, and chalk. *Gay.*

OA'TMEAL. *n. ſ.* An herb. *Ainſworth.*

OATS. *n. ſ.* [aten, Saxon.] A grain, which in England is generally given to horſes, but in Scotland ſupports the people.

It is of the graſs leaved tribe; the flowers have no petals, and are diſpoſed in a looſe panicle: the grain is eatable. The meal makes tolerable good bread. *Miller.*

The *oats* have eaten the horſes. *Shakeſpeare.*

It is bare mechaniſm, no otherwiſe produced than the turning of a wild *oatbeard*, by the inſinuation of the particles of moiſture. *Locke.*

For your lean cattle, fodder them with barley ſtraw firſt, and the *oat* ſtraw laſt. *Mortimer's Huſbandry.*

His horſe's allowance of *oats* and beans, was greater than the journey required. *Swift.*

OA'TTHISTLE. *n. ſ.* [*oat* and *thiſtle.*] An herb. *Ainſ.*

OBAMBULA'TION. *n. ſ.* [*obambulatio*, from *obambulo*, Latin.] The act of walking about. *Dict.*

To OBDU'CE. *v. a.* [*obduco*, Latin.] To draw over as a covering.

No animal exhibits its face in the native colour of its ſkin but man; all others are covered with feathers, hair, or a cortex that is *obduced* over the cutis. *Hale.*

OBDUC'TION. *n. ſ.* [from *obductio*, *obduco*, Latin.] The act

196

John Wilkes, 1727-97, was a distinguished member of the dissipated Hellfire Club founded by Sir Francis Dashwood at Medmenham Abbey. In 1757 he was elected MP for Aylesbury. Eleven years later he founded the notorious *The North Briton* as rival to Smollett's *The Briton*. In biting words, Wilkes criticised the Government until in Issue No. 45 he incurred a charge of seditious libel by attacking the speech from the throne. Although arrested and then released by reason of Parliamentary privilege, he was none the less expelled from the House of Commons on grounds of having issued an obscene publication, his *Essay on Woman*. He fled to Paris in December 1763, only to return five years later as MP for Middlesex. Rejected and re-elected three times more, he was finally allowed to enter the House in 1774. In the same year he became Lord Mayor of London, after serving as Alderman of the Ward of Farringdon Without. The Wardmote, so *St Bride's Fleet Street Vestry Minute Book* says, was held in the parish church of St Bride.

facing John Wilkes by R. Earlom. © *National Portrait Gallery*

That there was a need for a man like Wilkes seems indisputable. Johnson was not allowed any reports of Parliamentary speeches. He had to invent them. It was a breach of privilege to make known anything which happened in Parliament, but journalists with accurate memories were able to circumvent the prohibition of note-making – to the embarrassment of their printers, who were summoned to the bar of the House and made to crave pardon on their knees. Those who failed to appear were deemed liable to arrest. But Parliament had forgotten a privilege more ancient than its own. Parliamentary officers who dared pass Temple Bar to apprehend miscreants, were outraging the rights of the City – as the magistrates made clear. Parliament retaliated by summoning the Lord Mayor and Aldermen before the bar of the House of Commons and, on refusal, committed them to the

'The City Chanters', a scene in the 'Wilkes and Liberty' riots. Engraving by S. Okey 1775 from a painting by John Collett

The burning and plundering of Newgate Prison by rioters, 1780, painted by O'Neil, engraved by H. Roberts

Tower of London. When, shortly after, the power of Parliament to imprison was abolished, the City dignitaries were set free. Although this was a great victory for free speech and the freedom of the press, political reporting was still handicapped. Luke Hansard (1752-1828) began printing the *House of Commons Journals* in 1774, but these long remained privileged documents.

Nor did the Government hasten in other ways to help the press. Paper itself bore an excise duty. Stamp Duty of 4*d.* was imposed on every newspaper sold, while each advertisement, whether of two lines or a whole page, added 3*s.* 6*d.* to Government revenue. Newspapers were almost as valuable as family heirlooms. Each copy went round a considerable circle in town and then was usually dispatched to a country cousin. In 1833 came a great concession, when the advertisement tax was reduced to 1*s.* 6*d*. Three years later Stamp Duty was reduced from 4*d.* to 1*d*.

Robert Waithman (1764-1833) was another champion of freedom. His memorial, now in St Bride's crypt (where he was buried), records that he was a 'friend of liberty in evil times of Parliamentary reform in its adverse days'. Waithman, five times elected MP, was also commemorated by a statue in Ludgate Circus, an honour which he shared with John Wilkes. Incidentally Wilkes achieved this status, not so much for his Parliamentary career as for his service to the City – notably in 1780 when Lord George Gordon made his attempt to force Parliament to repeal the Act of 1778 for the relief of Roman Catholics. Once again the Fleet proved itself a focal point – the Ditch, the Prison and the Market were the scene of savage riots.

London had been four days under mob law when, on 7 June, came the culmination. The fuse of 'No Popery' had been lost in an explosion of pillaging and arson. Exultant at their success in burning Newgate Gaol, the mob next sent the Fleet Prison up in flames. At the foot of Fleet Street they encountered the Guards who, having no time to reload their muskets, set to with their bayonets. Twenty mutilated corpses were left on the street, and 35 more rioters were seriously wounded. A hundred yards away the tolls at Blackfriars Bridge were plundered, and a bonfire was fed with furniture looted from neighbouring houses. The troops fired volleys. Corpses were thrown into the Thames, and others were interred without identification. St Bride's burial register records two unknowns who were given the hospitality of a grave. One adventurous Fleet Street silversmith, named Brasbridge, determined to have a grandstand view. He climbed to the top of St Bride's steeple, only rapidly to come down again when brushed by live flakes from burning buildings.

Part of the crypt as rediscovered

This part of the crypt is now the Rector's study and is where this book was written

In his capacity as Alderman of the Ward of Farringdon Without, Wilkes sat in the Globe Tavern examining and committing to prison the rioters brought before him. In addition, he himself headed a party which beat back the rabble, and generally directed the strategy of a band of loyal volunteers, staying up much of the night to do so. He must have looked very dishevelled compared with the elegant Wilkes who during his mayoralty had paid a state visit to St Bride's, riding in the then new gilt coach and greeted by a band of young chimney sweepers, dressed with blue paper sashes and dancing in his honour. It all provided good material for Dickens in *Barnaby Rudge*, and it helped persuade Englishmen that an organised police force was necessary.

Wilkes' monumental companion in Ludgate Circus, Robert Waithman, once had an impressive calico shop at the south-east end of Fleet Street. The son of a Welsh furnaceman, he was of the rags-to-riches tradition so frequently encountered in London's history. According to his contemporaries he was arrogant, intolerant, conceited, ignorant, but completely honest and singleminded. He was a perfect subject for lampoons and caricatures. As a Radical, and committed to the campaign for the abolition of rotten boroughs and closed corporations, he needed all his powers. To him too fell the task of escorting the remains of Caroline, the unhappy wife of George IV, across the country from Hammersmith to Harwich for burial in Germany. He was one of the last great magnates who lived over his shop.

The City of London – already the centre of a growing colonial and industrial empire – depended in large part upon the enterprise of Fleet Street. It was newspapers which conveyed the intelligence needed by the builders of empire, whether financial or political. Without newspapers there could be little growth of the stock market or other City activities. Without newspapers how could, for example, a

These eighteenth-century figures which adorned St Bride's Parish School are now near the font

Lloyd's insurer be certain of sufficient reliable information to write a sensible insurance policy covering

> 'Seas, Men of War, Fire, Enemies, Pirates, Rovers, Thieves, Jettezones, Letters of Mart or Contre-Mart, Surprisals and Takings at Sea, Arrests, Restraints and Detainments of all Kings, Princes and People of what nation, condition or quality soever, Barratry of the Masters or Mariners and all other perils, losses and misfortunes'?

Without adequate information how could imperial development prosper? 'To use property agents' language', says Bernard Ash:

> 'the globe was ripe for development, and the only candidate for the job of developer was the Golden City. None of the older financial powers of Europe were any longer in the running. The world had always been the City's oyster: now the oyster was about to be opened. Its opening was to be Pandora's box as well as treasure-chest; unforeseen horrors, as well as unimagined wealth would flow from it, but a later time would reap the horrors, while the nineteenth century reaped the wealth.'[3]

Finally, at the very end of the century, close to St Bride's, emanated an enterprise of a very different kind, yet one that employed some of the same techniques as Paul Julius Reuter, or for that matter Karl Marx. For those who could handle the printed word could mould a century.

In 1799 was formed a group, largely consisting of laymen, troubled by the thought that heathen men and women were dying without a chance of hearing the name of Christ. So they set up 'The Society of Missions in Africa and the East'. Soon established in Salisbury Square, it was 'The Church Missionary Society'. For a century and a half (it moved to Waterloo Road in 1966) it held St Bride's as its parish church, and sent its messengers out to the ends of the earth. Its success (a word it would abhor) is to be measured, not in statistics nor yet in numbers of converts, but in the way in which it has conveyed the love of God, the compassion of Christ and the power of the Holy Spirit across great continents and tiny islands. Fleet Street has been the place for the communication of words. It has also communicated the Word.

10. The Nineteenth Century and after

By the end of the eighteenth century the pattern of the City of London as a world force had become clear. The point at which Roman merchants had exchanged their exotic ivory, apes, peacocks and wine for the homespun wool and the home-produced butter had become a unique global entrepôt. To its handling of visible products it had added a host of the invisible, such as banking and insurance services. The golden city had arrived. But, as Midas found, gold had to be paid for. The City of London, once a rabbit warren of rich burghers and human rabble, was to become a place of counters and desks with a nomad population which, in a morning flood and an evening ebb, moved as relentlessly as any tide.

In 1700 London had a population of some 600,000 out of a total of about 5½ million in England and Wales. It was already the biggest city on earth and it dominated the United Kingdom in a way that no other capital dominated its country. It was a remarkable concentration of urban wealth and labour, that handled more foreign trade than all the other English ports together.

Once a rich merchant had a motive for living in the City, since only through residence could he attain civic office. That proviso had been forgotten. The wealthy began building homes in Hackney or Bloomsbury, in Islington or Bromley. Those same magnates found that the space under the counter – where the apprentice slept – had become too expensive for human occupation, while the clerk who had once been treated as a member of the master's family could no longer be accommodated in the new mansion. The warehouse on the river bank had no room for a pallet of straw. The boardroom replaced the bedroom.

At the time of the Restoration, land in the City was worth about 15*s*. per square foot. In 1801, the same foot cost £54. And because of population migration, baptisms in City churches had dropped by 1800 to half the number of a hundred years before. Unhappily parents of the babies found few churches amid the drab rows of dwellings rushed up by speculators in the new suburbs. Those who travelled twice a day between home and office were wrestling with the dichotomy of two lives – the men they were at home and the clerks they were in the City.

'London going out of Town – or – The March of Bricks and Mortar', George Cruikshank, 1829

Was their real being the existence in a counting house or their brief evenings in Stepney or Camberwell? The integration of life and work, the community of labour and leisure, which mediaeval London had offered, had all but gone.[1]

The City was becoming one huge office. In the process it lost not only its residents but also its industries. The mediaeval blacksmith wanted but little room for his forge. The engineering works born of the Industrial Revolution needed acres. The Elizabethan weaver worked in his own kitchen. The power loom demanded a factory. The little ships that berthed at Blackfriars were replaced by giants that docked downstream. Only one important trade, with all the roaring machinery of industrialism, remained within or near the City boundaries – printing. Thus when silence invades the offices at 6.0 p.m., Fleet Street continues a 24-hour, 7-day bustle. In the advancing years of the twentieth century a man who stands near Ludgate Circus is necessarily struck by the anomaly of the daily intake of massive reels of paper, of tankers of ink, and other raw materials, followed by the frenzied vanloads of the finished product going out to a split-second schedule. Even with the new road systems, a remarkable number of long-distance lorries continue to treat Fleet Street as a trunk route. One wonders how all this traffic would fare if Temple Bar was still there. It was in 1878 that the City lost that ancient evidence of its separation from the rest of London, 'the pwincipal barwier between us and the horwid city' as a fop character in a *Punch* cartoon was made to say. The Thames Embankment road had been opened eight years before.

'Dirty Dick's'

left Charles Dickens, engraved from a photograph by Mason & Co

right William Cobbett, artist unknown

The industries left. The land became too valuable to live on. The people migrated. The City became a place for working hours. Yet Fleet Street still had its 37 taverns, not to mention the coffee houses (which sold far more than coffee), some of them enshrined in English literature. 'Dick's', for example, where Steele, so he tells us in the *Tatler*, took friends to dine and was embarrassed because each insisted that the other had precedence over himself, and he could not get them to enter. It was in 'Dick's' at breakfast time that Cowper read a newspaper which he thought criticised him whereupon, 'flinging down the paper in a strong fit of passion, he rushed from the room' determined to poison himself. 'Dick's', at 8 Fleet Street, was Thackeray's favourite resort – when he lived just round the corner in Brick Court.

'Peele's' was often visited by Charles Dickens, especially in 1845-6 when, for two weeks, he edited the *Daily News*.

> 'There he used to consult the files of the leading newspapers of the day. A veteran correspondent of that journal, recalling some recollections of Peele's in the first half of the nineteenth century, places the great Duke of Wellington among the company: he was frequently to be seen chatting over the files in the coffee room. Others at different times were Blomfield, Bishop of London, Lord Macaulay, Hone, the Fleet Street publisher, Alderman Waithman, William Cobbett, Nollekens, the sculptor, and

> Rundell and Bridge, the jewellers of Ludgate Hill, to whom the Court jewels of the day were entrusted for repair and resetting. The Society for Repealing the Paper Duty had its central committee room at Peele's.'[2]

The little backwaters around Fleet Street provided homes for exciting people. Charles Lamb (1775-1834), born in the Temple, spent much of his life around its sheltered courts. The advertising agency for which he once worked (he wrote copy about state lotteries), R. F. White & Co. Ltd, is still very much alive in Fleet Street. The imagination paints a tender picture of Elia taking his tragic sister around; or of his school friend Coleridge visiting him; or of the later visits from Wordsworth, Keats, Hood and Leigh Hunt. Then there was his erudite friend George Dyer who lived in Clifford's Inn and to whose chambers Leigh Hunt came, by invitation, to breakfast – only to find there was no butter, no knife to

left Charles Lamb. An early painting by William Hazlitt, engraved by Edward Smith

right S. T. Coleridge, artist unknown

left William Wordsworth, painted by W. Boxall, engraved by G. Cochran, 1842

right John Keats from a sketch by Severn engraved by Henry Meyer, 1828

cut the beef, and the teapot was without a spout. Thither came Sir Walter Scott and Southey; and in this same block, not long after, lived Samuel Butler, where he wrote *The Way of All Flesh* and dreamed nowhere into *Erewhon*. Across the road Mr John Murray, 'a young bookseller of capital and enterprise', had his shop; and it was he who insisted that Lord Byron should permit his name to go on *Childe Harold* as its author. In this same shop Byron frequently used his walking stick to practise fencing passes on bookshelves, causing Murray one day to admit 'I was often glad to get rid of him'. A few doors from Murray's was the office of the *London Magazine*. Its staff included Lamb, Hazlitt, De Quincey, Hood and Miss Mitford. There was great rivalry with Blackwood's, resulting in a duel of editors in which John Scott, first editor of the *London* was killed. In the same building were first published Lamb's *Dissertation on Roast Pig*, De Quincey's *Opium Eater* and Keats' *Endymion*, while nearby was the office from which Cobbett issued his *Political Register*. About this time Charles Knight, founder of the firm which published this book, started his *Penny Magazine*, to be followed rapidly by his *Penny Cyclopaedia* and other cheap series, all to have a remarkable influence on an increasingly literate public.

For such a large population of writers, 37 taverns were perhaps not excessive. Even so they had largely to depend (as did the churches) on the daily immigrant, for the City dwellers of a former day had gone. By 1829, the population within the old walls had declined to 56,000 (still a large number, considering they had no water closets until the 1840s, while the barges that brought in the vegetables each morning were the same that took out the night soil each evening). The attrition has proceeded steadily ever since, for the City today has barely 5000 permanent inhabitants. By the 1850s some of the little churchyards were being closed. In 1854 Parliament re-enacted what had been an inflexible law for the Romans: that there should be no more burials within the City boundaries – perhaps because of the cholera epidemic which killed 10,000 Londoners in the previous year. The banning of City burials was to have an unexpected result on St Bride's. Down the centuries the dead had been laid beneath its aisles, and its crypts had become packed – and odorous. Thereafter the crypts were sealed up and forgotten. A century later they were to be re-discovered as a result of wartime bombing.

left Sir Walter Scott, artist unknown

right Leigh Hunt by A. Croquis

left Lord Byron by H. W. Pickersgill. © *John Murray Ltd.*

right John Murray the Second by H. W. Pickersgill. © *John Murray Ltd.*

In 1862 came a measure for further reducing the number of churches, and proposals to unite some of the parishes. *The Times* said:

> 'You may walk through a score or two of parishes in an afternoon without being conscious of anything except some dreary churches, never open except for repairs. The names are so extraordinary that it is impossible to read them without a smile. The metropolitan saints must have been sadly mixed up with property, persons and institutions.'

Dickens made it even more vivid. 'As I stand at the street corner, I don't see as many as four people at once going to church, though I see as many as four churches with their steeples clamouring for people.'

Or again (from *The Uncommercial Traveller*):

> 'As a congregation, we are fourteen strong; not counting an exhausted charity school in a gallery which has dwindled away to four boys and two girls. In the porch is a benefaction of loaves of bread, which there would seem to be nobody left in the exhausted congregation to claim, and which I saw an exhausted beadle, long faded out of uniform, eating with his eyes for self and family when I passed in. There is also an exhausted clerk in a brown wig, and two or three exhausted doors and

Charles Knight. This book was published by the firm he founded.

> windows have been bricked up, and the service books are musty, and the pulpit cushions are threadbare, and the whole of the church furniture is in a very advanced state of exhaustion. We are three old women (habitual), two young lovers (accidental), two tradesmen, one with a wife and one alone, an aunt and nephew, again two girls (these girls, dressed out for church with everything about them limp that should be stiff, and vice versa, are an invariable experience), and three sniggering boys.'[3]

The Established Church, contrary to the persistent fallacy about nineteenth century Christianity, was in a bad way. Human souls sought sustenance elsewhere: for example, in the warm but meaningful service held in the Moravian Chapel in Fetter Lane (where Richard Baxter preached), the headquarters of the Moravian Brethren in England since 1742, and earlier an Independent Chapel. To it, on 1 January 1739, had gone a certain ordained Anglican clergyman who recorded in his *Journal*:

The Moravian Chapel, Fetter Lane

John Wesley aged 63, engraved by Fry from a print by Bland

> 'Mr Hall, Kinchin, Ingham, Whitefield, Hutchins and my brother Charles were present at our love-feast in Fetter Lane, with about sixty of our brethren. About three in the morning, as we were continuing instant in prayer, the power of God came mightily upon us, insomuch that many cried out for exceeding joy and many fell to the ground.'

John Wesley wrote those words, evidence of the spiritual dynamic that was to result in a world-wide movement. Wesley and the Moravians parted, but their Fetter Lane meeting house remained.

The nineteenth century depopulation of the City caught the Church in general, and many churches in particular, unawares. Nobody knew what to do with a

June Holiday at the Public Offices. George Cruikshank

church bereft of its congregation. For decades many of them became little more than museums. Not until 1867 did it occur to anyone to start midday services for office workers.[4] Changing office conditions, not least the shortening of the lunch hour to enable an earlier closing and home before the rush hour, have now made even these services less valuable than in the past. Today the problems of the City churches are greater than ever, but due not so much to an indomitable ecclesiastical conservatism as to the force of public sentiment. The Church authorities may say, 'St X is superfluous. Let it come down so that we can use the money to feed the hungry in Asia' – only to be confronted with a great outcry from people who never go to church as worshippers, and yet cannot bear the thought of the building not being there for them to neglect.

One church in St Bride's parish, however, *was* pulled down – in 1904 – Holy Trinity, Gough Square. It is a curious story. The City was already losing its residents when, in 1837, the year of Victoria's accession, the Gough Square-Whitefriars part of the parish of St Bride became a parish on its own. True, all the accounts of life in St Bride's at that time suggest the church was uncomfortably packed and there was clearly an immediate but temporary need for further accommodation. The Goldsmiths' Company gave the land for Holy Trinity, together with the sum of £500 for endowment. The building was an excrescence in

facing Holy Trinity, Gough Square, 1913. © *Royal Commission on Historical Monuments*

THE TATLER
TO LET

'The Queen' *c.* 1840 painted by W. C. Rop. Drawn on stone by R. J. Lane

every sense, designed in a mongrel style and executed in brick of a 'flaring yellow'. Closed in 1904, then a gradually deteriorating eyesore, it was eventually pulled down in 1913. It had been the last attempt to create a new ecclesiastical parish in the City and was born well out of season.

Holy Trinity happened because St Bride's was always crowded, even though the residential population was dwindling – possibly because for the first time for centuries, St Bride's could be seen from Fleet Street.

facing St Bride's seen from Fleet Street, 1829, drawn by Thomas H. Shepherd and engraved by J. Tingle

About 3.0 a.m. on Sunday 14 October 1824, a fire started in the premises of a linen draper, next a druggist on one side and a barber on the other. An hour later an oilman's stock added fuel to the flames. Before long Mr Marriott's furniture shop and showroom were involved. At one stage, eight buildings were ablaze and they were all lost. The feeling of Fleet Street for St Bride's was then given a unique

BOOKSELLER

opportunity of expression. At a public meeting held on 4 January 1825 at the London Tavern, the Lord Mayor called for £7000 to buy the land where the burned-out buildings had stood, in order to make 'the view of the beautiful steeple of St Bride's church, which had lately burst upon the public, permanently visible'. It would, said the Lord Mayor, only be an act of justice to the great architect to let people enjoy his work.

The appeal was successful – not least due to the generosity of John Blades, member of the great printing dynasty whose name still occurs in many cheque books as well as elsewhere. That, however, was not the end of the matter. One of the houses was owned by Richard Carlile, well known for his antipathy to the Church, and as the publisher of Tom Paine's revolutionary *Rights of Man*, likewise of works by the atheistical Shelley, 'systematic poet of seduction, adultery and incest, the contemner of patriotism, the insulter of piety, the raker into every sink of vice and wretchedness', as Bishop Heber ('From Greenland's icy mountains') wrote in 1822. Carlile crystallised his thoughts and hates, when he adorned his shop window with 'a jolly fat bishop in canonicals linked arm in arm with the devil'. Carlile had no strong desire to go to any trouble to make St Bride's visible. But there was another consideration. According to a manuscript note by the late Horace Sanders:

> 'Richard Carlile's shop was burned out in 1824, while its owner was in Dorchester Gaol, for what he called upholding the right of free discussion, but what the Law called selling blasphemous works. The Vicar and Wardens of St Bride's wanted this site. Carlile offered to sell if the churchmen would secure his release. They saw the Prime Minister: Carlile was released: the site was secured.'

Because of a fire, a public subscription and a Prime Minister, there is many an expression of delighted surprise on the face of a passer-by nowadays, as he looks between the Press Association and the *Birmingham Mail*. Or as, on a sunny day, he catches a luminous reflection of St Bride's steeple in the black glass of the *Daily Express*.

Another reason why St Bride's remained full was the phenomenon of large families. Dr Dale, for example, curate of St Bride's in 1826, and subsequently (with the support of Sir Robert Peel) the vicar, could always rely on the nucleus of a congregation in his wife and ten children sitting near the wealthiest parishioner, who also had a dozen siblings. An account of their Sunday-by-Sunday triumphal entry was written by a Mrs Carr, who must have been an authority on the subject for she was superintendent of the parish school. Any inference that Dr Dale spent all his time in domesticities is, however, unfair. He was a noted preacher. He translated the tragedies of Sophocles. He wrote some seventy books. And for a time he was Professor of English language and literature at University College, Gower Street. He ended his career as Dean of Rochester.

A third reason was that St Bride's has always maintained a strong connection with a recognisable and identifiable segment of our public life. A church near Threadneedle or Lombard Streets has little inevitable link with banking, any more than has a church near Billingsgate with fish. Furthermore, banking, the fish trade, and almost any profession or craft other than printing and its ancillaries, have no obvious connection in their own right with the Church as a whole. On the other hand, the theological statement of the importance of communication was honoured by the Church throughout history. The sayings and doings of Jesus were carefully recorded. Carefully the letters Paul wrote were preserved and re-read. Generation by generation the corpus of writing grew, and age by age it was faithfully handed on. Great bodies of monks became specialists in scriptoria, copying secular manuscripts no less faithfully than the sacred ones. As Rome fell and the barbarians came, they copied; and so when Europe learned about printing, it was alongside monasteries that the first presses were set up. As this book has tried to show, it was because mediaeval churchmen clustered around this

John Thaddeus Delane

A PENNY NEWSPAPER FOR ONE HALFPENNY.

Daily Mail.

THE BUSY MAN'S DAILY JOURNAL.

NO. 1. [REGISTERED AS A NEWSPAPER.] LONDON, MONDAY, MAY 4, 1896. ONE HALFPENNY.

BUSINESS NOTICES.

PRIVATE ADVERTISERS

RATES FOR ADVERTISEMENTS.

BIRTHS.

MARRIAGES.

DEATHS.

COOK'S WHITSUNTIDE CONDUCTED TOURS AND EXCURSIONS.

A WEEK IN SWITZERLAND FOR FIVE GUINEAS.

WHITSUNTIDE HOLIDAY TOURS.

NATIONAL SUNDAY LEAGUE.

SPLENDID COASTING TRIPS.

WEST AUSTRALIAN GOLD FIELDS.

MARGATE COLLEGE (BOYS).

PERSONAL.

HOTEL CECIL.

MR. WILLIAM WESTON.

POOL'S ADVERTISING OFFICES.

TRACKED BY A TATTOO.

THE WAR IN EGYPT.

CASSELL'S DICTIONARY OF COOKERY.

CHATTO and WINDUS'S NEW NOVELS.

MESSRS. LONGMANS & CO.'S LIST.

LONGMAN'S MAGAZINE.

THE EDINBURGH REVIEW.

UMBRELLAS, WALKING STICKS.

HARNESS.

THE ILLUSTRATED CARPENTER AND BUILDER.

BOW BELLS.

REYNOLDS'S NEWSPAPER.

1892 CERTIFICATE.

1893 CERTIFICATE.

1896 CERTIFICATE.

SWAN SONNENSCHEIN & CO.

DICTIONARY OF QUOTATIONS.

PROS AND CONS.

PARTS OF THE PACIFIC.

HISTORY OF THE PARIS COMMUNE.

ALLOTMENTS AND SMALL HOLDINGS.

ST. JAMES'S HALL.

WILLY BURMESTER'S VIOLIN RECITAL.

MLLE. CLOTILDE KLEEBERG'S.

HERR FRITZ MASBACH'S.

MISS MURIEL ELLIOT'S.

HANS BRONSIL'S THURSDAY SUBSCRIPTION CONCERTS.

MADAME GRIMALDI.

MISS ISABEL HIRSCHFELD.

GORDON TANNER'S VIOLIN RECITAL.

MLLE. SZUMOWSKA AND MR. JOSEPH ADAMOWSKI.

RICHTER CONCERTS.

EMIL SAUER.

JONES AND HIGGINS, LIMITED.

THE CYCLE MANUFACTURERS' TUBE COMPANY, LIMITED.

bank of the Fleet Ditch that Wynkyn de Worde brought Caxton's press to Fleet Street, and here in Fleet Street the Church in general was represented by the church of St Bride in particular. Thus did the life of St Bride's become a singular thread in the tapestry of the history of English letters and therefore of English life.

Thus, too, does any attempt to record the life of St Bride's become infinitely complex, not least in that nineteenth century when British newspapers multiplied in number and magnified in influence. The eighteenth century journalist had not been an honoured figure, Samuel Johnson and Oliver Goldsmith had small opinion of him: 'You must not imagine that they who compile these newspapers have any actual knowledge of the politics or the government of the State'. Richard Brinsley Sheridan felt even more strongly. 'The newspapers! Sir, they are the most villainous – licentious – abominable – infernal – Not that I ever read them – no – I make it a rule never to look into a newspaper!' Byron expressed himself more moderately: 'London journalists have no merit but practice and impudence.'

The nineteenth century was to improve conditions and alter the image – so that the public would come to assume that the Editor of *The Times* was as naturally a member of the 'Athenaeum' as the Prime Minister. John Thaddeus Delane, the man chiefly responsible for the changed status, lived for 31 years in Serjeants' Inn where, until overtaken by sickness, he conducted – or should it be wielded? – *The Times*. Then came the Harmsworth brothers, who captured mass readership with the *Daily Mail* in 1896, and loosed a power unrivalled until television made possible the immediacy of news and attracted away advertising – thus attacking newspapers at their two vital points. Before the Harmsworths, there was hardly anything that a present-day reader would recognise as advertising. The word 'display' was ostentatious and unacceptable. The man who had something to sell had to speak in a hushed voice. The newspaper provided the medium. The advertising made the newspaper possible. The techniques of mass production both demanded a newspaper as a platform for sales and made that platform possible. The twentieth century was on its way, and Britain was to become uniquely a country of newspapers.

In the first place, Britain has truly *national* newspapers. You expect your *Times* or *Mirror* to be available with your breakfast wherever you are in the British Isles. The Frenchman, the German (though *Bild-Zeitung* is making this statement less true), the American does not expect to see the same newspaper in the morning in whatever part of his homeland he may be. He must make do with a local product. Because the British have the choice of national as well as regional newspapers, they have a far wider range. This is partly due to the fact that, by the turn of the nineteenth century, Britain already had an unrivalled system of internal communications. One result is that, at the time of writing, while Britain's ten national daily newspapers have a total daily circulation of fifteen millions, her regional dailies have only two millions.

Herein perhaps lies the reason why the British are the world's largest newspaper buyers. The figures of copies sold per hundred of the population are: Britain 50, Sweden 46, Germany 30, Belgium 28, Holland 27, France 27.

British newspapers, too, are the cheapest in Europe (each copy being sold for far below the cost of the raw materials and production), though how long they can remain at their present prices is a question people are always asking. Contemporary conditions threaten. Year by year the minimum viable circulation rises, and the demand for more and more advertising to meet economic necessities is

left Anthony Hope

right The Prince of Wales, later Edward VII

met by tight advertising budgets already squeezed by rivals like television. Newspapers are not as strong as they were. And they are already caught up in a technological revolution which is the greatest – and most painful – since Gutenberg.

St Bride's has witnessed it all, sustaining its dual task as the home of a regular congregation and acting as the pressmen's friend. It has always had its family gossip. In 1894, for example, when the Rev. E. C. Hawkins was vicar, 'The vicar's son is writing a novel. He calls it *The Prisoner of Zenda* and he's using the pseudonym Anthony Hope'. And just before that, 'Mr Keating who lives in Bride Lane has invented a powder. It's supposed to kill bugs'. One moment of excitement occurred in 1893 when the Prince of Wales laid the foundation of the new St Bride's Institute, fruit of the commutation of ancient charities and public generosity, giving the City, among other things, its first swimming bath. About the same time Sion College found a site on the then new Thames Embankment. It is both the City parson's club and a storehouse of learning. It was preceded by the opening of the City of London School, its neighbour, in 1882 – which traces itself back to John Carpenter, Town Clerk in 1442 and executor of Mayor Richard

Alfred Harmsworth, Lord Northcliffe. © *National Magazine Co.*

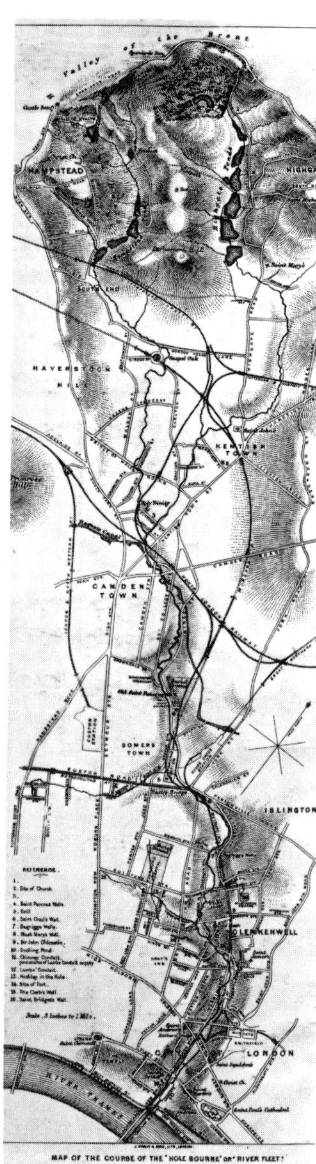

The course of the River Fleet

Whittington's will. In 1886 the Guildhall School of Music was built close by in John Carpenter Street.

Another contemporary event was the birth in 1882 of the London Press Club, the prime mover being the magnificent George Augustus Sala. 'We shall become a power in the land', he said, and he was not exaggerating. For years the Club was as travel-stained as some of its wandering members, moving from home to home and including, for a brief stay, 'Fagin's Kitchen' in a candle-lit beer cellar in Bride Court. They were the golden days of Bohemian journalists whose personal idiosyncracies and dress were as vivid as their prose styles. In 1923 the Club found a home in St Bride's House.[5] Since that date almost everyone who is anyone in British – and indeed, international – public life has climbed the Astor staircase with its glazed teak panels setting off *Vanity Fair* cartoons. Its guest-lists at dinners provide fascinating juxtapositions – an ex-President of the United States next to Jam Sahib of Nawanagar ('Ranji'), Winston Churchill near J. Ramsay MacDonald, Paderewski, Jack Hobbs, Kreisler, Sir Oliver Lodge, Steve Donoghue, Lord Reith . . . the list is endless and infinitely diverse. All of them have glanced through the windows on to the lovely line of Wren's church whose incumbent is the Club chaplain. It has even been suggested that there should be a chute from the Club windows to the Rectory to facilitate the chaplain's return home at the end of a long evening. It is fitting that a Club, whose library has the Bible sitting next to the *Guide to the Turf*, should thus rub shoulders with a church.

At some date in the last century, St Bride's Well disappeared. The explanation is hard to find, but the fact remains that this ancient landmark has gone.

In his gossipy *Everyday Book*, published in 1831, William Hone says:

> 'The last public use of the waters of St Bride's Well drained it so much that the inhabitants of the parish could not get their usual supply. The exhaustion was caused by a sudden demand on the occasion of King George IV being crowned in Westminster in July, 1821. Mr Walker, of the hotel at number ten, Bridge Street, Blackfriars, engaged a number of men in filling thousands of bottles with the sanctified fluid from the pump.'

St Bride's Well, it seems, had long been the source of water used in some way at coronations – perhaps for sprinkling the royal route. Mr Walker, who had the monopoly at the time, was obviously a very greedy person and the Well, after thousands of years of service, dried up. However one further report is to be found in the Vestry Minutes of 29 August 1850. Contractors excavating for a new sewer in Bride Lane had cut off or diverted the spring that fed the well. In search of water, the well had been made deeper at great expense, but what was found was unfit for use. Mr Mason, Churchwarden of St Bride's, took pains to tap a fresh source nearby, which yielded 300 gallons a day, but a high percentage of saline water made it unusable for domestic purposes.

The rest is silence.

Here a little and there a little, the Victorian St Bride's was 'improved' until it became a repository of well-varnished, dark, furniture whose seasoned timbers were perfect tinder for a fire bomb. The night of Sunday 29 December, 1940 at a time when St Bride's was acting as host to the congregation of the City Temple which had already been bombed, coincided with one of the great incendiary raids

The Evening News

LARGEST EVENING NET SALE IN THE WORLD

LATE EXTRA

NO. 18,390 — SIXTIETH YEAR — LONDON: MONDAY, DECEMBER 30, 1940 — ONE PENNY

TO-NIGHT'S BLACK OUT
5.27 p.m. to 8.38 a.m.

COURTS Day by Day —See Page 4

CITY CLOSING PRICES On Page 6

GIGANTIC GERMAN ATTEMPT TO SET THE CITY OF LONDON ABLAZE

Guildhall in Flames: St. Bride's a Blackened Ruin: Old Bailey Damaged: St. Paul's Saved Just in Time

NINE FAMOUS CITY CHURCHES DAMAGED

Flaming Buildings Had To Be Dynamited

R.A.F. ATTACK RAIDERS IN GLARE-LIT SKY

A gigantic attempt to set the heart of London ablaze was made by the German Air Force last night. It was the greatest fire-raising raid of the war.

SEVERE damage has been done to the City. The historic Guildhall—one of the most famous buildings in the world—was set on fire. A Wren church—St. Bride's in Fleet-street—was reduced to a blackened ruin. The Old Bailey was damaged.

In addition to St. Bride's, eight other famous City churches were damaged. They were St. Lawrence Jewry; St. Stephen's, Coleman-street; St. Vedast's, Foster-lane; St. Mary Aldermanbury; St. Andrew by the Wardrobe, in Queen Victoria-street; St. Anne and St. Agnes, in Gresham-street; Christ Church, Greyfriars (another Wren church); and St. Mary Woolnoth, in Lombard-street.

St. Bride's spire. It is still standing.

The wrecked interior of St. Bride's Church.

RECORDS SAVED

St. Lawrence Jewry and St. Vedast's were completely burned out.

The Rev. J. R. Sankey, rector of St. Andrew by the Wardrobe, rushed into the flaming church and rescued the registers, dating back to 1566, plate, vestments and some altar linen.

Damage was also done to the Guildhall School of Music and several well-known buildings in Cheapside, Fleet-street, Ludgate Hill, Bunhill Row, Moorgate, Queen Victoria-street and Aldermanbury. The ancient hall of the Girdlers' Company in Basinghall-street also suffered severely.

"DELIBERATE"

The Air Ministry and Ministry of Home Security communique, issued to-day said:

"Last night the enemy dropped a large number of incendiary bombs on the City of London in a deliberate attempt to set fire to it. Damage was done to many famous buildings, including the Guildhall and several of the City's churches.

"St. Paul's itself was endangered but the neighbouring fires were extinguished in time.

"THERE WAS NOWHERE ANY ATTEMPT TO SINGLE OUT TARGETS OF MILITARY IMPORTANCE. FIRES WERE ALSO CAUSED IN OTHER PARTS OF THE LONDON AREA, WHERE DAMAGE WAS DONE TO COMMERCIAL BUILDINGS.

"London's fire services worked heroically and with success throughout the night. Casualties were few."

FIREMEN KILLED

Never since the raids began have incendiaries cascaded down as they did last night. In one district alone 40 fires could be seen burning at one time. Whole areas of London were lit up. In some neighbourhoods, even miles from the flames, it was possible to read a newspaper by the glare.

At one hour of the night, the biggest of all London shelters was circled with flaming buildings. There were 15,000 people in the shelters.

Two London hospitals were hit. Two theatres and a museum were damaged and a hotel was bombed, while many shops and offices and other buildings were on fire.

New fires were continually breaking out. It was a stupendous test of the London Fire Service, but, yet again, it came through brilliantly. But several firemen were killed.

In some parts of London drastic measures had to be taken. Buildings were dynamited to prevent the flames spreading.

In addition to the threat to St. Paul's by the number of fires spreading around it, incendiaries fell through the roof. The cathedral staff, using stirrup pumps, put out the fire-bombs before any serious damage could be done.

NIGHT FIGHTERS

R.A.F. fighters were in action over London. Many people watched air battles in the glare-lit sky.

The sudden end to the attack on London after a few hours is believed to have been due to bad weather conditions on the Continent.

A full description of the great fire raid is on Page 3.

HOW THE CITY WENT TO WORK

ALL the fires in the City were under control by the time the rush-hour began.

Londoners arriving for work before daylight saw the eastern sky aglow with a vast radiance. The air was filled with smoke.

The glow in the sky was like a halo round the dome of St. Paul's.

St. Paul's had had an extraordinary escape. At one time the cathedral was ringed with fires. Buildings within a stone's throw still blazed and cracked as daylight approached.

Trailer pumps were dotted about Ludgate Hill. St. Paul's Churchyard was aglow with several devastated buildings.

Building after building in Cheapside had been reduced to a scarred and blackened shell. The spire of a church rose in the background against a pall of smoke.

The Guildhall was alight like a vast bonfire, but against the ruddy glow a Union Jack still flew.

Around it thousands of fire and A.R.P. workers picked their way over miles of hosepipe, floundering through pools of water, avoiding heaps of glass and charred rubble.

Typists Unable To Reach Offices

Along Moorgate shops and offices had their windows blasted or broken by fire.

The junction with London Wall became an impromptu "clearing house" for typists and other City workers who found their normal means of access to their places of occupation inaccessible.

"Can't get through" was the frequent answer to agitated inquiries. Police and firemen advised workers as to alternative routes to their places of business. Parts of London Wall were closed to the public.

TWO ON LOOTING CHARGE

William Robert McClintock (47), [illegible], North Kensington, and Philip Richard Kaiser ([illegible]), dealer, [illegible], were remanded for trial when charged at [illegible]minster to-day with stealing [illegible] from bombed premises.

IN THE GUILDHALL TO-DAY—a heap of charred ceiling rafters in the main hall.

The main hall used to look like this.

SEVEN AIRMEN "BAG" 58 PLANES

ALL DECORATED

Seven airmen who, between them, have destroyed at least 58 enemy planes appear in the latest R.A.F. awards list, which was issued to-day.

The D.S.O. is awarded to Acting Squadron Leader R. R. Tuck, D.F.C. (No. 257 Squadron) of Catford. His total victories are at least 18 planes.

A Long Chase

A bar to the D.F.C. is awarded Acting Flight-Lieutenant J. C. Dundas, D.F.C. (A.A.S. No. 609 Squadron), of Doncaster, who chased an enemy plane from Winchester to Cherbourg before finally destroying it. He has now destroyed at least 12 planes.

The D.F.C. is awarded to Squadron Leader M. V. Blake (No. 234 Squadron), a 27-year-old New Zealander; Flight Lieut. Billy Drake (No. 421 Flight), a Londoner, of 23, who now lives at Chatham; Pilot Officer E. S. Marrs (No. 152 Squadron), 19, a Dover boy, whose parents live at Hawkhurst (Kent); and Pilot Officer W. D. Williams, R.A.F.V.R. (No. 152 Squadron), of East Grinstead.

The D.F.C. is also given to Sergeant D. A. S. McKay (No. 421 Flight), an ex-bank clerk, of Yorkshire, who has shot down at least eight enemy planes.

GOEBBELS TO-MORROW

Goebbels, German Propaganda Minister, will broadcast to Germany at 6 p.m. (B.S.T.) to-morrow, New Year's Eve.—Reuter.

ROUND AND ROUND

"I ought to have kept to what I sell—that would not have let me down," said a milkman charged at Highgate to-day with drunkenness.

ROOSEVELT'S NEW PLEDGE WELCOMED

President Roosevelt's historic broadcast announcement during the night that the United States will give more and more aid to Britain despite all the threats of the Dictators is warmly welcomed in London.

OFFICIAL circles regard it as a further proof of the courage and realism of America's attitude towards the dangers which confront democracy, no less in the Western Hemisphere than in Europe and Asia.

Here are the reactions to the President's speech reported from other capitals:

BERLIN.—Ribbentrop, Hitler's Foreign Secretary, is now personally studying the speech.

It is significant, however, that the German Press has called off its campaign of warning to Roosevelt not to intensify the help to Britain.

WASHINGTON.—"A moral declaration of war" was how some diplomatic circles described the speech.

There was much speculation as to whether Germany will sever diplomatic relations with the United States.—B.U.P.

Speech reported on Page Five.

Rome Says:—

R.A.F. BOMB NAPLES AGAIN

RAIDS OVER GERMANY AND THE PORTS

Naples was bombed by the R.A.F. last night, according to to-day's official Italian communique.

Two waves of aircraft are said to have dropped bombs and leaflets. Buildings were damaged and a number of casualties were caused.

THE raid was apparently carried out by the R.A.F. Middle East Command.

An Air Ministry communique issued in London this afternoon:

Very bad weather seriously restricted R.A.F. bombing operations last night. In spite of this, small forces of our aircraft attacked an objective in Germany and invasion ports and aerodromes in enemy-occupied territory. Two of our aircraft are missing.

Attacks on Lorient

The German news agency to-day admitted that British planes have repeatedly attacked Lorient, the German U-boat and air base on the French coast.

The agency added: "Once again a British bomber attempted an attack on the vital military installations there, but was shot down soon after it appeared.

"Germans describe it as typical of British military amateurism and the stupidity of their strategy that they send single planes against this vast armed front, thousands of miles long, while Germany, in large-scale attacks, systematically makes very heavy raids on England's centres of military importance."—Reuter.

FIRE WATCHERS

Govt. to Appeal Urgently for Voluntary Action

From Our Political Correspondent

A Government announcement on fire watchers will be made to-morrow, it is expected, by Mr. Herbert Morrison, Minister of Home Security.

I understand that he will make an urgent appeal to all owners and occupiers of buildings not covered by the existing compulsory Order dealing with fire precautions to organise voluntary protection for premises now left untenanted and unguarded at night.

MORE FIRE BOMBS TO-DAY

A solitary raider dropped fire bombs and oil bombs on an East Anglia town to-day.

Commercial premises were hit: it is believed there were no fatal casualties.

The raider machine-gunned roof-tops.

LONDON TRAM HIT BY BOMB

Several passengers as well as driver and conductor of tramcar killed by H.E. bomb in London street last night.

Bomb struck centre of car and crashed through it on to track below. Tram was hurled through air and landed shattered against pavement 20 yards away.

THREE WARDENS KILLED

Three wardens—A. A. Collins, H. A. Bush and J. W. Pockall—were killed on duty in one London district.

H.E. bomb near them. Ten people were rescued from nearby house.

'UNDECLARED WAR' —ROME ON ROOSEVELT

Rome, Monday. — "Roosevelt, the man of undeclared war against the Axis and Japan, side by side with England."—Description of Roosevelt to-day by Virginio Gayda ("Mussolini's mouthpiece") in "Giornale d'Italia."—B.U.P.

U.S.A. ACCLAIMS ROOSEVELT

American comments on Roosevelt's speech include: Senator Alben (Kentucky), leader of Democratic majority in Senate: "A magnificent clarification of our objectives."

Senator Austin (Republican), leader of Republican minority: "Remarkably fine presentation of situation."

Mr. William Allen White, chairman of Committee to Defend America by Aiding Allies: "President's statement was calm and magnificent."—B.U.P.

HITLER TO REPLY TO ROOSEVELT

Berlin, Monday.—Stated in Berlin German reply to Roosevelt will come direct from Hitler himself—either in speech or in statement.

German officials refused any comment pending Hitler's reply. "We have no instructions, and have absolutely no comment to make," it was stated.—B.U.P.

R.A.F. BOMB VALONA TWICE MORE

Athens, Monday. — Valona attacked for 21st and 22nd times yesterday by British bombers, R.A.F. headquarters in Greece announce.

In first raid bombs exploded among troops and transport near jetty. In second raid bombs burst between military transport park and military stores.—Reuter.

PENSIONERS' POSTAL DRAFTS BURNED

War Office said to-night that some postal drafts prepared for despatch to Army pensioners who normally receive quarterly pensions on January 1 destroyed by fire at Manchester.

Pensioners possessing certificates of identity issued by Regimental paymasters at Barnet, Canterbury or Manchester should go to nearest Post Office on or after January 1 to obtain pensions.

The morning after, looking west (*left*) and east (*right*)

of the war. That evening Verger Leonard Morgan had chosen 'The year has gone beyond recall, with all its hopes and fears' to play on the bells. It was a natural choice but it had a prophetic irony. The bells rang for the last time over a darkened Fleet Street (blackout was at 5.27 p.m.). The congregation, some forty or so, attended the last evensong. After the doors were locked, they all went home – but not to bed. Few Londoners had any sleep that night. 'The dome of St Paul's', said *The Times*, 'seemed to ride the sea of fire like a great ship lifting above the smoke and flames the inviolable ensign of the golden cross.' But below the smoke there were no noble metaphors. Only steel being melted, stone being calcined, a city being consumed.

A bomb, or maybe bombs, pierced the roof of St Bride's, and the inside was soon ablaze. Good neighbours from the Press Association, Reuters and the Press Club rushed in, grabbed what they could – including the brass lectern which

tradition said had already been rescued from the same blazing church nearly 300 years before. St Bride's famous bells fell in molten ruin but the steeple in which they hung had its night of greatest glory, for, though flames were ravening out from its every opening, it stood, a triumphant affirmation of Wren's engineering mastery.

pages 229 *and* 230 Beauty from ashes: Tony Dyson

Arthur Taylor had already been vicar for 22 years. He was 72 years old. He had loved St Bride's. He was left with a charred ruin. War restrictions made any attempt to restore parish life almost impossible. Yet somehow he carried on. First the Church Missionary Society, distinguished parishioner of St Bride's for nearly a century and a half, gave St Bride's congregation a home. Then Prebendary Taylor was able to restore a vestry, and a remnant of the former parish could once more pray on familiar ground. So a thin thread of the long tapestry was maintained until, an octogenarian, Taylor died in 1951.

Six years later St Bride's would be rebuilt, but not even the wildest imagination could have foreseen what that rebuilding would reveal. So far as was known, St Bride's had begun its life somewhere in the twelfth century. All that the eye had been able to discern for a century was the Wren church. People suspected that somewhere below the floor level there would be remains of the church which had preceded the Fire of London. There were good grounds for such suspicions. To quote Professor Grimes:

Commercial Cables

PLEASE SEND YOUR REPLY
VIA COMMERCIAL
TELEPHONE FOR MESSENGER
TO COLLECT YOUR CABLEGRAMS.

All America Cables

Postal Telegraph U.S.A.

480

Cablegram

TELEPHONE:
LONDON WALL 5678
(PRIVATE EXCHANGE)

HEAD OFFICE.
27/33. WORMWOOD STREET.
LONDON, E.C.2.

1941 JAN 5 PM 9 56

WXY.4. LX435 NYK 50 3

NLT PASTOR SAINT BRIDES CHURCH LDN

MEMBERS OF NIGHTWORKERS MASS ASSOCIATION OF CHURCH OF SAINT ANDREW
THE PRINTERS CHURCH NEWYORK ARE SHOCKED TO LEARN OF DESTRUCTION OF
SAINT BRIDES CHURCH AND OFFER OUR HEARTFELT SYMPATHY RIGHT REVEREND
MONSIGNOR WILLIAM E CASHIN SPIRITUAL DIRECTOR

DANILE B OSHEA PRESIDENT
JOHN MACKENZIE SECRETARY

No Inquiry respecting this Message can be attended to without the production of this form. Repetitions of doubtful words should be obtained through the Company's Offices, and not by *direct* application to the Sender.

The world Press showed ecumenical sympathy

Human remains re-discovered subsequently proved of exceptional scientific interest

> 'A drawing by the Rev. John Pridden, curate of St Bride from 1783 to 1803, had preserved the record of a mediaeval vault which had been retained by Wren and incorporated; and when in 1952 the church authorities were preparing to rebuild the church, the Excavation Council was invited to look for the vault which was no longer visible but could be assumed to be still in existence below the present day floor.'[6]

There may, too, have been vague memories (though constant questioning of those around at the time has failed to reveal any) that the vault had been used for burials up to 1854. Few people had the remotest idea of what Professor Grimes would soon bring to light. He dug for a vault a few hundred years old, and found nearly 2000 years of embalmed history. To write this book before the 1950s would have been impossible. Any London guide book published little more than a decade ago is necessarily misleading about St Bride's. Our knowledge today owes much to Hitler who, by destroying a surface, revealed a great depth. Nor are historians and archaeologists the only scholars who share that debt. For below St Bride's floor was found a mediaeval charnel house with its bones laid in chequerboard pattern. This probably points to a custom of burying in the churchyard for a limited time, then removing the bones and carefully placing them in the charnel

facing The tower and steeple suffered little war damage

house before re-using the churchyard for further burials – evidence that London has long had a land shortage problem.

Edmund Evans related how this practice extended into the nineteenth century:

> 'From the engraving room in Bride Court we overlooked the Churchyard of St Bride's. We used to see some gruesome sights of funerals in this place, open to the public on three sides. We used to see the old gravediggers explore the small burying-ground with a long iron rod with a "T" piece handle on top, which we called a "Cheese Tester"; he tried place after place to find a sufficiently clean place to dig a grave, and as soon as he began to dig he had to erect a screen to hide from view the large amount of human bones he turned up.'[7]

In addition to the charnel house, St Bride's possesses one of the most important groups of identified human remains known in Europe, described as 'the greatest skeletal find of the century'. During the eighteenth and nineteenth centuries, nearly 300 bodies had been buried in that vault. Their coffins had crumbled but the coffin plates remained. Accordingly the sex and age at death of each skeleton was accurately known; and thanks to Verger Leonard Morgan this knowledge was preserved. None of these human remains are open to the general public, but by special arrangement accredited medical researchers are allowed to examine them if it can be established that such examination will be to the benefit of humanity. This procedure was made possible by gifts from the Royal Society (founded in St Bride's parish), the Royal Anthropological Institute, Cambridge University and the Wellcome Foundation. The British Museum (Natural History Department) gives continuing advice. Already many items of medical knowledge have been enriched or revised as a result.

The crypts are open to all visitors who range from school children to highly sophisticated international tourists. There, thanks to the generosity of Sir Max Aitken in 1969, a permanent exhibition of the history of the site is on display, including panels about the origins of printing and the beginnings of newspapers.[8]

Through dying by fire, St Bride's rose again to become a yet more significant and enthralling place. The new church cost more than its predecessors. To the war damage compensation of £110,000 was added a further £140,000, contributed for the most part by those who communicate in print – representing national, regional, and even overseas and allied interests. Eventually on 19 December 1957, anniversary of the very day on which the Wren church had been dedicated nearly three centuries before, the new St Bride's, eighth church on this site, was rededicated in the presence of H.M. the Queen and the Duke of Edinburgh. By an inspired thought, the workmen who had constructed the new St Bride's were taken to a feast in the Old Bell Tavern, which Wren had built for *his* workmen. Fleet Street takes little account of any rampart between sacred and secular, perhaps because – with the quiet maturity of the centuries – it knows that so much in Fleet Street which the world calls secular has been born out of its own side. The sacred and the secular are one.

Olymp
TYPEWR

facing Seen from the Press Association – Reuter Building

The mechanics of restoration

Wren's St Paul's looks on as Wren's St Bride's is restored

Buttresses were put in to keep ancient masonry *in situ*

facing Twentieth-century craftsmen

facing Each to his own trade

The Royal Arms, carved by Kenneth Gardner from a single block of Beer stone weighing nearly two tons

The carver is working from the model on his left

facing David McFall, RA, with early designs for his statues of St Bride and St Paul. © *Evening Standard*. The statues now in St Bride's are eight feet tall

Bride
Paul

facing David McFall (sculpture), Alfred Banks (drawings), Glyn Jones (artist), W. Godfrey Allen (architect) inspect progress. © *Sport and General*

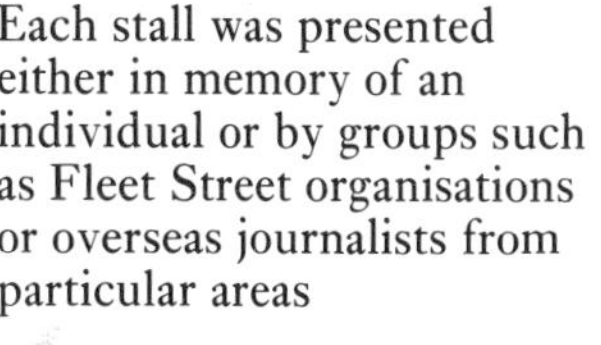

Each stall was presented either in memory of an individual or by groups such as Fleet Street organisations or overseas journalists from particular areas

H.M. The Queen, H.R.H. The Duke of Edinburgh, Lord Astor of Hever and the Revd Cyril Armitage at the re-dedication in 1957. © *The Times*

The reredos is unveiled at the re-dedication

facing The Crucifixion, being a historic event, is in traditional idiom. The Risen Christ, being ever-present, is given contemporary treatment. The apogee is the Heavenly Dove

11. A Phoenix again

Sunday, 5 June 1951, was a perfect summer evening in London. It was an augury of the incumbency of Cyril Moxon Armitage, who for 21 years had been Precentor of Westminster Abbey and was Chaplain to four monarchs. In a ruined nave, amid bracken and willowherb and alongside a small plum tree planted by no human hand, he stood where once had been the pulpit and delivered his inaugural address. Among the long line of St Bride's clergy, few had gifts more appropriate to their particular moment. He had the right natural qualities and they were enhanced by a peculiarly relevant experience. He could visualise the new church that was to be, he could work persistently to make it a reality, and he could inspire others to work with him.

The parson was matched by a man no less distinguished in his own field. W. Godfrey Allen was a successor of Wren himself as Surveyor of the Fabric of St Paul's Cathedral. Together, they recruited the services of a team of craftsmen of a quality rarely found in the twentieth century. At the outset they agreed not to attempt the recreation of the St Bride's that Hitler had destroyed – a church which in several ways had been altered from Wren's original ideas – but to go to the master's original sources and give twentieth century substance to a seventeenth century concept. To stand in St Bride's today, and let the eye rove around delight after delight is to know how well they succeeded.

In 1940 the church had heavy galleries along three sides, that on the west being loaded with a great organ case which completely hid Wren's minstrel gallery, a delicate sonata in its own right and the only one Wren put in a church. The east wall, lacking the distance effect created by a chancel, was abrupt, flat, and uninspiring – while the whole church was cluttered with dark brown pews. Wren's superlative statement of beauty had been bloated with cumulative prolixity.

St Bride's, as Armitage and Allen left it, is not an assemblage of bricks and mortar but space enclosed by art and animated by light into an ever-subtle change. The building has the curious capacity of never seeming to be the same twice, however often you see it. It is a living thing, ready to respond to the affec-

facing Gifts of the faithful over the centuries (not available for viewing)

tion of those who love it, ready to adapt to the silence of a quiet soul at prayer in a corner, to the pageantry of a great Fleet Street occasion, or even to the gossipy intimacy of a village green.

facing Cyril Moxon Armitage, whose inspiration recreated St Bride's

In 1967 the Press Association, to celebrate its centenary, gave to the west end of St Bride's a magnificent glass screen and doors, incised with the invitation ENTER WITH PRAISE. Designed by John Stammers, it has had the effect – by opening it up – of presenting the whole church to the Fleet Street which has so long cherished it. This is therefore an appropriate point at which to begin a description of the building itself.

The immediate impression on entering St Bride's is one of silence rather than speech. The mind of man seeking the mind of God is caught here in a climactic moment. Newton was alive when Wren was designing this church, and of him Pope said:

> 'Nature and Nature's Laws lay hid in Night:
> GOD said, *Let Newton be!* and all was Light.'

The West End

A
ω

facing and above Details from the reredos by Glyn Jones

Wren's genius breathed the same air and he took Nature's laws and gave them shape in stone. Wren did not drop his mathematics and his science, when at the age of 30 he took up architecture. Instead he remembered them in a new and eloquent language, in architecture which is the least evasive of all the arts.

We are just inside the glass doors. We are, so to speak, *in camera*, in our own small but perfectly proportioned apartment, which is the ground level of the steeple.

Its north and south walls are curved and in the curves are stone benches. Its ceiling is a dome, small but not inadequate, intimate yet preserving an aloofness. This dome stands on four arches, but it is the eastern arch which makes this truly a camera, for it is a lens through which is focussed a vista of great beauty. You look, first over a few feet of Purbeck and then over a geometrical pattern of black

facing 'A madrigal in stone' (Henley)

marble from Belgium and white from Italy until, 90 feet away, it reaches the architectural altar-piece with its pairs of Corinthian columns and its curved pediment crowned by flaming urns. At its heart is the Crucifixion painting by Glyn Jones, a rare concept with the sturdy legs of the two thieves, firm symbol of the strength of sin, seemingly daring a dying Lord to try to escape, and the rude soldiery, the rough mob, and the rigid Establishment looking mindlessly on. That Lord has ginger hair, an audacious way of making the viewer revise hackneyed ideas of the Jesus of Victorian sentimentality. Above the painting – traditional in style, for the Crucifixion is a historic event now past – is a stained glass representation of the Risen Lord, modern in idiom, for he remains forever above.[1]

The Incarnation was the culmination of the Old Testament. The Jesus who was incarnate always pointed beyond himself to the Father, and the east end of St Bride's says all that. The eye goes from the free-standing reredos to the wall a few feet behind it, to find both the past of the Old Covenant and the everlasting

The Press Association Centenary Service. © *Press Association*

future of the Infinite. The wall above the reredos and at its sides is 'painted Nebulous and above the Clouds appears (from within a large Crimson Velvet Festoon painted Curtain) a Celestial Choir or Representation of the Church Triumphant'. The Crucified and Risen Christ of the reredos is in the setting of his glory. No attempt is made to depict the Father. The final resting point is the Dove, symbol of the Holy Spirit whom Jesus promised and sent. Flanking the altar are Moses, the prophet, figure of man alone with God, and Aaron, the priest, figure of corporate man engaged in the Opus Dei.

The quotation above is from Edward Hatton's *New View of London*, published in 1708 and showing the east end as Wren wanted it. Yet this east end is one of the most striking differences between the 1939 St Bride's and its present successor. For the dull flat east end which Hitler destroyed has been replaced by what all but the most eagle eye accepts as a perfect half-domed apse. Glyn Jones achieved a brilliant *trompe d'oeil.* The solid structure of the free-standing altar and the mothering curve of the apparent apse somehow assert both the immanence of Jesus and the transcendence of Christ, without any heretical element of separating the two natures.

facing and below Details of the stalls

View from south aisle

The line from the glass doors, open to the world, and the east end, opened up to God, is an axis about which the rest of the fabric balances. For those who want it more technically expressed we quote from the London Survey Committee Monograph:

> 'Each side of the central compartment is filled by the five semicircular arches of the arcades, springing from piers and responds formed of coupled Doric columns with a section of entablature above each pair. The bases of the columns stand on semi-octagonal plinths, well above the seating, the capitals have an egg-and-tongue enrichment to the echinus, and the only relief to the entablature is given by the dentils of the cornice bed-mould and the water-lily leaf of its upper member. The face-mould of the arches is plain, but each has a delightful little key block of a winged cherub's head beneath a feathered headdress. A rich character is given to the arcades by the coffering of the soffits, with carved mouldings to the panels and roses in the centre of each panel.

Above the arcades runs an inconspicuous cornice from which springs a segmental (almost semicircular) plaster vault that spans the church from side to side and extends from east to west, some 45 feet in height. This vault is divided into bays which echo the arcades not only in number but in their transverse arches that are similarly coffered and enriched. These arches are carried on skilfully designed corbels in the arcade spandrels formed of elaborate escutcheons with a boldly carved cornice member that stands out from the unemphasized springing of the vault. In each bay the vault opens at the sides to provide for the large elliptical windows of the clerestory, the effect of which depends solely on their concentric and radiating glazing-bars. These large windows flood the church with light and give value to the whole arcuated scheme of the interior. In the centre, between the sections of cross-vaults that admit the clerestory, the vaulted ceiling is furnished with simple rectangular panels with carved bolection mouldings.'[2]

Apart from the opening in the reredos there is no stained glass in St Bride's. The east window is glazed in leaded lights to a geometrical pattern designed to reduce glare. Incorporated in the design is a large cross, in reeded glass. When the church is lit at night this makes a striking feature from Bride Lane. All other windows are glazed with plain reamy antique glass set in wrought-iron frames. This allows daylight to remain natural and yet to have its nature enhanced.

One major change between the present St Bride's and its predecessor is in the seating. The high box pews, like the galleries, have gone. In their place are collegiate-type stalls set within waxed natural oak screens, consisting of columns and entablature in the composite order, enriched with carvings and cartouches bearing armorial devices. On the north and south sides the screens are open, but

The churchyard, fountains in foreground presented by the Fleet Street branch of the British Legion

The Royal Arms

at the west end they are closed, and finish with terminals surmounted by David MacFall's statues of St Paul – recalling the mother church of the diocese – and St Bride. The symbols of the four Evangelists are represented over the stalls. These stalls, like the reredos, are triumphs of twentieth century woodcarvers. (There are people who come into St Bride's and insist that this work was done by Grinling Gibbons.) The designs for the carvings were by Alfred Banks. To the backs of the stalls are attached uniform teak plaques, either recording the gift of the stall (at the time of rebuilding) or commemorating an individual. The lettering here, as everywhere else in the church, up to the time of writing, was designed by William Sharpington.

The stalls in St Bride's are impressive. Their arrangement encourages a feeling of community among the congregation (and St Bride's is proud of its reputation for friendliness). The arrangement does, however, have one disadvantage, in that the preacher feels he is addressing a row of noses. There is no pulpit in the church and it is difficult to know where one could be put. An amplification system, gift of the Berry family in memory of the first Lord Kemsley, has therefore proved of especial value.

The beauty of the east end of St Bride's is compulsive. More gentle, but no less lovely, is the west end with its pensive minstrels' gallery. It is this west wall which best shows off the Portland stone, primary material of the building (both Wren and Godfrey Allen went to the same firm for their stone). Immediately below the minstrels' gallery is a single block of Beer stone weighing nearly two tons, carved by Kenneth Gardner into the Royal Arms, coloured and gilded.[3] These are a reminder, not only of St Bride's past association with monarchs, but also of the great day in 1957[4] when the Queen and the Duke of Edinburgh came for the re-dedication.

The west end has one other distinction. Behind the minstrels' gallery, and in the north-west and south-west corners where once the stairs mounted to the galleries, there are the 3606 pipes of the superb organ, gift of the first Lord Astor of Hever who was Master of the Guild of St Bride at the time. The console is in the south aisle. Rarely has there been a greater opportunity for an organ builder, and rarely better taken. The present instrument is a worthy successor to the work of Renatus Harris.[5]

Since the church was being re-built, the problem of accommodating the organ could be solved afresh – and by a group of men peculiarly fitted to do so. Cyril Armitage, the rector, had been responsible – as mentioned – for services at Westminster Abbey, including great occasions such as a royal wedding and a coronation. The Director of Music was the talented Gordon Reynolds, journalist and teacher, as well as virtuoso. Lord Astor was distinguished, not only by his

The dedication of the fountains

generosity to the church, but as a music lover and organist, adding personal interest to his gift. A committee of professional musicians, including Sir Ernest Bullock, Dr O. H. Peasgood, and Dr George Thalben Ball, gave their enthusiastic advice. Wren had designed a building which can be seen as the perfect extension of the organ chamber, and which enhances any music – curiously, its acoustics honour music but deride the spoken word, a great trial to a preacher, especially if he is a Welshman.

facing Gordon Reynolds, Osborne Peasgood and George Thalben-Ball at the organ console

Throughout the planning of the organ, St Bride's choir was kept in mind. The result is a blend of instrument and voices which is as rare as the visual splendour of the church. Eye and ear can worship together.

St Bride's is not a mere gem for the aesthete. It is also a place where human warmth can legitimately be expected. The simple things are there, such as the figures of the charity school boy and girl in the south-west corner.[6] Near them is Meg Meggitt's effigy of Virginia Dare, first Anglo-American baby–see page 108. St Bride's is homely. After a service, the west end seems to become a family meeting place with cheerful conversation before departure for home or office.

On leaving the north-west corner of the nave, the visitor first sees an aerial photo of the neighbourhood. Descending the stairs, he can study plans and diagrams of the area in the nineteenth, eighteenth, seventeenth and sixteenth centuries. Entering the main crypt he can examine a variety of objects, beginning

Leonard Morgan, verger for 43 years, at the console of the carillon

The crypt exhibition presented by Sir Max Aitken in memory of Lord Beaverbrook, 1969

with Roman pottery and oyster shells, which were the litter after some legionary's picnic. He can stand on the line of a first century Roman ditch and peer at the second century Roman pavement. He can touch the walls of a church which was probably here before St Augustine, and study remains of walls of the churches which succeeded it – all *in situ*. In the eastern end of the smaller crypt he can sit in a chapel hardly touched for 600 years. And back in the main crypt he can see an exhibition of the history of Fleet Street throughout its lifetime as the home of print.

In St Bride's even the mechanics of church heating have their message – though they were designed as a matter of practical convenience, not a sermon. It is the theme this whole book has tried to convey. The inextricable entwinement between church and community in Fleet Street extends even to the physical. Running from the boiler room of the Press Association headquarters is an umbilical cord consisting of hotwater pipes. The same flow of warmth embraces both the ancient Roman remains and those who on Press Association and Reuter staffs help to mould the minds of all mankind in tomorrow's mass media. It is a conjunction of

facing The north aisle of the crypt today

facing A new life together

A new life

THE SCOTSMAN
PETER EVANS EATING

ancient and modern, of sacred and secular, of symbolism and expediency which can surely not often be surpassed.

When Wordsworth stood on Westminster Bridge composing:

> 'Earth has not anything to show more fair . . .
> This city now doth, like a garment, wear
> The beauty of the morning . . .'

perhaps he had St Bride's in his vision. It is certainly visible from there as it is from Hampstead Heath and many other places. It is a superb example of how Wren grasped an opportunity. For centuries St Bride's neighbours had pressed as close as possible to the church. They had hidden it. Wren would rise above them all and let his church be a burgeoning flower in a bed of roofs. Today from ground level the Press Association building is a towering piece of Portland stone cliff. From the top of the steeple it is reduced to its proper proportions. Perhaps the finest of all tributes to Wren's genius as an engineer is that after nearly three centuries, after assaults by lightning, and after an orgy of bombing with flames issuing from its apex, his tallest steeple[7] smiles serenely into the sun and remains 'a madrigal in stone'.

The steeple is the crown and glory of St Bride's, however regarded. In December 1940 it shone like a filament incandescent in a furnace. Thirty years later surveyors paid a tribute to its strength and stability. The physical resurrection of the church is the outward sign of its spiritual permanence; and this has been its message ever since St Bride's began.

facing The Winston Churchill funeral, 1965. St Bride's was packed with people at a service almost identical with that which was simultaneously happening in St Paul's Cathedral

Fleet Street is a village

facing A village set in a city

Silver-gilt mace 'For the use of the Parish of St Bridgett in the Ward of Farringdon Without'. Among the names inscribed on it are John Wilkes Esq., Alderman, and Sir Francis Child. Dated 1703

Mace used by liverymen of the Guild of St Bride at Sunday services

There is a moving story behind the Paul Boston silver – see page 135

facing Heads of two staves representing State *(left)* and Church

274

facing A silver-gilt flagon

A fifteenth-century Spanish processional cross, a gift from Sir Bruce Ingram

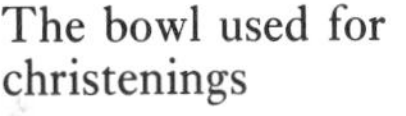

The bowl used for christenings

page 276. A reminder of the number of religious houses once in the parish

Carmel alias white Fryers LONDON

Appendix

The Tower and Steeple are described on p. 45 of the *London Survey Committee Monograph No.* 15.

'The ground stage of the tower projects about a foot from the main walls above and is capped with a bold string course and curved weathering which covers the projection. The angles have quoins and in the centre is the main west entrance with a square-headed opening set in rusticated masonry with flat arch having a large keystone bearing a cartouche with the words, 'Domus Dei' beneath a cherub's head. The door is flanked by Ionic columns supporting an entablature and segmental pediment, the latter rising above the course which divides the storeys.

'The second stage consists of a plain block, 47 feet in height, without projecting quoins but with emphasised ashlar joints. The centre, for rather more than a third of the whole width is recessed and arched at the top within a distance of three courses of the cornice. This contains a circular window above a large rectangular one finished with entablature and pediment. Each window is surrounded by a broad architrave in three faces and there is a sunk panel beneath the lower light. A well-marked cornice furnished with modillions surrounds the tower between the second and third stage, and above it the lower surface is extended for four courses to serve as base for the structure of the third stage. The other faces are plain except for a small circular opening north and south, the former having been covered by a modern clock. The third storey (bell chamber) has all four faces alike. At each angle is an engaged (three quarter) column, flanked on each side with pilasters, of the Corinthian order, carrying a continuous entablature that surrounds the tower. This entablature breaks forward slightly on each face above the pilasters to carry a segmental pediment. The columns and pilasters have moulded bases resting on pedestals that stand on the podium above the cornice of the storey below. Within a rectangular recess between the pilasters is an arch, framing the louvred openings of the bell chamber. This arch springs from moulded responds on plain jambs and beneath the cills of the openings is

page 277. The Arthur Stratton measured drawing

placed a projecting panel or table capped with a moulded cornice. On the north and south faces small circular windows are inserted in the centre between the pedestals of the main pilasters. Above the pediments each face of the tower is carried up the width of the central feature only, leaving re-entrant angles at the tower corners, to assist in the transition to the octagonal spire. A panelled parapet follows the contour of this uppermost section of the tower and eight vases, each carved with demons' heads and flame finials, stand on the parapet angles.

'The steeple stands on a circular base with a simple cornice. Above this are four stages, octagonal in plan, treated in the lower three with arched openings on each face in the fourth with rectangular openings with a small circular hole above each. The angles of the stages, which diminish in size as they ascend, have single pilasters, Doric in the first two, Ionic in the third and Corinthian in the fourth. Each stage has a full entablature, breaking round the pilasters and the three top stages have similar bases beneath both pilasters and arches. The arches have moulded responds and carved key blocks. In the centre of the spire is a stone newel stair which serves as a spinal support, terminating in the spirelet which has a panelled and pierced base. It is an obelisk in form, octagonal on plan, and carved with a ball at each angle above the base. The whole is surmounted by ball and vane. There were originally eight vases at the foot of the obelisk.'

left Erosion on the tower decoration, 1972

right The weathervane during exterior cleaning of the church, 1972

NOTES

Chapter One
1. *The Excavation of Roman and Mediaeval London* by Professor W. F. Grimes, p. 197, Routledge & Kegan Paul, 1968.
2. *Roman Britain* by R. G. Collingwood and J. N. L. Myers, pp. 308-9, O.U.P., 1937.

Chapter Two
1. *History of the Church of Ireland* by W. A. Phillips, Appendix K, p. 390, O.U.P., 1933.
2. Article, *St Bride*, p. 197, O.U.P., 1957.
3. *Lives of British Saints*, Vol. 1, p. 272, Honourable Cymmrodorion Society, 1907.
4. *England and the Continent in the Eighth Century* by W. Levinson, p. 3, O.U.P., 1946.
5. *The Church and the Nation* by Charles Smythe, p. 31, Hodder, 1962.

Chapter Three
1. The Convent of the Blackfriars was on the site of Blackfriars railway station; that of the Whitefriars was a forerunner of the *News of the World* building.

Chapter Four
1. See page 323 of the edition published by O.U.P. in 1958.
2. *The Black Art*, Vol. 1, No. 2 – a magazine, now alas defunct.
3. *Five Hundred Years of Printing* by S. H. Steinberg, p. 40, Pelican, 1955.
4. Op. cit., p. 72.
5. *English Books and Readers, 1475 to 1535* by H. S. Bennett, p. 186, C.U.P., 1952.
6. *Wynkyn de Worde: Father of Fleet Street*, published for Wynkyn de Worde Society, 1960.
7. Steinberg, op. cit., pp. 73-4.
8. Quoted in *Annals of Fleet Street*, Beresford Chancellor, p. 65, Chapman & Hall, 1912.
9. Op. cit. Stow's *Survey of London*, Ed. Kingsford 1:69 Clarendon Press, 1908.
10. In 1867 the school moved out to become the King Edward VI School at Witley, Surrey. On the second Tuesday in March each year, it returns to its old parish church in company with the Lord Mayor and the Lord Bishop.
11. London Survey Committee Monograph No. 15, p. 14, 1944.
12. Henry Machyn's Diary (Ed. Camden Soc. 1848), p. 95.
13. Op. cit., p. 291.
14. Stow, op. cit., p. 45.

Chapter Five
1. Machyn's Diary, op. cit., pp. 300-1.
2. *Poems of Ben Jonson*, Ed. G. B. Johnston, pp. 73-74, Routledge & Kegan Paul, 1954.
3. John Stow, 1525-1605, see Chapter Four, Note 8.
4. *Aubrey's Brief Lives*, Ed. O. L. Dick, p. 201, Secker & Warburg, 1949.

Chapter Six
1. See Chapter 4, Note 11.
2. *A History of the Church of England* by J. R. H. Moorman, p. 241, A. & C. Black, 1953.
3. London Survey Monograph, op. cit., p. 27, quoting churchwardens' accounts.
4. *Fleet Street in Seven Centuries* by Walter G. Bell, p. 331, Pitman, 1912.
5. See Anthony Burgess's Introduction to the Penguin edition of Daniel Defoe's *Journal of the Plague Year*, Penguin, 1966.
6. Diary of John Evelyn, p. 496, O.U.P., 1959.

Chapter Seven
1. It seems that £150,000 of books alone, exclusive of printing presses and other equipment, were destroyed by the Great Fire. Pepys suggests that all the great booksellers were ruined.
2. From an unpublished MS, part-sequel to Walter G. Bell's work, see Chapter Six, Note 4.
3. Dr Fell was the subject of the jingle:

'I do not love thee, Dr Fell,
The reason why I cannot tell.'

In consequence, says the *Oxford Companion to English Literature* he 'has come to be used to describe a type of vaguely unamiable person against whom no precise ground of dislike can be adduced'.

4. Steinberg, op. cit., p. 137.
5. In its preamble, this Act described itself as 'an act for the encouragement of learning by safeguarding authors'.
6. The reputation of Birmingham due to the activities of John Baskerville was shortlived, for after his death all his equipment was removed to France.

Chapter Eight
1. Steinberg, op. cit., p. 151.
2. *Mist's Weekly Journal*, 5 April 1718.
3. *The Romance of Bookselling* by F. A. Mumby, p. 252, The Scarecrow Press, 1968.
4. A Bibliography of English Corantos and Periodical Newsbooks 1620-1642, Folke Dahl English Bibliographical Society, 1952.
5. Steinberg, op. cit., p. 165.
6. Steinberg, op. cit., p. 168.
7. *The Church and Parish of St Bride, Fleet Street* by the Rev. E. C. Hawkins, p. 18, St Bride's Foundation Institute, 1905.

Chapter Nine
1. Some people question whether such a shortening occurred, but no one appears to have made the hazardous climb with a yardstick. It is said that the removed portion of the steeple lay for a long time in a stonemason's yard in Old Street, before being transferred to Kingsgate Castle, Isle of Thanet. At the accession of Queen Victoria, it was moved again to Park Place, Remenham, near Henley.
2. *Annals of Fleet Street* by Beresford Chancellor, p. 79, Chapman & Hall, 1912.
3. *The Golden City* by Bernard Ash, p. 136, Phoenix, 1964.

Chapter Ten
1. Certain notable improvements characterised the City during the nineteenth century. For example, the pillory was abolished in 1843, and public executions after 1867. In the latter year the invention of the typewriter (in practical form) led to the influx of women into offices, and this in turn introduced a number of revolutionary changes. One was the patronage of tea and bun shops – to the detriment of the old trencherman eating-houses.
2. Bell, op. cit., p. 506.
3. *The Uncommercial Traveller*, p. 122, R. E. King edn., 1906.
4. At St. Edmund the King, Lombard Street.
5. At the time of writing the Press Club is preparing to move to the International Press Centre.
6. Grimes, op. cit., p. 182.
7. *The Reminiscences of Edmund Evans*, pp. 15-16, O.U.P., 1967.
Edmund Evans was the colour printer responsible for the Kate Greenaway and other Victorian children's books.
8. This exhibition was honoured by the award of a 'highly commended' certificate presented by the British Travel Association.

Chapter Eleven
1. The stained glass is also the work of Glyn Jones, and the reredos is intended partly as a memorial to Edward Winslow. See p. 97.
2. See Chapter Four, Note 11.
3. The block of Beer stone was presented by the Bath and Portland Stone Firms Ltd.
4. 19 December 1957.
5. The organ was built by The John Compton Organ Company Ltd. It has 51 ranks of pipes, eleven of them extended. It has 97 speaking stops, four manual (cc-c 61 notes) and a pedal board (ccc-g 32 notes). The enclosed great and swell organs are in the south chamber, the solo organ is in the north chamber with an unenclosed tuba beside it, along with the contrabass and subbass pedal ranks. Behind the minstrel gallery stands the unenclosed positive organ and behind that the unenclosed choir organ.
6. These two figures once adorned the parish school, but since the closure of the latter in 1937, they have found an appropriate and permanent home inside the parish church.
7. See also Appendix.

SOURCES OF ILLUSTRATIONS

A large number of the pictures in this book have been taken from the files of St Bride's Church. Sources of the other pictures are as follows: Mary Evans Picture Library for the illustrations on pages 8, 15 (right), 18 (right), 19, 27 (left and right), 28 (left and right), 30, 32, 33, 46, 50, 52 (left), 54, 66, 67, 68, 72, 73, 75, 82, 84, 85 (left and right), 92, 99, 110, 112, 113, 115, 119, 120, 121, 122, 124 (left and right), 125 (left and right), 126 (left and right), 127, 128 (right), 130 (above and below), 133, 134, 135, 137 (left and right), 140 (left), 143 (above and below), 152, 153, 155, 165, 166 (left and right), 167, 174, 182, 186, 187, 191, 193 (left), 197, 204, 206 (left and right), 207 (left and right), 208 (left and right), 209 (left and right), 211, 212, 213, 214, 216, 219, 222 (left and right); British Museum, 5 (bottom right), 10, 18 (left), 20, 31, 43, 52 (right), 63, 80 (left and right), 138, 188 (right); London Museum, 6, 9, 41 (below), 48, 60 (below), 61, 90, 91, 101, 136, 157; Guildhall Museum, 7 (below), 21; Guildhall Library, 106, 114, 117, 150, 151, 198, 205, 224; Bord Failte Eirean, 13, 14; National Portrait Gallery, 41 (top left and right), 42, 58, 59, 60, 69, 79, 87 (left), 93 (left and right), 95, 96, 103, 104, 105, 128 (left), 172, 184, 185, 188 (left), 192 (right), 196; Ashmolean Museum, 141; Bodleian Library, 65, 158; National Monuments Record, 89; *Mirror*, 94; Science Museum, 140 (right); Courtauld Institute of Art, 145 (top right); London Survey Monograph No. 15, 146-7, 153; National Galleries of Scotland, 179; John Murray Ltd, 210 (left and right); Royal Commission on Historical Monuments, 29, 215; National Magazine Co., 223; Press Association, 236 (Reuter photo), 254, 278; Sport and General, 160, 161, 226, 244; *The Times*, 245 (below); *Evening Standard*, 242 (below); Unilever, 38; Dulwich College, 87 (right); Sir John Soane's Museum, 123; Associated Newspapers, 220; Keystone Press Agency, 232, 233, 246, 268; London News Agency, 233, 238 (below), 255, 256; Aerofilms, 270; Aldus Books, 195 (right): Tallis's *London Street Views*, 1838-40, ed. Peter Jackson, published by London Topographical Society in association with Nattali and Maurice 1969, ii and iii; National Museum of Ireland, 12.

INDEX

Page numbers in italic refer to illustrations

Adamites, 112
Adams, John, 188
Addison, Joseph, 164, *166*, 181, 182
Aitken, Sir Max, 235
Alban, St, 9
Alcuin, 19
Alençon, Duke of, 91
Alfred, King, 21, *21*
All Hallows', Barking, 21, 25
Allen, W. Godfrey, *244*, 249, 261
Alsatia, 121-2, 124, 126, 131, 183
American Revolution, 186, 187-8
Angelico, Fra, 53
Anne, Queen, 181, 194
Archer, Thomas, 168
Arles, Synod of, 8
Armitage, Cyril Moxon, 44, *245*, 249, *250*, 261
Ash, Bernard, 202
Ash, Simon, 90, 115
Ashmole, Elias, 128
Astor of Hever, Lord, *245*, 261
Athanasius, St, 9
Atherton, Charles, 148
Atterbury, Francis, 118, *119*
Aubrey, John, 108, 128, *128*, 156
Audley, Sir Thomas, 70
Augusta, 9
Augustine of Canterbury, St, 15, 18, *18*, 265
Augustine of Hippo, St, 9
Aula, William de, 35
Ayala, Peter de, 70

Backwell, Edward, 146
Bagley, Henry, 40
Ball, John, 46
Bangor, Bishop of, 31
Banks, Alfred, 260
Bankside, 81
Baptists, 112
Barebones, Praise-God, 110
Baring-Gould, Sabine, 14
Barrow, Dr, 157
Barry, Mrs, 125
Bat, Robert, 35
Bathe, William de, 40
Baxter, Richard, 212
Beaker, Bronze Age, *7*
Beale, John, 97
Beauclerk, Topham, 194
Beaumont, Francis, *85*, 87, 88
Becket, Thomas à, 31
Bede, Venerable, 10, 17, 21
Bedlam (Bethlehem), Hospital of, 43
Beeston, William, 124
Behn, Mrs Aphra, 124, 125, *126*
Bell, W. G., 153
Bennett, H. S., 56
Berthelet, Thomas, 72, 74
Besant, Sir Walter, 133
Bessarion, John, 53
Betterton, Thomas, 88, 124
Bible, printing of, *63*, 65, 92, 159
Bills of Mortality, *129*
Birch, Peter, 156, 159
Bird, Edward, 148
Black Death, 44, 129
Black Friars (Dominicans), 27, 31, 33
Blackfriars, 3, 7, 31, 32, 81, 87, 88, 204
Blackfriars Bridge, 183, 199
Black Prince, 31
Blackstone, Sir William, 154
Blades, John, 218
Blomfield, Bishop, 206
Bloomsbury, 203
Boccaccio, 81
Boleyn, Ann, *67*, 67, 90
Boniface, St, 19
Boniface VIII, Pope, 28
Bonner, Bishop, 74
Book of Kells, 19
Book of St Albans, *52*
Booth, William, 83
Boston, Paul, 135
Boswell, James, 192, *193*, *194*, 194
Boyle, Abraham, 126
Brace, Hannah, 148
Bradford, John, 74
Break-neck Stairs, *192*
Bride Court, 224, 235
Bride Lane, 186, 259
Bride, St, 3, 10, 11, 13-14, 19, 44, *243*
Bride Well, 1, 3, 7, 8, 224
Bridewell Palace, 34, 68, *68*, 70, *71*
Britannia (title-page), 138
British Museum, 235
Brito, 52
Bromley-by-Bow, 203
Brooch, Anglo-Saxon, *10*
Brotseach, 11
Browne, Edward, 128
Browne, Sir Thomas, 128
Brownrigg, Mrs, 178
Buckingham, Duke of, 93
Buke, Henry de, 26-7
Bullock, Sir Ernest, 263
Burbage, James, 81, 82
Burgess, Anthony, 128
Burke, Edmund, 193, 194
Burney, Charles, 194, *194*
Burton, John de, 47
Busby, Dr, 139
Butler, Samuel, 208
Butter, Nathaniel, 168, 175

Byddell, John, 65
Byrd, William, 94
Byron, Lord, 208, *210*

Caesar, Julius, 8, *8*
Calvin, John, 81
Camberwell, 204
Cambridge University, 235
Campe, J. H., 168
Campeggio, Cardinal, 67, 70
Canesby, Sir John, 39
Canterbury, Archbishopric of, 18
Canterbury Pilgrims, *30*
Cardmaker, John, 72, 74
Carlile, Richard, 218
Carmelite Friars, 31, 33, 47, 121
Caroline, Queen, 201
Carpenter, John, 222
Carr, Mrs, 218
Carteret, Lady, 131
Catherine, St, 32
Caumpeville, Maude de, 29
Cave, Edward, 194
Caxton, William, 34, *50*, 51, 54-5, 56, 164
Cecil, Sir Robert, 91
Celtic Christianity. *See* Christianity
Celtic remains, 4, 15, *15*
Censorship, 100, 106-8
Chancery Lane, 31, 65, 147
Chapman, George, 88
Charles I, *110*, 110, 112, 136
Charles II, 112, 115, 120, *120*, *121*, 124, 134, 144, 146, 148, 154
Charles V (Emperor), 32, 70
Charles Martel, 21
Chatham, Matilda, 44
Chaucer, Geoffrey, 31, *31*, *32*, 39
Cheapside, 154
Chesterfield, Earl of, 153
Chichester, Bishop of, 31
Child, John, 132
Child's Bank, 153, 154, *155*
Christ Church, Newgate, 148
Christianity,
  British,
    early, 7-10, 15
    seventh-century, 18-19, 21
  Celtic, 4, 15, 17, 18, 19, 21
    Irish, 11, 13-14, 21
  Friars and, 47
  Romans and, 8-10, 15, 17-18, 19
Church, 81, 219
  printing and, 49, 51-5, 61, 62, 65, 100, 106, 107, 108, 221
  Puritanism and, 109, 112-13, 115
  rebuilding in City (1670), 144, 147-51
  reduction in City (1862), 210, 212-14
Church Missionary Society, 202, 231
Churchill, Sir Winston, 224, *268*
Cirencester, Abbot of, 30
'City Chanters, The', *197*
City of London School, 126, 222
Civil War, 94, 109, 175
Clarke, Henry, 132
Clarke, William, 132
Cleeve, William, 148
Clifford's Inn, 207
Clinton, Governor, 189
Cobbett, William, 107, 206, *206*, 208
Cobham, Eleanor, 39
Cole, John, 148
Coleman, Thomas, 118
Coleridge, Samuel Taylor, 128, 176, 207, *207*
Colet, Dean, 56, 61, 70
Columba, St, 19
Columbanus, St, 19, 21
Congregationalists, 112
Congreve, William, 118, 181
Constantine I (Emperor), 8
Coster, 52
Convocation of Canterbury, 30
Coverdale, Miles, 65
Cowley, Abraham, 126
Cowper, William, 37, 39
Crane, Court, 128
Cranmer, Archbishop, 65
Cromwell, Oliver, *59*, 98, 110, *111*, 112, 151, 153
Cromwell, Thomas, 65
Croppe, Elizabeth, 61
Croppe, Gerard, 61
Crowmere, William, 37, 39
Curll, Edmund, 166
Cutpurse, Moll, *122*, 124

Dahl, Folke, 175
Daily Mail, 220, 221
Dale, Dr, 218
Danes, 21
Dare, Ananias, 77
Dare, Elenor, 77
Dare, Virginia, 77, 97, *108*, 263
Dashwood, Sir Francis, 197
Davenant, William, *124*, 124, 125
Defoe, Daniel, 107, 124, 128, 132, 174, 175, 181-2, *182*
Dekker, Thomas, 88, 124
Delane, John Thaddaeus, *219*, 221
De Quincey, Thomas, 208
Dickens, Charles, 154, 178, 200, 206, *206*, 210
Dicks, John, 118
Diggers, 112
'Dirty Dick's', *205*, 206
D'Israeli, Benjamin, 195
D'Israeli, Isaac, 194-5
Dodd, Dr, 157
Dominican Friars, 27, 31, 33
Domitian (Emperor), 7
Donatello, 53
Donne, John, 95

Donoghue, Steve, 224
Dorset Garden Theatre, 124-6, *127*
Dove, Dr, 150-1
Downs, Bryan W., 191
Drake, Sir Francis, *95*
Drayton, Michael, 88, 94
Drew, George, 148
Drinkworth, Henry, 94
Drury Lane, 126
Dryden, John, 87, *124*, 124, 125, 126, 136, 139, 153, 156, 164, 166
Dubthach, 11
Dürer, Albrecht, 53
Dyer, George, 207 ll

Earthquake Council, 46
Easter, date of, 17
Edinburgh, Duke of, 235, *245*, 261
Edward I, *28*, 28, 34
Edward II, *29*, 29, 30, 35
Edward III, 44
Edward IV, 39
Edward VI, 70, 100
Elizabeth I, *41*, 76, 77, 79, 81, 90, 91, 92, 100, 123, 151
Elizabeth II, 235, *245*, 261
Elizabeth of York, 62
Ely, Bishop of, 31
Ely Place, 31
Empson, Elizabeth, 71
Empson, Sir Richard, 71
Erasmus, 61
Erconwald, St, 18
Essex, Earl of, 77, 79, 91
Essex Street, 31
Ethelbert, King, 18, *18*
Eton College, 74
Evans, Edmund, 235
Evans, Rhys, 137
Evelyn, John, *128*, 128, 135, 153
Evening News, 225
Exeter House, 31

Fabian, Henry, 44
Faraday, Michael, 176
Faux, Thomas, 40
Faversham, Abbot of, 30
Fawkes, Guy, *92*, 93
Fawkes, William, 62, 65, 168
Fell, John, *158*, 159
Felton, John, 93-4
Fetter Lane, 31, 94, 95, 97, 135, 146, 212, 213
Field, Richard, 83, 88
Fire engine, *135*
Fisher, Samuel, 118
Fisher, William, 85
Fitz-Stephen, William, 30
Flatman, Thomas, 95
Fleet Street, 33, 39, 62, 175
'Fleet parsons', *177*, 177-8
Fleet Prison, 33, 43, 46, 74, 98, *123*, *152*, 154, 175, *176*, 176-8, 199
Fleet river, 1, 8, 25, 26, 31, 32-3, *61*, 68, 70, 88, 92, 116, 125, *151*, 176, 183, *183*, 186, 199, 221, *224*
Fleet Street, *ii*, *iii*, *v*, 14, 26, 31, 32, 37, 39, 44, 46, 56, *60*, 77, 90-4, 99, 108, 121, 123, 125, 126, 131, 135, 136, 139, 153, *157*, *191*, 193, 194, 199, 206, 207, 216, 235, *269*
  arts and, 77, 79, 81-2, 85, 88
  Press and, 1, 55, 56, 59, 62, 65, 70, 74, 91-2, 159, 164, 189, 190, 201-2, 204, 221
  publishing and, 164, 166, 168
  rebuilt, 144
Fletcher, John, *85*, 87, 88
Florio, John, 95
Foliot, Gilbert, 25
Forster, John, 193
Fourth Lateran Council, 27
Fox, Georgiana, 178
Fox, Henry, 178
Franciscan Friars, 47
Franklin, Benjamin, *184*, 186-8
Frith, Mary, *122*, 124
Frost fair, *60*, *90*
Fuller, Thomas, 118, 133

Gardiner, Bishop, 74
Gardner, Kenneth, 261
Garrick, David, 194, *194*
Gauntbrigge, William, 39
Geary, Sir Francis, 153
Geoffrey, Archbishop of York, 32
George I, 124
George II, 124, 190
George III, 159, *185*, 186-7, 188
George IV, 201, 224
Germanus, St, 10
Gibbon, Edward, 187
Gibbons, Grinling, 181, 260
Gibbons, Orlando, 94
Gifford, Nathaniel, 97
Glastonbury, 7
Globe Theatre, 70, 81, *82*, 87
Gloucester, Duchess of, 39
Gloucester, Duke of, 39
Godfrey, Sir Edmundsbury, 146
Goldsmith, Oliver, 191, *192*, 193, 194, *194*, 221
Gordon, Lord George, 199
Gosling's Bank, 153
Gough, John, 62
Gough Square, 195
Grafton, Richard, 65
Great Fire of London, 76, *101*, 133-6, *134-5*, *142*, 154, 176, 231
Great Plague, 128-9, *129-30*, 131-3, *132-3*, 136, 175
Green Ribbon Club, 146
Greene, Robert, 82

Gregory the Great, Pope, 17, 18
Gregory IX, Pope, 47
Grimes, W. F., 3, 7, 231, 233
Grosseteste, Robert, 47
Guildhall School of Music, 224
Gunpowder Alley, 137
Gunpowder Plot, *92*
Gutenberg, Johann, 52-3, 100, 222
Gwynne, Nell, 126, 154

Haberdashers' Company, 32
Hackney, 203
Hales, Mr, 70
Hall, 213
Halley, Esmond, 181
Hammersmith, 201
Hampstead Heath, 269
Hampton Court Conference, 92
Handel, 156
Hansard, Luke, 178
Harmsworth brothers, 221
Harris, Renatus, 153, 261
Harvey, William, 97
Hatton, Sir Christopher, 31
Hatton, Edward, 149, 257
Hatton Garden, 31
Hawkins, E. C., 178, 222
Hawkins, Sir John, 194
Hawksmoor, Nicholas, 146
Hawksworth, 194
Hayton, Thomas de, 37
Hazlitt, William, 125, 208
Heber, Bishop, 218
Hellfire Club, 197
Henley, W. E., 156
Hennenbert, Archbishop, 100
Henry I, 22, *27*
Henry III, 35
Henry IV (of France), 93
Henry VI, 39
Henry VII, *58*, 62, 70, 71
Henry VIII, 32, *41*, 44, *58*, 61-2, 65, *66*, 67-8, 71, 74, 151
Henry, Prince of Wales, 93
Herbert, George, 94
Herring, John, 118, 120
Hertford, Council of, 17
Heywood, Thomas, 88
Hildebrand, Pope, 22
Hitler, 133, 134, 249, 257
Hoare's Bank, 153, 154
Hobbes, Thomas, 95, *96*, 97, 106, 108
Hobbs, Jack, 224
Hogarth, William, 123, 178, 190, 194
Holborn, 183
Holborn Bridge, 33, 183
Holder, William, 139
Holland, Henry, 88
Holy Trinity, Gough Square, 214, *215*, 216
Hone, William, 206, 224
Hood, Thomas, 207, 208
Hook, Robert, 139
Hooker, Richard, 95
Hooper, Bishop, 74
Hope, Anthony, 178, 222, *222*
Hopkins, John, 81
Howard, Thomas, 72
Howe, Timothy, 93
Hughes, Owen, 93
Hulsun, Master, 74, 77
Hume, David, 168, 187
Hundred Years War, 29
Hunt, Leigh, 207, *209*
Hutchins, 213

Indian chief and camp, *80*
Industrious apprentice, *113*
Ingham, Benjamin, 213
Innocent VIII, Pope, 62
Iron Age craftsmanship, *5*
Islington, 203

Jam Sahib, 224
James I, 79, 91, 92, 93, 97, 123, 128, 151
James III (of Scotland), 107
Janock, Richard, 37
Jenner, Sir William, 180
Jewel, Bishop, 90
John, King, 25, 27, *28*
John II (of France), 31
John de Barnes, 25
John de Flete, 26
Johnson, Dr, 159, *172*, 187, 190, 192-5, *193*, *195*, 197, 221
Jones, Glyn, *244*, 254, 257
Jonson, Ben, 82, *86*, 87, 88
Joseph of Arimathea, 7
Judas Bible, 159
'June holiday at the Public Offices', *214*

Katherine of Aragon, *41*, 65-6, *66*, 70
Keating, 222
Keats, John, 207, *208*
Kempis, Thomas à, 53
Kemsley, Lord, 260
Kildare, 11, 15
Kinchin, 213
King's Head Court, 136
Kinnon, James, 94
Kit-Kat Club, 166
Kneller, Sir Godfrey, 166, 181
Knight, Charles, 208, *211*
Knights Hospitallers, 31, 71
Knights Templars, 22, 31
Knyvet, Sir John, 37
Kreisler, Fritz, 224
Kyd, Thomas, 82

Lamb, Charles, 1, 207, *207*, 208
Langton, Bennet, 194

Langton, Stephen, 27
Latimer, Bishop, 76
Laud, Archbishop, 98
Leather Lane, 32
Leaver, Stephen, 148
Lecky, William, 191
Lee, Alexander, 39
Leicester, Earl of, 79, 81
Leo X, Pope, 62
Leonardo da Vinci, 53, 187
Lettou, Johannes, 62
Leveland, Nathaniel de, 33
Levinson, W., 18
Lilly, William, 136-7
Lily, William, 56, *57*, 74
Linacre, Thomas, 56
Lincoln, Earl of, 33
Lincoln's Inn Fields, 22, 154
Lindisfarne Gospels, *20*
Lippi, Fra Lippo, 53
Livingston, William, 189
Locke, John, 106, 139
Lodge, Sir Oliver, 224
Lollards, 39, 61
Lombard Street, 218
London, 21, 47, *48*, *81*, 106-7, *114*, *117*, *150*, *270*
  bishopric, 8, 10, 15-16, 18
  eighteenth-century, 201-9
  Great Fire, *see* s.vv.
  Great Plague, *see* s.vv.
  name, 6, 9
  rebuilding plans after Fire, *143*
  Roman, 1, 4, *4*, 7-10, *9*, 203, 209
London, Bishop of, 27, 35, 68, 70, 133
London Bridge, 22, 27, *91*
London Gazette, 175
'London going out of town', *204*
London Museum, 134
London Press Club, 224, 226
London Wall, 4
Longland, John, 148
Loppedelle, Thomas de, 35
Louis XV, 186
Lovelace, Richard, *87*, 88, 95
Lucy, Thomas, 71
Ludgate Circus, 77, 183, 199, 200, 204
Ludgate Gaol, 43
Ludgate Hill, 8, 10, 62, 135, 180
Lupus, St, 10
Luther, Martin, 62
Lyly, John, 82

Macaulay, Lord, 106, 191, 206
MacDonald, Ramsay, 224
MacFall, David, *244*, 260
Macgenius, Constantine, 178
Machlinia, William de, 62
Machyn, Henry, 74
Magazines, 175, 182-3
Malcolm, Sarah, 178, *179*
Malory, Thomas, 53
Mansion House, 183
Mantua, Marchioness of, 67
Mare, Matilda de la, 37
Marlborough, Duchess of, 181
Marlborough, Duke of, 153, 181
Marlowe, Christopher, 82
Marriott, Richard, 94
Marshall, Joshua, 146
Marshalsea Prison, 79
Marston, John, 88
Marx, Karl, 202
Mary, Queen, 72, *73*, 74, 79, 91, 100, 151
Matthews, John, 107
Mauritius, Bishop, 68
Mee, Thomas, 115
Meggitt, Meg, 108, 263
Mellitus, Bishop, 15-16, 18
Merchant Taylors' Company, 88
Metropolitan Railway, 183-4
Michaelangelo, 53
Middle Temple Lane, 128
Middleton, Thomas, 88, 124
Millington, Francis, 156
Milton, John, 100, *105*, 108, 109, 134, 164, *167*
Mitford, Mary Russell, 208
Mithras, 8
Moeza, Gerado, 67
Monk, General, 115
Montague, Marquis of, 39
Montague, Lady Mary Wortley, 153
Monument, 147, 156
Moore, Sir Gerald, 144
Moorman, Bishop, 112
Moran, James, 62
Moravian Chapel, *212*
Moravians, 212-13
More, Thomas, 56
Morgan, Leonard, 226, 235, *263*
Morley, Thomas, 94
Morton, Cardinal, 65
Moxon, Joseph, 49-50
Muggletonians, 112
Murray, John, 208, *210*
Myles, Nicholas, 70-1

Nashe, Thomas, 82
Nechtone, Sir William, 37
Needham, Jasper, 153
New England, 97, 98
Newgate Gaol, 43, *198*, 199
Newsbooks, 168, 175
Newspapers, 168, 175-6, 182, 187-9, 198, 201, 221-2
New Street Square, *173*, 195
New Temple, 32
Newton, Sir Isaac, 128, 139, *140*, 181, 251
Nicaea, Council of, 9

Nicholas, St, 32
Nicholas of Cusa, 53
Nollekens, Joseph, 206
Northcliffe, Lord, 175, *222*
Norton, Thomas, 81
Norwich, Bishop of, 31

Oates, Titus, 146, 154
Ogilby, John, 136, *137*
Old Bailey, 135
Ollyver, Magdalene, 97, *98*
O'Neale, 118
Origen, 7
Osborne, Thomas, 190
Otway, Thomas, 125, *126*, 164
Overton, Nicholas, 40
Oxford, Earl of, 153, 154

Paderewski, Jan, 224
Paine, Thomas, 107, 218
Palmer, James, 88, *89*, 90, 97, 115-16, 118
Paoli, Pascal, *194*
Paris, Matthew, 25
Parliament, 88, 107, 132, 146, 178, 181, 198, 199, 209
  House of Commons, 90, 92, 109, 156, 190, 197
  Long, 100
  Rump, 110
Paston family, 29
Patrick, St, 11, 13, *15*
Paul, St, 7, *243*
Peasgood, Osborne H., *262*, 263
Peel, Sir Robert, 218
Peele, George, 82
Peirson, Richard, 132
Pelagian heresy, 9, 10, 15, 17
Pelagius, 9, 15-16
Pen case, eleventh-century, *18*
Penn, William, 144
Pepys, John, 116-18, 120, 134, 151
Pepys, Margaret, 116
Pepys, Samuel, 88, 106, 116, *116*, 117, 118, 120, 125, 128, 131, 133-4, 151, 156-7, 175
Pepys, Thomas, 117
Peterborough, Abbot of, 30
Peter de Rupibus, 27
Pettigue, Simon, 44
Philip, Prince (of France), 31
Philosophical Society, 126
Pilgrim Fathers, 77, 97, 99
Plaque, eighth-century bronze, *12*
Playing cards, *112*
Playter, Sir William, 146
Poore, Richard, 27
Pope, Alexander, 118, 136, 164, 166, 181, 191, 251
Powell, Mary, 108
Prayer Book, 76, 109
Presbyterians, 112
Press Association, 226, 251, *254*, 265, 269
Pridden, John, 233
Pride, Thomas, 109-10
Prince Henry's Room, 93
Pringle, Sir John, 187
Printer's Bible, 159
Printing, 168, 181, 190
  Bible, *63*, 65, 92, 159
  Caxton types, *55*
  censorship, 100, 106-8
  Church and, *see under* Church
  Fell type, *159*
  magazines, 175, 182-3
  newsbooks, 168, 175
  newspapers, *see* s.v.
  office, *54*
Publishing, 164, 166, 168, 188
Pudding Lane, 133, 137
Purcell, Henry, *93*, 94, 156
Puritans, 72, 90, 95, *112*, 115, *115*, 118, 124
Pynson, Richard, 56, 65

Quakers, 112

Raleigh, Sir Walter, *42*, 77, *78*, 79
Ram Alley, 91
Ramsay, Alice, 117
Ranters, 112
Rede, Thomas, 40
Reformation, 47, 74
Reith, Lord, 224
Restitutus, 8
Reuter, Paul Julius, 202
Reuters, 226, 265
Reynolds, Gordon, 261, *262*
Reynolds, Sir Joshua, 193, 194
Rich, Susannah, 180
Rich, William, 180
Richard I, *27*, 32, 33, 35, *43*
Richard of Dunstable, 27
Richardson, Samuel, *180*, 187, *188*, *189*, *190*, 191
Richmond, Countess of, 56
Richmond, Duke of, 178
Ridley, Bishop, 70, 76
Rievaulx, Abbot of, 29, 30
Rimini, Council of, 9
Rivington, Charles, 189, 190
Rivington, James, 189, 190
Rivington, John, 189
Robinson, Jacob, 168
Rochester, Earl of, 154
Rolle, Samuel, 134
Roanoke Island, 77
Romans
  Britain and, 1, 4, 7, 8-10, 265
  Christianity and, 8-10, 15, 17-18, 19
  foundations, *3*
  Mithraism, 8
  pavement, *1*

Romans *(cont.)*
  wall and tesserae, *7*
  woman's burial, *5*
Rose, 164
Royal Anthropological Institute, 235
Royal College of Physicians, 56
Royal Exchange, 118, 134
Royal Society, 126, 128, 175, 186-7, *187*, 235
Rudhall, Abraham, 151, 153
Russell, Lady Rachael, 153
Russell, Lord William, 153

Sackville House, 91
Sackville, Sir Richard, 90, 91
Sackville, Thomas, 81, *87*, 91
St Albans, Duke of, 154
St Andrew's, Holborn, 195
St Bride's Avenue, *169*
St Bride's, Fleet Street, 94, 97, *102*, 133, *170-1*, 191, 195, 200, 202, 214-15, *217*
  apse, ninth-century, *16*
  bells, 151, 231
  benefice, 25, 27, 70-2, 115
  burials *and* churchyard, 4, 7, 55, 67, 74, 79, 91, 94, 95, 108, 117, 118, 124, 132, 136, 142, 148, 199, 209, 233, *233-4*, 235, 259
  chancel, 15, 22, 249
  chapel, *38*
  charnel house, 233, 235
  christening at, *267*
  christening bowl, *275*
  Commonwealth period and, 109, 115, 120
  cross, processional, *275*
  crypts, 1, *2*, *5*, *15*, *23*, *35*, 191, 209, 235
  date, 3-4, 14-15, 17, 21
  destruction,
    (1666), 133, 135
    (1940), 224, *225-8*, *231*, 231, *236*
  earliest building, 3-4, 14-15, 17
  exhibition in crypt, *265*
  figures, Parish School, *201*
  flagon, *274*
  floor, 15, 233
  fountains, *261*
  gifts to, *248*
  gilds, 44, *45*, 47, 55, 72
  interior
    post-war, *229-30*
    pre-war, *160-3*
  maces, *271*
  marriage in, *266*
  minstrels' gallery, 249, 261
  name, 14-15
  nave, 43
  Norman tomb, *16*
  north aisle, *264*
  organ, 153, 261, *262*, 263
  pews, 249, 259
  position, 7

St. Bride's *(cont.)*
  Press and, 52, 55, 218-19, 221-2, 224, 235, 251, 265
  rebuilt (1957), *229-30*, 235, *237-40*, 242, 249, 251, *251*, 253-4, 257-61, 258, 263, *264*, 265, 269
  rectory, 71-2, 224
  roof, 36
  Royal Arms, *241*, *260*
  screens, 43, 76, *246-7*, 251, *252-3*, 259
  second church, 21-2
  silver, *272*
  stalls, *245*, *256-7*
  staves, *273*, *276*
  steeple, *145*, *147*, 149, 153, 154, 186-7, 218, 231, *232*, *255*, 269, 277, *277-8*
  third church, 22, 25, 26-47
  tower,
    curfew, *24*, 25, 136, 140
    Wren, 140, 148, 151, 154, *232*, *255*, *277-8*
  Vestry meeting, 118, 120, 134, 149, 197
  Virginia and, 77
  walls, 17, 34, 148
  weathervane, *278*
  west end, *251*
  windows, *36*, 148, 259
  Wren's rebuilding, 15, 124, 135, 136, 139-40, 144, *145-7*, 146-51, *148-9*, *153*, 153, 154, 156, 159, 181, 231, 235, 249, 251, 257, 261, 269
St Brigid's Shoe, shrine of, *14*
St Brigid's Well, *13*
St Clement Danes, 22, 142
St Dunstan's, Fleet Street, 94, 142
St David's, Bishop of, 30
St Etheldreda's, Ely Place, 31
St Giles's, Cripplegate, 25
St James's, Westminster, 156
St Lawrence Jewry, 148
St Margaret's, Westminster, 90
St Mary-le-Bow, 25, 148, 156
St Mary, Spital, 156
St Paul's Cathedral, 7, 18, 21, *26*, 30, 62, 72, 123, 134, 135, 144, 150, 168, *170-1*, 186, 226, 249, 260
St Paul's School, 56, 74
Saintsbury, George Edward, 190
Salisbury, Bishop of, 28, 30, 33, 37, 67, 90
Salisbury Cathedral, 144
Salisbury Court, 39, 176
Salisbury Square, 28, 88, 94, 202
Sanders, Horace, 218
Saxey, William, 74
Saxons, 15
Scott, John, 208
Scott, Sir Walter, 121, 125, 208, *209*
Seacoal Lane, 33
Secret Confederation of London Rectors, 35
Serjeant's Inn, 136
Serrate, John de, 74

Shadwell, Thomas, 121, 124, 125, *125*
Shaftesbury, Earl of, 146
Shakespeare, William, 31, 70, 71, 79, 81, 82, 83, *84*, 85, 87, 125, 128, 164
Sharpington, William, 260
Sheldon, Joseph, 151
Shelley, Percy Bysshe, 218
Sheridan, Richard Brinsley, 176, 221
Shire Lane, 166
Shirley, James, 135-6, *137*
Shoe Lane, 4, 29, 31, 32, 61, 93, 136, 137
Shoreditch, 82
Siddons, Mrs, 194
Sion College, 222
Skarle, John, 37
Smithfield, 32, 74, 76
Smollett, Tobias, 178, 197
Society of Antiquaries, 128
Society of Arts, 128
Society of St Cecilia, 156
Somerset, Duke of, 41
South Sea Bubble, 183
Southey, Robert, 208
Spenser, Edmund, 79
Spratt, Thomas, 128
Staël, Madame de, 190, 191
Staines, Sir William, 186, *186*
Stammers, John, 251
Star Chamber, Court of, 100, 168
Stationers' Company, 76, 83, 97, 100, 156, 168, 175
Steele, Sir Richard, 164, *166*, 181, 182, 206
Steinberg, S. H., 166, 175
Stepney, 204
Sternhold, Thomas, 81
Steven, Henry, 39
Still, Bishop, 81
Stow, John, 67, 68, 70, *75*, 76, 93, 164
Strahan, William, 187, 195
Strand, 31, 43
Straw, Jack, 46
Streeter, Robert, 148
Swift, Dean, 181

Tarleton, Richard, 79
Taylor, Arthur, 231
Telescope, Newton's reflecting, *140*
Temple, 22, 46, 70, 82, 95, 118, 121, 132, 142, 207
Temple Bar, 61, 77, 92, 118, 126, 147, 154, *155*, 166, 181, 197, 204
Tennyson, Lord, 79
Tertullian, 7
Tewkesbury, Abbot of, 30
Thackeray, William, 118, 206
Thalben-Ball, George, *262*, 263
Thames, river, 4, *60*, *90*, *114*, *117*, *150*, *151*, 183, 199
Thames Embankment, 204, 222
Theodore of Tarsus, 17
Theodosius, 9
Thomas of Merton, 27
Threadneedle Street, 218
Throckmorton, Job, 100
Throgmorton, Elizabeth, 77
Times, The, 3, 176, 210, 221, 226
Tonson, Jacob, *104*, 164, 166
Torquemada, 54
Tower of London, *46*, 198
Trevelyan, G. M., 110
Trippelowe, William, 44
Tunstall, Bishop, 62
Tusser, Thomas, 79
Tyburn, 94, 157
Tyler, Wat, 46
Tyndale, William, *64*, 65

Udall, Nicholas, 78
Ulsthorpe, Isabell, 40, 43
Ulsthorpe, John, 39-40

Vanbrugh, Sir John, 181
Van Dyck, 87
Venor, William, 41
Verrochio, Andrea del, 53
Victoria, Queen, *216*
Villiers, Barbara, 154
Villiers, George (Duke of Buckingham), 93
Villon, François, 53
Vinegar Bible, 159
Viner, Sir Robert, 146
Voltaire, 118

Waithman, Robert, 199, 200-1, 206
Waldvogel, 52
Wales, Prince of, 93, 222, *222*
Walker, Henry, 87
Walker, Mr, 224
Waller, Edmund, 128, 156
Walpole, Sir Robert, 181
Walton, Izaak, *93*, *94*, 94
Walworthe, John, 37
Ward, Ned, 156
Wareham, Bishop, 70
Wars of the Roses, 22
Warton, Joseph, *194*
Washington, George, 189
Webster, John, 88
Weelkes, Thomas, 94
Wellcome Foundation, 235
Wellington, Duke of, 206
Wels, John, 39
Wesley, Charles, 213
Wesley, John, 212-13, *213*
Wesley brothers, 187
Westminster, 32, 47
Westminster Abbey, 1, 21, 25, 51, 54, 61, 67, 70-1, 72, 125, 156, 194, 249
Westminster, Abbot of, 25, 27, 43, 70, 72
Westminster Bridge, 269

Whichcote, Sir Jeremiah, 151
Whig Party, 147
Whitby, Synod of, 17, 19, *19*
Whitchurch, Edward, 65
White, John, 77
White, R. F. & Co., 207
Whitefield, George, 213
Whitefriars, 88, 121, 136
Whitgift, Archbishop, 83
Whittington, Richard, 224
Wicked Bible, 159
Wihtred, 18
Wilfrid, St, 19, 21
Wilkes, John, 107, *196*, 197, 199-200
William the Conqueror, 22, 68
William III, 123, 153
Willibrord, St, 19, 21
Wilmot, Robert, 81
Wilson, 186
Winchcombe, Abbot of, 30
Wine Office Court, 153, 192
Winslow, Edward, 97-9, *98*, *99*
Winsor, Kathleen, 121
Wolsey, Cardinal, 39, 67-8, *69*, 70, 72, *72*
Wordsworth, William, 207, *208*, 269
Worcester, Earl of, 79
Worde, Wynkyn de, 34, *52*, *53*, 54-6, 61, 62, 65, 67, 221
Wren, Sir Christopher, 15, 95, *103*, 124, 126, 134, 135, 136, 139-40, *141*, 144, 148, 149, 150, 154, 156, 183, 235, 249, 251, 253, 257, 261, 263, 269
Wren, Faith, 139-40
Wycherley, William, 124, *125*, 139, 164
Wycliffe, John, 44, 46, 65
Wye, John, 44
Wyrley, Humphrey, 156
Wyrley, Sybil, 156

York, Duke of, 134

South of England
BUILDING SOCIETY
SOUTH OF ENGLA D BUILDING SOCIETY
WIMP